Shakespeare and Religion

SHAKESPEARE and RELIGION

| *Early Modern and Postmodern Perspectives* |

Edited by

KEN JACKSON and **ARTHUR F. MAROTTI**

University of Notre Dame Press
Notre Dame, Indiana

Library of Congress Cataloging-in-Publication Data
Shakespeare and religion : early modern and postmodern
perspectives / edited by Ken Jackson and Arthur F. Marotti.
p. cm.
Includes bibliographical references and index.
ISBN-13: 978-0-268-03270-8 (pbk. : alk. paper)
ISBN-10: 0-268-03270-X (pbk. : alk. paper)
1. Shakespeare, William, 1564–1616—Religion.
2. Christianity and literature—England—History—16th century.
3. Christianity and literature—England—History—17th century.
4. Drama—Religious aspects—Christianity.
5. Religion in literature. I. Jackson, Kenneth S., 1965–
II. Marotti, Arthur F., 1940–
PR3011.S32   2011
822.3'3—dc22
2010049949

Contents

PART TWO

Introduction

KEN JACKSON & ARTHUR F. MAROTTI

The topic of Shakespeare and religion has been a perennial one, though since the recent "turn to religion" in historical and literary scholarship it has come to the foreground.[1] In every era, the treatment of this subject has used the available critical and scholarly discourses to make sense of the dramatist's awareness of, relation to, and use of religious beliefs, religious culture, and religious conflicts from both historically specific and transhistorical points of view. In an era in which history-of-ideas scholarship was prominent, investigations of theological and philosophical elements in the plays could be pursued independent of social, political, or economic history. During and after the heyday of cultural materialist and new historicist criticism, it was impossible to ignore the affiliations of religious traditions, beliefs, and ideas with specific social, political, and economic realities. Now, in the wake of postmodern philosophy and theology, it is inevitable that scholar-critics consider, within a variety of historical frames, the deep religious and philosophical issues surfacing in early modern religious culture at a time of religiocultural conflict many find relevant to contemporary religious struggles and awareness.

In 2004 we published "The Turn to Religion in Early Modern English Studies," an essay that gave significant attention to the ways in which recent Shakespearean scholarship had readdressed the topic of religion and the dramatist's relationship to the religious culture(s) of his time. This essay has evidently helped to stimulate subsequent conversations in the field, including three sessions at the 2007 convention of the Renaissance Society of America and a seminar at the 2007 Shakespeare Association of America. The individual essays in this collection were first presented in shorter form in either of these two venues. All are by specialists in the field, and the collection combines historical and theological/philosophical perspectives as well as early modern and postmodern contexts to interpret the place of religion and religious issues in Shakespearean drama.

We have chosen to arrange the essays in this collection not by the rough chronological order of the Shakespeare canon but rather in two sections corresponding to their emphases—the first on historical analyses of the religious material in the plays, the second on postmodern theological, ethical, and philosophical interpretation of the dramas. Those scholars who attempt to situate Shakespeare's plays within their immediate historical contexts usually attempt to use the religious and philosophical vocabularies of the time, even as they bring modern critical methods to bear in their interpretations. Those who use modern philosophy and postmodern theology to interpret Shakespeare attempt to use Shakespearean texts to think through issues that have contemporary urgency, thus, in a sense, assuming that it is possible to see Shakespeare as addressing perennial theological and philosophical problems that unite his time with ours. Those who concentrate on the early modern contexts of the dramas emphasize the distance of that historical moment, even as they assume the importance and value for modern (and postmodern) readers of understanding it. Contributors to this collection gravitate toward the early modern or postmodern historical polarities, though all of them share the belief that the Shakespearean texts and what can be said about them or through a discussion of them have both general and specific relevance to our world. The more theoretically charged discussions of the plays are not innocent of history, and the more historically grounded ones are influenced by literary and cultural theory—in some cases, by postmodern philosophy and theology.

In examining the intellectual work done by the individual essays in this collection, we come up against the distinctness of two basic approaches to the religious: the first, most clearly embodied in those analyses that focus upon the relationship of Shakespearean texts to their immediate local or general cultural contexts, sees religion and sectarian religious differences and conflicts as part of cultural, social, and sociopolitical history; the second treats the religious as a transhistorical reality that enables us to think thoughts we otherwise would not be able to formulate or to treat a writer such as Shakespeare as a religious thinker whose insights could transcend their own cultural matrix. One of the contributors to this collection, Julia Lupton, has elsewhere argued that the current "turn to religion" in literary study has made clear that "religion is not identical with culture" and that "it is a testing ground for struggles between the universal and the particular," that it is "a form of thinking."[2] She argues that "religion names one strand of those forms of human interaction that resist localization and identification with a specific time, place, nation, or language, installing elements of thought that stand out from the very rituals and practices designed to transmit but also to neutralize them."[3] This is a timely reminder of some of the limits, and shortcomings, of new historicist and cultural materialist analyses. Fortunately, however, even when their interpretations are most historically specific, the scholars in this collection offer ways of thinking about Shakespeare and religion that open out onto the broader field of experience and understanding toward which Lupton points.

The two methodological orientations actually lead to some common conclusions. That is, both theory-centered interpretation and historical scholarship rather consistently point to the multiple ways in which the playwright dismantles religious practices only to end in a position, paradoxically, that still can be termed "religious." Both theory-centered interpretation and more distinctly historical scholarship are on the cusp, as it were, of developing a new and surprisingly compatible understanding of this simultaneous binding and unbinding of religion in the plays, an understanding that challenges the still standard Enlightenment divisions between the religious and the secular, faith and reason, the transcendent and the immanent.

The notable difference in methodological orientation might be in how these distinct forms of scholarship began to arrive at these similar conclusions. For the historically oriented critic, the results can be traced back to assaults on the Whig interpretation of English history. Historians writing about early modern England have reexamined the religious dynamics of the period, questioned the bottom-up theory of religious change, and emphasized the ways that residual, dominant, and emergent religious cultures coexisted in unstable hybrid forms. This hybridity long has posed a challenge for scholars, but again, in addition to this collection of essays there seems to be a recent trend toward developing new language and paradigms to understand this. Jean-Christophe Mayer states that Shakespeare's plays "have the power to pose pressing questions but also to allow potential contradictions to remain. This is a logic which is largely alien to us."[4] Beatrice Groves argues: "Only once we have come to recognize the influence of the competing strands of Christianity on theatrical presentation in this period will we understand how religion was assimilated into the ostensibly secular drama of early-modern England."[5]

Literary scholars have been particularly influenced by the historical reexamination of the often marginalized history of early modern English Catholicism, and Shakespeareans have been unusually preoccupied with the question of Shakespeare's religious identity: whether he remained committed to a familial Catholicism, retained only an attachment to some of its enduring cultural forms, was a "church papist," was a Protestant, or became a skeptic or agnostic about things religious. The first group of essays in this collection try to treat Shakespearean plays in this immediate and newly complex historical and religious context. They take a long view of the religious inheritance of early modern secular drama, highlighting both residual Catholic and newer reformist elements of the culture. All the essays are scrupulously cautious about embracing calls for "Catholic" Shakespeare. In that, they are aligned with Groves when she suggests that some calls for a Catholic Shakespeare are infused by a now common desire to find some identifiable "exciting marginality" in Shakespeare.[6] Perhaps the central "theoretical" point of our 2004 essay was to warn against the overuse of the term and concept of "otherness" or "alterity" without an awareness of how complexly that term is bound to the religious. Correspondingly, the essays here all portray the dramatist as a religious skeptic who was critical of his own religiously conflicted society and also both intellectually and emotionally attached to some of the features of the "old religion" as he sought ways to translate some of them into psychologically and ethically powerful theater. As suggested, Shakespeare's critique of or skepticism about religion, again, never breaks completely from what can be understood as religious impulses, but those religious impulses are not easily described by traditional markers such as "Catholic" or "Protestant" or even "skepticism," as John D. Cox recently has shown.[7]

The more theoretically oriented critics in this collection arrive at similar conclusions, primarily, but not exclusively, from an engagement with Continental philosophy and, in particular, with the later work of Jacques Derrida. In a collection intended primarily for early modernists and Shakespeareans, this engagement with Derrida still requires some explication. Derrida's deconstruction is mainly (and provocatively) concerned with ontology, the philosophical study of what *is* or *what exists*. Deconstruction focuses on the ancient ontological tension between Being and non-Being, a tension that for many should not even be a tension. Western thought always has tried to purge the very notion of non-Being or the notion that there is something *other* than or outside of Being. For there *to be* non-Being, the pre-Socratic Parmenides first suggested in his poem "On Nature," implies some minimal participation in Being. To talk of the being of non-Being, then, is to talk nonsense; correspondingly, to talk of something "other" is also nonsense because that other will always be some version of what we already know and therefore not other in any thoroughgoing way. Nonetheless, the notion of the other or an otherwise than Being continues to exert an incredible pull on human thought and activity. Any serious talk of justice, to take the critical example, always involves a "justice" that cannot be fully realized, one that can be only gestured toward rather than achieved. Any talk of justice always involves a justice yet to come, something absolutely other that haunts us but cannot be reached.

One of the forms in which the call of something other than Being has always manifested its (non)presence is religion. Derrida came to recognize the connection between his philosophy and a whole set of religious discourses, including those in the wide-ranging tradition of negative theology. Negative theology works vigorously to think of and pray to "God" without imposing any anthropomorphic or other distortion on this divine other. The task is not easy. Negative theology requires extraordinary rigor and patience in dealing with contradiction and paradox. This rigor is best expressed, perhaps, in Meister Eckhart's short prayer: "I pray God to rid me of God." But Derrida also always made it quite clear that a distinction was absolutely necessary between deconstruction and negative theologies. Any negative theology, he argued, no matter how rigorous and exacting, always has a specifically divine other in mind, whereas deconstruction dreams of an "absolute heterogeneity that unsettles all the assurances of the same."[8] Like Shakespeare, Derrida is interested in religion stripped of religion, a "religion without religion," that presses for a sustained attention to otherness, to non-Being, to that which cannot be thought—in short, the impossible.

What the contributors in the second part of this collection assume, then, is that the analogous relationship between Derrida's deconstruction and any number of religious practices provides a useful calculus to understand the "mystery" of Shakespeare's religion: the playwright's seemingly systematic and fastidious refusal to identify with certainty and clarity his relationship (if any) to a divine other. Derrida himself used Shakespeare's spiritual dimensions to explicate his own positions. As we wrote in 2004, Derrida turned "to Hamlet and Hamlet's ghost, and he relies on Shakespeare to create a word, 'hauntology,' that helps describe the irreducible space between religion as anthropological residue and as something absolutely other. Although, from one point of view, this might be an example of savvy nescience, it is a space that some scholars and critics are beginning to occupy as they readdress religion, religious traditions, religious culture, and religious agents in their studies of the early modern era—a period that is and is not like our own."[9] Derrida was drawn to *Hamlet* because the play is able to address the "spirit" of King Hamlet's ghost without seizing possession of the spirit in a violent gesture that renders "it" either this or that, something of this world that our reason can manage effectively. Importantly, this spirit of King Hamlet is not an inconsequential, ephemeral distraction in the world of the play but a driving force, blurring the lines, again, between material and immaterial, transcendent and immanent.[10]

Derrida and Shakespeare both press religiously against religion, so hard in fact that "religion" seems to collapse into an immanent materialism, prompting Michael Whitmore, following Spinoza, to argue recently for a Shakespeare who is a "dramaturgical monist."[11] Indeed, one could ask if religion as a category is still even useful. In *Specters of Marx* Derrida was not addressing what might be called the religious or the religiously minded. On the contrary, he was writing specifically for Marxist thinkers who deplored his repeated attempts to raise the specter of non-Being. From a Marxist perspective, to think of something "other" than or outside Being is to engage in potentially dangerous idealism that distracts our attention from the material conditions of existence.

Derrida was trying to remind Marxist thinkers that Marxism/ materialism has its own ghosts and a sort of spiritualism ("A specter is haunting Europe—the specter of Communism" is the first line of the *Manifesto*), that the tension between Being and non-Being persists in all Western metaphysics, including Marxism. Despite its best efforts to exorcise ghosts and purge the nonsense of non-Being, a nonpresence of an unrealizable better and more just world animates Marxism, and this "spirit" of Marxism is what can be retained—in a somewhat ghostly fashion—after the events of 1989. This attention to non-Being is not a kind of dangerous idealism but a more accurate ontological take on Marxism, *what it in fact is*, a take that includes its animating but impossible-to-grasp spirit. Derrida insists that this attention to non-Being is still an ontology (*hauntology* is a pun on the French pronunciation of *ontologie*):

This logic of haunting would not be merely larger and more powerful than an ontology or a thinking of Being (of the "to be," assuming that it is a matter of Being in the "to be or not to be," but nothing is less certain). It would harbor within itself, but like circumscribed places or particular effects, eschatology and teleology themselves. It would *comprehend* them, but incomprehensibly.... Can the extremity of the extreme ever be comprehended? And the opposition between "to be" and "not to be"? *Hamlet* already began with the expected return of the dead King. ... Oh, Marx's love for Shakespeare![12]

Derrida thus located in Shakespeare's *Hamlet* and its animating spirit—King Hamlet's ghost—a way to articulate a new ontological understanding, one he hoped would be conducive to a spirit of Marxism if not exactly in line with the strict materialist ontology sought after by Marxist thinkers.

Not long after the publication of our 2004 essay, Ewan Fernie edited an inspired collection of essays, *Spiritual Shakespeares,* including an elegant introduction that realized in part the paradoxical potential for Derrida's "spiritualism" to reinvigorate Shakespearean materialist criticism. He rightly cautioned, though, that if one is going to draw attention to the analogies between Shakespearean spirituality and Derridean deconstruction, the Derridean tendency to hint at infinite deferral needs to be balanced by the Marxist/materialist critique of that tendency. Like Derrida, Shakespeare is driven by "the impossible," but in Shakespeare "the impossible assumes specific form and invades the reality of the poems and the plays time and again."[13] In short, Shakespeare very often "contravenes the French thinker's fastidious deferral of the absolute into a region beyond the real world of history."[14] Shakespeare is capacious enough to stage the Derridean gesture and its Marxist critique.

There is much truth to this claim, and it is elegantly expressed in Fernie's introduction. But it is difficult for us to see how Fernie's stance does not ultimately point us back in the direction we started—that is, toward a position that translates the strangeness of religion into something else entirely: spirituality, for example. Is Shakespearean drama really spiritual but not religious? Fernie writes: "Though it is religion's heart and inspiration, spirituality precedes religion and may well take place outside it. Spirituality is an experience of truth, and of living in accordance with truth, but it is concerned with the truth not of this world but of a world that has not yet and perhaps never will come to be. Spirituality is a mode of opposition to what is."[15]

It is not clear to us that the term *religion* can be dispensed with so readily in dealing either with the early modern past or with the present. As already suggested, many of the essays in this collection seek to address the "heart and inspiration" of religion, but none deems it necessary to detach the heart and inspiration of religion from religion itself—whatever historical and institutional forms it may take.

While it may now be a common habit to decry "institutional" religion to get at the heart and inspiration of religion, it simply seems a critical and scholarly mistake to turn our attention away from the history of established religions and religious institutions to get at this "heart and inspiration." The dialectic between the two is the thing. For Derrida, the relationship between religion in terms of the history of revelation and its "heart" is an aporia that should be respected, not somehow solved.[16] Shakespeare is both a living thinker accessible for "presentist" concerns, as Fernie suggests, and a critical interlocutor between the ancient past, the medieval and early modern world, our current times, and the future. And he does most of his dramatic thinking in religious terms that cannot be disconnected from the long and rich history of religious practices and set of interpretations that were available to him.

All the essays in this collection show that at its most profound, Shakespeare's dramatic religious questioning presses against what we normally tend to think of as constituting religion—its dogmas, institutions, beliefs, and practices—to the point where one is asked to question what, if anything, "religion" can mean. The lines between secular and sacred, transcendent and immanent blur so continuously that we begin to doubt our own vocabulary and historical paradigms in our attempts to describe the strange otherness of Shakespeare's religion, the way in which he can, again, deliberately and systematically strip away the layers of religion until nothing is left—nothing except the desire for something more or better that cannot be fully disentangled from religion.

Perhaps the figure that emerges most distinctly to clarify this religious unbinding of religion is Job. As Lupton writes here, the Jobean text illuminates a "force beyond human sociality that is drawn into the framework of civility not by trauma itself (the loss of wealth, health, and offspring), but by the failure of neighbor love, understood locally and globally, to effect its own rebindings." This force is at the very heart of religious experience, and it is this religious experience—a religious experience tied "to the event of its own disarticulation"—that fascinates Shakespeare and produces some of his most compelling and often disturbing work. We find it particularly useful, then, to link our two sets of essays here with two different essays on Job, one more distinctly "historical" by Hannibal Hamlin, and one more distinctly "theoretical" by

Lupton. This ancient narrative reveals religion pushed to its extremes, to its own destruction. But of course one would be hard pressed to describe the Jobean text as nonreligious.

Part One

In the first essay of the collection's first part, Robert Miola re-explores two familiar scholarly topics in a new way: the allusions, by way of Samuel Harsnett's polemical distortions, to William Weston's exorcisms in *King Lear* and the shadow presence of Henry Garnet as an evil Jesuit "equivocator" in Shakespeare's *Macbeth*. With regard to the first case, he uses Weston's biography to illustrate that priest's use of the situation of exorcism to effect a psychotherapeutic pastoral cure of a suffering sinner. Instead of being a malicious trickster, William Weston is depicted as a caring minister whose concern for his suffering fellow human being is analogous to Edgar's care of the blinded and despairing Gloucester in Shakespeare's tragedy. In the second case, Miola deals more directly not only with the distorted critical presentation of Jesuit equivocation's relationship to *Macbeth* but also with the ways in which the myth of the evil Jesuit has permeated both English historiography and critical interpretations of that play. He broadens our understanding of Garnet's thinking and of the carefully limited uses of equivocation and mental reservation by embattled Catholics in late Elizabethan and Jacobean England, tracing some of the historical and intellectual roots of this thinking and freeing it from its simplistic portrayal in the language of the prosecutors in Gunpowder Treason trials and in subsequent and long-lived anti-Jesuit polemic.

In writing against the grain not only of mainstream historiography but also of Shakespearean criticism, which often reflects the anti-Catholic and anti-Jesuit prejudices hardwired into English culture, Miola rehabilitates the images of Weston and Garnet, whose social and religious functioning was decidedly more benign and pastorally sensitive than their polemical caricatures would lead us to believe. His essay allows us to see the persecuted Catholic figure from the inside, as it were, committed to a universally understandable pursuit of human sociality rather

than a religious war. His nuanced approach to Weston's missionary behavior creates an interesting friction with Harsnett's depiction of the
priest-exorcist and complicates our understanding of *King Lear*. Miola
examines sympathetically Garnet's carefully circumscribed endorsement
of equivocation for reasons of protecting one's life or the life of another
as well as the Jesuit's anguish over the conflict between confessional
secrecy and the need to avoid misprision of treason. A politically loyal
Shakespeare may have responded imaginatively to the demonizing of
Garnet in the Gunpowder Treason trials and in the subsequent government propaganda, but Shakespeare need not be used to validate anti-
Catholic myths that have had brutal consequences in his time and later.

Gary Kuchar's essay on the politics of ceremony in *Titus Andronicus*
focuses on the broken and interrupted ceremonies in the first and fifth
acts of the play to show how the play breaks the classical association of
decorum and morality as it points to the instabilities and contradictions
within the Elizabethan religious settlement. Using as touchstones Cranmer's "Of Ceremonies" and "precisian" or Puritan critiques of Anglican
ceremonialism, he demonstrates how the play's Roman features are used,
not primarily to associate Catholicism with paganism, but rather to expose the ways official Elizabethan culture was politically and religiously
self-divided and incoherent: "Titus's Rome mirrors, albeit in a distortedly
hyperbolic form, how Elizabethan liturgical policies threatened to reiterate the social antagonisms they were designed to mitigate." The 1549
and 1559 Prayer Books and the Elizabethan religious settlement were
incoherent attempts to cover over cultural self-division. In identifying the
"politics of ceremony" as central to Shakespeare's play, Kuchar discusses
the problematic relationship of the sacred and profane, the civilized and
the barbaric, in both the fictional Rome of the drama and the all-too-
immediate world of late Elizabethan England, making a disturbing and
disorienting connection between both ancient and contemporary Roman
violence and that of Elizabethan culture.

Kuchar argues that Shakespeare dramatically, and counterintuitively,
associates indecorum with the ethical, here and in many of his later plays.
Rather than accepting the traditional Ciceronian association of decorum
with justice or the religious use of decorous ceremonialism as the basis
for a kind of social order, Shakespeare dismantles these constructs to

uncover the violence and barbarity they precipitate—those religious state murders, for example, that were justified as punishments for treason. Kuchar argues that the formal operations of indecorum encourage genuine political thought, leading the audience to recognize not only the conflicts between individuals and society but the conflicts within both individuals and society. The dramatist emerges as one who is neither recusant nor conformist, but rather religiously, ethically, and politically critical. Kuchar gives the dramatist's stance a final religious quality when he states: "For Shakespeare, genuine ethical action seems more in sympathy with St. Paul's conception of Christian life as a form of divine foolishness than with the ostensibly Ciceronian values of order and decency seen by Tudor authorities to be voiced in 1 Corinthians."

Kuchar's essay shows how intensely self-conscious Shakespeare and Elizabethan culture were about the competing strands of Christianity, the ways in which the playwright and his audience could meditate on rather than simply engage in religious war and polemics. The "orgy of indecorum" in *Titus Andronicus* that demystifies almost all religious ritual, Kuchar suggests, stems from a deep awareness on the part of Elizabethans that Tudor authorities could engage in torture and barbaric rituals even as they condemned Catholics for such practices—all the while remaining within a certain broader religious framework. The play is decidedly unwilling to pit one religious stance against the other because the playwright seems acutely aware that doing so would nullify the underlying purpose of religion itself—although what that underlying force of religion is is decidedly unclear.

Richard McCoy's reading of Shakespeare's *Comedy of Errors* concentrates on the play in the context of its performance as part of the Gray's Inn Revels in 1594, in which the festive atmosphere of misrule encouraged a debunking of magic and enchantment. The first recorded review of a Shakespeare play, then, found in the *Gesta Grayorum*, was not good. A highly stylized "Masque of Amity" quickly followed at the Gray's Inn to help calm the audience reaction to this "Night of Errors." McCoy deftly shows that *Comedy of Errors* had the "last laugh" in this short-lived artistic competition because the play's creation of feelings of goodwill and harmony reproduce the feeling of communion associated with a "Eucharistic miracle." The essay moves, by way of Coleridge's notion of the "willing suspension of disbelief," Reformation debates about the Eucharist, Keats's idea of "negative capability," and a reconsideration of the play's Pauline Ephesian resonances, to a double vision of its religious elements: on the one hand conjuration and exorcism are mocked, but on the other the play, like a medieval miracle play such as the *Croxton Play of the Sacrament*, reaffirms the miraculous even as it effortlessly restores amity. After all, Shakespeare's original audiences were religiously heterogeneous, and many Elizabethans and early Jacobeans practiced a hybridized religion with elements of the old and the new faiths. As we can see in the essays by Miola and Kuchar, Shakespeare opts not to exploit some of the possibilities for anti-Catholic satire in the situation and action of the play; instead, he recuperates, as he does in later dramas, some of the aura of the miraculous implicit in the "old religion." McCoy implicitly argues, then, for Shakespeare's continuing attachment to residual Catholic culture even as he portrays him as a skeptic escaping religious dogmatism.[17] But what McCoy identifies as at work in the play's long-term success is its ability to inspire affections at the core of any understanding of the "religious."

Working with Stanley Cavell's notion that, in Shakespeare's tragedies, "acknowledgment" is central to the particular relation of characters to others, Sarah Beckwith in her essay turns to that dramatist's post-tragic dramas or romances to explore the presence in them of the languages of penance as a vital component of Shakespeare's theater of recognition. Focusing on *Cymbeline*, she reexamines the familiar critical perception of "the comedy of forgiveness" in the late romances, relating elements of the traditional sacrament of penance to the dynamics of forgiveness and reconciliation dramatized in these plays. Not unlike McCoy, she argues that the final social reconciliations result in a "Eucharistic community" in which personal renewal and societal recreation are related. She reveals the richness and importance of Shakespeare's sacramental language and its dramatic uses, specifically of the playwright's transformation of the inherited languages of forgiveness.

Taking the long view of penance and confession by going back to the medieval understandings of the sacrament, Beckwith also looks at the work of important Protestant reformers to highlight the social dimension of both confession and communion. At the same time, she argues that the change from auricular confession (addressed to another person, the priest) to a general confession or to private confessional prayer to God left a kind of social void in the dynamics of reconciliation that became "an opportunity for Shakespearean theater" to fill and dramatize. In the late plays human bonds need to be renewed. Beckwith uses speech-act theory to deal with the phenomenon of passionate utterance, which she sees as crucial to the romances. In the last scene of *Cymbeline*, she discerns five confessions through which community is restored: "the deathbed confession of the queen; the long, cluttered, self-interrupting confession of Giacomo; the confession of Pisanio, completed by the outburst of Guiderius; and the confession of Belarius." She sees these confessions as "part of a shared story" and confessional speech, as Augustine defined it, as a gift of language that returns to an original giver, God. In her account, Shakespeare's sacramentalist dramaturgy kept him in touch with a religious and cultural past that many of his contemporaries found it necessary to reject.

Beckwith's sacramentalist reading, oriented toward the medieval world, recasts and reenergizes religion—and social relations—in a historical moment when religious institutions are violently shifting. In her essay we can see the link between a specific religious practice, confession, and the heart and inspiration of that religious practice, the desire to renew always fragile human bonds. Part of Shakespeare's enduring appeal is his ability to stage this difficult-to-grasp and ever-shifting process as acutely experienced in his world, a process that, in turn, cannot be completely disentangled from an ancient past or our contemporary world. It is possible, in our post-post-Enlightenment world, relatively free from a widespread insistence that religion can be clearly identified and walled off in its strangeness, that we are just now learning to see and hear what Shakespeare can reveal to us about this transhistorical process of binding and unbinding.

In reexamining the much-discussed relationship of *King Lear* to the book of Job, which centers on questions of human suffering and providential justice, Hannibal Hamlin introduces more intertexts for an understanding of the play than one usually finds in critical discussions of this drama as he illuminates the crucial religious and ethical issues at stake in the play. Referring to the common practice of connecting biblical texts with one another, he brings into the discussion the Epistle of James, which discusses the Job story. He also makes use of John Calvin's *Sermons on Job*, along with the dedicatory epistle written by the work's English translator, Arthur Golding; John Florio's translation of Montaigne's "An Apologie of *Raymond Sebonde*"; and Robert Parsons's *A Booke of Christian Exercise*, in the popular expurgated Protestant edition produced by Edmund Bunny. Using convincing verbal evidence, he demonstrates Shakespeare's employment of the important themes as well as the specific language found in these works.

Hamlin's explorations of Shakespeare's "reading practice and the gestation process of his plays" result in a deeper understanding of the interpretive cruxes of this drama. He shows how Shakespeare responds to the theological and moral problems of the Job story—particularly those of unmerited suffering and of a tyrannical and/or absent God. Although Hamlin also cites some of Luther's thoughts on Job, he argues that Calvin's extensive interpretations of the Job story influenced the playwright more. By the end of the essay, however, the Protestant reading of *Lear* is undermined as Shakespeare emerges as a religious skeptic addressing a religiously heterogeneous audience on whom the final burden of interpretation rested. Shakespeare insists, as Hamlin puts it, on "probing the anxieties about Job that the reformer was not quite able to argue away." The play, in other words, pushes us closer to the Job text rather than to one side or another of religious polemic.

Part Two

In the first essay in the second part of this collection, Lupton (like Hamlin) turns to Shakespeare's use of the figure of Job to explore Shakespeare's religion, and her more distinctly theoretical findings corroborate much of Hamlin's historicism. Lupton argues that Shakespeare turns to the book of Job, not for a "positive religious program," but for a figure of "commutativity" whose cries of suffering and protest point toward a universality older than even Paul's promise, a universality disturbingly marked by its open wounds and scars in *The Merchant of Venice*, *Othello*, *King Lear*, and *Timon of Athens*. According to Lupton, it is not simply our ability to empathize with Job's pain that suggests this universality.

Rather, the Jobean text recalls minimal claims of obligation, care, and respect that are due a sufferer when more elaborated institutional forms of addressing his misfortunes have been destroyed or disabled. That is, the Jobean text illuminates a "force beyond human sociality that is drawn into the framework of civility not by trauma itself (the loss of wealth, health, and offspring) but by the failure of neighbor love to effect its own rebindings." This force is at the very heart of religious experience, and it is this religious experience—a religious experience tied "to the event of its own disarticulation"—that fascinates Shakespeare and produces some of his most compelling and often disturbing work. As suggested earlier in our introduction, Job is perhaps the figure in its various Shakespearean renditions that, as Lupton says, "challenges the norms" of both the religious and the secular not to land on one side or the other but to call us "to the work of rebuilding such norms anew."

Abraham is, in many respects, a figure comparable to Job. In *"Richard II*, Abraham, and the Abrahamic," Ken Jackson suggests that Shakespeare's political theology, the extent to which theological concepts underwrite and determine political understandings, can be understood not in terms preferred by the critical tradition that distances itself from religion—the "King's two bodies" or the "law-in-parliament"—but in terms of a narrative that points to the very heart and origins of the "Abrahamic" religions: Abraham's sacrifice of Isaac in Genesis 22. Jackson takes seriously both Gaunt's and Richard's expressed commitment to a divine other that cannot be approached or fully comprehended. Both are shocked, however, when that expressed commitment asks them to give everything, absolutely, all at once. Gaunt is asked to give up his son, Bolingbroke, and the sonless "sun king" Richard II is asked to give up his divinely sanctioned rule. In these scenes, Shakespeare conjures a form of sovereignty that is based on absolute selflessness of the sort that exceeds our conception of self-sacrifice. Shakespeare's sophisticated return to the still relevant narrative of Genesis 22, pitting a commitment to an absolute, unknowable other against a commitment to a loved one, also explains the strange and seemingly comic figure of York, on whom the play's politics pivot. York's attempted "sacrifice" of his own son, Aumerle, in the fifth act for defying the new king Henry IV is drawn straight from the cycle play renditions of Abraham and Isaac.

Lisa Freinkel addresses *Timon of Athens*, a critical text for us in that Shakespeare uses the word *religion* three times in that work, more than in any other play. Freinkel, too, reveals the strange way in which Shakespearean drama unsettles the line between transcendent and immanent, material and immaterial. She does so, however, in a rather idiosyncratic and brilliant fashion that manages, remarkably, to connect with other essays in the collection. Freinkel uses Buddhist thought and the work of William Empson, including that critic's own Buddhist explorations. She suggests that what we find in *Timon of Athens* is nothing less than the problem or paradox "of [Christian] dualism laid bare," a problem that prompted Empson's interest in Buddhism. In brief, the Christian God is utterly independent from his own creation, but for that creation to have meaning "he" must enter into it in some form. When God does enter his creation, though, he negates his own independence and thus disappears or empties himself into the impermanence of this world. This "embodiment" of God in the world is expressed, of course, in the mystery of the cross, but Empson is repulsed by a religion that relies on such sacrificial logic and is instead drawn to Buddhism because it eschews such "dualism." Buddhism is religiously "indifferent" to the difference between Being (God) and outside or other than Being that is so often expressed in Christian thought.

Empson never published his manuscript on Buddhism, but Freinkel tracks his "Buddhist" thought in his reading of *Timon of Athens*, specifically of *Timon*'s dog. Empson notes that there are two contradictory uses of the word *dog* in the play: one suggests a flatterer and the other a snarling cynic. Freinkel points out there are also "two *gods* in *Timon*, just as there are two *dogs* in *Timon*." This is no coincidence: the two senses of *dog* "precisely articulate the discontinuity central to the play's vision of divinity." The first god of the play is *Timon*'s god of giving. This god is forced to reveal his mortality, as his "divinity" is bound up in the temporal arc of the promise, one that is necessarily broken in the material world. The second god is money. This god is capable of leveling and exchanging everything, and it is visible. It is also indestructible, since money, in some sense, embodies the eternal. But this visible and eternal god can be known only through the eyes of a cynic—that is, etymologically speaking, the dog (as opposed to the flattering dog linked to the first god of *Timon*). It can only be known cynically, as it were, in the world of material things that is, paradoxically, impermanent. As Freinkel writes, "There is no eternal life that isn't also life that dies. There is no divinity—no buddha nature—apart from the frail appearance of all things." *Timon*'s dog, then, is "not a symbol at all, but a cipher: a placeholder for a division—what Derrida might call a *différance* that cannot, by definition, be embodied."

In what is in many respects a comparable critical gesture, Joan Linton employs the work of Walter Benjamin and Eric Santner to argue that the "absent presence" of Falstaff in *Henry V* constitutes something of a miracle of the everyday. Falstaff is resurrected throughout the play as various figures tell and retell his story, one that counters the official Tudor myth of Henry and reveals in Falstaff the abandoned "creaturely" life that sovereignty excludes. In Falstaff an audience discovers a "differently imagined redemptive future" than is available in Tudor mythology. Falstaff's continued (non)presence is not that of a ghost but, in Santner's terms, "part of a past" that, because it is unrecorded, "never achieved ontological consistency" and thus "in some sense has not yet been but remains stuck in a spectral, protocosmic dimension." Falstaff's continued return throughout the play, then, can be read as something of a counter-miracle. Linton, too, shows how Shakespeare completely blurs the lines between the material and the immaterial, the secular and the sacred, to the point that our standard use of those terms is practically useless: "In staging the passing of Falstaff, Shakespearean theater discovers the extraordinary amid the ordinary, the sacred in the everyday, the miracle that never appears, yet to which one can bear witness, embedded as it is in the fabric of lived historical experience."

The way in which Shakespeare thinks through rather than around religion is suggested as well in James A. Knapp's "Penitential Ethics in *Measure for Measure*." Knapp argues that, despite the title, Shakespeare's play resists settling for a prescriptive ethics, a system where a particular sin must be compensated for by a particular action. "Rather than parrot Christian views on repentance, ethics, justice, and mercy," Shakespeare "reserves judgment on every system that would proscribe, or prescribe, a particular course of action" and rejects the "most obvious correctives to Vienna's morally depraved state—the Puritan Angelo's law, the ascetic Isabella's withdrawal, and ducal responsibility." These correctives

determined by state law and religion are revealed to be life-denying delusions. Yet the corruption of a life guided by desire is shown to be equally
untenable. Shakespeare deconstructs the systems on which both Angelo
and Isabella rely, leaving them to face their experiences without the armor
of a specific religious piety or state law. This reading resolves some of
the tension in the play's problematic ending by suggesting that the play
takes seriously the transformations that Angelo and Isabella undergo.
This interpretation, we note, does not negate religion but, as we have seen
so many times so far, dismantles religion to press toward its inspiration
and heart. This essay implies how deeply and seriously Shakespeare read
the call in the Sermon on the Mount to "judge not that ye be not judged."
For Shakespeare, the "judgment of any course of action must be deferred
to an inaccessible future." Judgment is always retrospective, while ethical
action is always looking forward to an unknown future. As Knapp shows,
Shakespeare again points to the heart of scripture, but in a way that unsettles preconceived or predetermined interpretations of scripture. There
is none of the political quietism here feared by Fernie and others, but a
rapt attention to lived experience and the process of judgment.

IN THE EARLY TWENTIETH-FIRST CENTURY, MOST EUROPEAN AND AMERICAN
Shakespeare scholars are probably agnostic, atheistic, or religiously
indifferent—hostile to confessional apologetics, as well as resistant to
criticism that mystifies real-world economic, political, and social relations
by accepting early modern religious languages and religious points of view
as intellectual frameworks adequate to understanding the culture and the
literature of a time distant from our own. Living in religiously pluralist
or secular societies with intellectual elites that are rightly antagonistic to
any manifestation of religious fundamentalism, but also uncomfortable
with religion in general, they find it hard to take a fresh look at manifesta-
tions of the religious in the work of a dramatist whose openness to interpretation has facilitated modern secular understandings of his plays. If
they deal with religious subject matter, they prefer to analyze it historically
as just one feature of the cultural context of Shakespearean drama. The
problem with this approach is that it does not allow us to take seriously
the religious thought, beliefs, or crises that both energized and disturbed

Shakespeare when he wrote and that, in transformed shapes, still manifest themselves in our own world. In the wake of the current "turn to religion" in literary studies, however, and in response to the writings of postmodern theologians and philosophers, including Jacques Derrida in the final phase of his career, Shakespeare scholars have been more sympathetically responsive to the presence of the religious in that author's work, if they have not also used it to think through perennial philosophical and religious issues of which we have become more aware. As the essays in this collection demonstrate, there are serious religious stakes for Shakespeare in his plays and for us in our scholarship.

Notes

The following are abbreviations used in chapter notes:

CRS   Catholic Record Society
EETS   Early English Text Society

1. See Ken Jackson and Arthur F. Marotti, "The Turn to Religion in Early Modern English Studies," *Criticism* 46 (Winter 2004): 167–90. For examples of recent studies of Shakespeare and religion, see Jean-Christophe Mayer, *Shakespeare's Hybrid Faith: History, Religion and the Stage* (London: Palgrave, 2006); Ewan Fernie, ed., *Spiritual Shakespeares* (London: Routledge, 2005); Beatrice Groves, *Texts and Traditions: Religion in Shakespeare, 1592–1604* (Oxford: Oxford University Press, 2007); John D. Cox, *Seeming Knowledge: Shakespeare and Skeptical Faith* (Waco: Baylor University Press, 2007); Julia Reinhard Lupton, *Citizen-Saints: Shakespeare and Political Theology* (Chicago: University of Chicago Press, 2005). See also Donna Hamilton, *Shakespeare and the Politics of Protestant England* (Lexington: University Press of Kentucky, 1992); Stephen Greenblatt, *Hamlet and Purgatory* (Princeton: Princeton University Press, 2001); John E. Curran Jr., *"Hamlet," Protestantism and the Mourning of Contingency: Not to Be* (Aldershot: Ashgate, 2006); Lisa Freinkel, *Reading Shakespeare's Will: The Theology of Figure from Augustine to the Sonnets* (New York: Columbia University Press, 2002); and Debora Shuger, *Political Theologies in Shakespeare's England: The Sacred and the State in "Measure for Measure"* (New York: Palgrave, 2001). There are some studies of Shakespeare's particular relationship to Catholicism: see, for example, Richard Dutton, Alison Findlay, and Richard Wilson, eds., *Theatre and Religion: Lancastrian Shakespeare* (Manchester: Manchester University Press, 2003), and *Region, Religion, and Patronage: Lancastrian Shakespeare* (Manchester: Manchester

University Press, 2003); Richard Wilson, *Secret Shakespeare: Studies in Theatre, Religion, and Resistance* (Manchester: Manchester University Press, 2004); Dennis Taylor and David N. Beauregard, eds., *Shakespeare and the Culture of Christianity in Early Modern England* (New York: Fordham University Press, 2003); Velma Bourgeois Richmond, *Shakespeare, Catholicism and Romance* (New York: Continuum, 2000); David N. Beauregard, *Catholic Theology in Shakespeare's Plays* (Newark: University of Delaware Press, 2008); and Phebe Jensen, *Religion and Revelry in Shakespeare's Festive World* (Cambridge: Cambridge University Press, 2008).

2. Julia Lupton, "The Religious Turn (to Theory) in Shakespeare Studies," *English Language Notes* 44 (Spring 2006): 146–47.

3. Ibid., 146.

4. Mayer, *Shakespeare's Hybrid Faith,* 155.

5. Groves, *Texts and Traditions,* 188.

6. Ibid., 5.

7. For instance, Cox suggests we are not yet in a position to distinguish between a historically determined skeptical materialism and a hidden God in Shakespeare's writing. Cox, *Seeming Knowledge,* 250.

8. John Caputo, *The Prayers and Tears of Jacques Derrida: Religion without Religion* (Bloomington: Indiana University Press, 1997), 5.

9. Jackson and Marotti, "Turn to Religion," 182.

10. See Elizabeth Williamson, *The Materiality of Religion in Early Modern English Drama* (Farnham: Ashgate, 2009).

11. Michael Whitmore, *Shakespearean Metaphysics* (New York: Continuum, 2008), 25.

12. Jacques Derrida, *Specters of Marx: The State of Debt, the Work of Mourning, and the New International,* trans. Peggy Kamuf (New York: Routledge, 1994), 10.

13. Fernie, *Spiritual Shakespeares,* 16.

14. Ibid., 18.

15. Ibid., 9.

16. "Is revealability *(Offenbarkheit)* more originary than revelation *(Offenbarung)*, and hence independent of all religion? Independent in the structures of its experience and in the analytics relating to them? Is this not the place in which 'reflecting faith' at least originates, if not this faith itself? Or, rather, inversely, would the event of revelation have consisted in revealability itself, and the origin of light, the originary light, the very invisibility of visibility?" Derrida, "Faith and Knowledge: The Two Sources of 'Religion' at the Limits of Reason Alone," in *Acts of Religion,* ed. Gil Anidjar (New York: Routledge, 2002), 55.

17. For another version of this line of argument, see Arthur F. Marotti, "Shakespeare and Catholicism," in Dutton, Findlay, and Wilson, *Theatre and Religion,* 218–41.

PART ONE

Chapter 1

Two Jesuit Shadows in Shakespeare
William Weston and Henry Garnet

ROBERT MIOLA

The current furor of revisionist confabulation, special pleading, and spurious association has apparently reached its *ne plus ultra*. Peter Milward's *Shakespeare the Papist* (2005), Clare Asquith's *Shadowplay: The Hidden Beliefs and Coded Politics of William Shakespeare* (2006), and Joseph Pearce's *The Quest for Shakespeare* (2008) all read Shakespeare and early modern culture variously, and sometimes contradictorily, to support the same predetermined thesis, namely, that Shakespeare was a secret Catholic. All too often lost in the controversy over this unproven and, barring the unlikely appearance of new documentary evidence, unprovable idée fixe has been the opportunity to reexamine Shakespeare's work in light of important scholarly developments. In recent decades historians such as Eamon Duffy, Christopher Haigh, Alexandra Walsham, and the members of the Catholic Record Society have largely dismantled the old view of a reformist Protestant religion providentially triumphing over a moribund and medieval Roman Catholicism. Researches into private archives, manuscripts, local registries, and Continental imprints have revealed a vigorous and effective Catholicism that effectively guided and served its flock. These researches have also highlighted the instabilities and contradictions of early modern religious identity and practice. Such developments have prepared the way for literary critics, who, for a variety of reasons, have contributed to "the turn to religion" in early modern studies. The best of these critics, like those in this volume, especially Hamlin, Jackson, and Beckwith, use documentary evidence to rehistoricize the theology of the period and illuminate its literature.

Two members of the Society of Jesus claim such historical reexamination in this essay. They were probably more shadow than substance for Shakespeare, ghosts known through gossip, rumor, slander, and screed, but they flit behind two of his greatest plays, *King Lear* and *Macbeth*. They are, of course, William Weston and Henry Garnet.

What do we know of the substance behind the shadow? "If I spoke with the tongue of Father Campion," declared a popular saying recorded in a Valladolid archive, "and wrote with the pen of Father Persons, and led the austere life of Father Weston, and yet had not charity, it would avail me nothing."[1] Called to the English Mission from Seville, William Weston (1549/50–1615) sold the horse he was given for the journey, donated the money to the poor, and walked to Paris. In 1584 he began his extraordinary activities of the next two decades, converting souls (among them, Philip Howard), ministering the sacraments, and visiting the imprisoned (including Jasper Heywood with Heywood's nephew, the young John Donne). "At no hour are we certain to survive, but as we make no account of living, the expectation of death only puts an edge on our zeal."[2] He endured long periods of imprisonment (during which he refused a bed and all attempts to buy his freedom), including five years in solitary confinement, along with insomnia, headaches, and failure of sight. Exiled to the Continent in 1603, Weston recovered sufficiently to teach theology, Greek, and Hebrew in the English College of Rome and then returned to Seville, where in 1611 he recorded his English experiences.

To moderns William Weston lives on largely in the diatribes of his enemies: he is the deceitful manipulator excoriated by the appellant priests for supporting the appointment of George Blackwell as archpriest of England. Christopher Bagshaw characterizes him and Henry Garnet as "indeed condemned for their Machiavellian practices against their brethren, being (under pretence of their fatherhoods) so puffed up with pride and arrogancy as it is scarce possible to relate." Weston also stars as the stager of fraudulent exorcisms in Samuel Harsnett's *A Declaration of Egregious Popish Impostures* (1603). There "Ignatius his great grand-childe" produces puppet-play exorcisms to deceive the gullible and win them to His Holiness the Pope and to hell.[3] Lewis Theobald first saw that Harsnett contributed to Shakespeare the devils' names, perhaps the name of Edmund (Weston's pseudonym was Edmunds, in tribute to Campion), and Edgar's dissembled lunacy, possession, and role as Poor Tom (probably from the account of Nicholas Marwood). There are also many verbal echoes, assiduously collected by Kenneth Muir.[4] In addition, Harsnett supplied details for Lear's madness, the storm, the images of a tortured body, and the sexual nausea. Possession, madness, and evil lie at the heart of play. In the *Declaration* Shakespeare read Weston's Latin accounts of the exorcisms, Harsnett's translation (not always accurate), and a consistently shrill, satirical commentary.

Harsnett's thesis that possessions and exorcisms are really theatrical charades has seemed to many to be reflected in Edgar's pretended obsession with the devil, fake exorcism, and phony miracle for his despairing father, Gloucester. After leading his blind father to a nonexistent cliff and allowing him to "fall," Edgar, in a different persona, celebrates the miraculous rescue from the devil:

> As I stood here below, methought his eyes
> Were two full moons; he had a thousand noses,
> Horns whelked and waved like the enridgèd sea.
> It was some fiend. Therefore, thou happy father,
> Think that the clearest gods, who made them honors
> Of men's impossibilities, have preserved thee.
>
> (4.6.69–74)[5]

Unlike Weston, Edgar has won much admiration for his theatrical exorcism, especially by those who read *King Lear* in light of Harsnett's *Declaration*. According to Stephen Greenblatt, Edgar courageously confronts "a free-floating contagious evil more terrible than anything Harsnett would allow." His fiction, F. W. Brownlow declares, makes us wonder what miracles really are; it "saves the old man from suicidal despair by proving more real than his suffering"; it shows that "love is as strong as death." Amy Wolf writes that Shakespeare's portrayal of the compassionate Edgar allows him to "transcend Harsnett's cynicism to explore suffering and the tragic consequences of evil. . . . There are devils in the world of *King Lear*, yet they are not supernatural but human ones, and their exorcism has little to do with superstition, priests, popery, or even religion." And finally, Richard Dutton characterizes Edgar's false exorcism as an "act of love" that shows theater to be "a form of compassionate magic, which helps to hold things together as society falls apart."[6] Shakespeare is no Harsnett, many agree, and the admirable Edgar no William Weston.

Or is he? To be sure, Weston's own account of the exorcisms in his autobiography and in one surviving letter clearly reveals his belief in Satan as an active malignant presence in the world. But early moderns of virtually all religious persuasions shared in this belief. In his prayers and commentaries John Calvin, like many Protestants, continually admonished believers to guard against the wiles and incessant assaults of Satan. Luther famously threw an inkhorn at the devil in the Castle of Wartburg. He saw demons everywhere: "Many devils are in woods, in waters, in wildernesses, and in dark pooly places, ready to hurt and prejudice people; some are also in the thick black clouds, which cause hail, lightnings, and thunderings, and poison the air, the pastures and grounds."[7] In such a devil-haunted world, humans variously fell victim to demonic influences, becoming sinners, witches, and, most seriously, individuals possessed by devils. In such extreme instances Catholics and many Protestants looked to the scriptures, to the many instances where Christ cast out demons (Matt. 12:22–28; Mark 9:14–29; e.g.) and exhorted his followers to do likewise (Matt. 10:1, 8; Mark 6:7; Luke 9:1, 10:17), and thus practiced exorcism. Luther retained the exorcism rite in baptism. The Puritan John Darrell sensationally performed exorcisms and sparked Harsnett's *Declaration*. In 1603 six Church of England clergymen performed an exorcism on one Mary Glover. The following year Archbishop Bancroft issued the following decree: "No minister or ministers shall . . . without licence or direction *(mandatum)* of the Bishop . . . attempt upon any pretence whatsoever either of possession or obsession, by fasting or prayer, to cast out any devil or devils."[8] The official attempt to control the rite through licensure, rather than through denial and prohibition, constitutes powerful de facto affirmation.

In this context, it is all the more remarkable that Bancroft's enemy the archexorcist William Weston at least once portrays exorcism not as a rite of dispossession but as a practical, compassionate response to pastoral urgencies. In a remarkable instance from his autobiography, written not for publication but at the request of the Jesuit general, Weston, like Edgar, confronts a dying, despairing man. The man says, "I am condemned and handed over, for good and all to the devil. I have no hope of forgiveness." Weston counters, "What nonsense! . . . No one, as long as there is life left in him, no one can say he is cut off from God's goodness, or so abandoned by his grace that when he craves and beseeches God's helping mercy it is refused him outright. You know—your faith teaches you—God's mercy is infinite. It is mightier than all our sins and all the wickedness and power of the devil."

The man grows increasingly agitated and claims possession: "Can't you see," he says, "the room is full of devils? Yes, here where we are. They are in every nook and cranny. In the ceiling, in the walls. A thousand. More. Terrible black devils, with fearful faces. They mutter and terrify me. They go on and on. They never stop. They're savagely cruel. They say they'll drag me down to the bottom of hell. I have the cursed creatures inside me. In my bowels. I am full of them. They claw me to pieces. They tear me in all directions—torture me, body and soul, with a thousand torments. It's not as if I were going to be snatched away instantly and smothered in pain. I seem to be hurled into hellfire already. Clearly God has abandoned me. He has barred me for ever from all hope of mercy."

Weston listens patiently without assent or denial and tries a new tack: "Look," he tells the man, "you may be damned. I am not going to ask you to make a confession. But just recollect yourself a moment. Answer briefly. Don't worry yourself at all. Say 'yes' or 'no' to the questions I ask. That's all I want you to do."

Weston goes on to recite the commandments and ask the man to nod if he has sinned against them. After a short while he asks him about the devils. The man replies, "They are quieter now. . . . They don't seem to be raging so much as before." Weston continues calmly until the man reports that the devils have retreated, throwing stones, making faces, and

threatening hideous things. Finally, he makes a full confession and receives absolution. "Are the devils troubling you still?" Weston asks. "No
not at all," the penitent answers, "they have all fled. Not a trace of them
is to be seen, thanks be to God."

The next day Weston brings communion to the man, who is now
resting peacefully, and asks him why he was so troubled. The man reports
that he had fallen into sin and away from the sacraments, especially confession: "I concealed my sins and hid them from my father confessor.
The devil convinced me that I had to seek pardon and help from God,
not through confession, but by penance and austere living. Therefore
I used either to make an insincere confession or no confession at all,
and found myself cast into this anguish of soul and most tormented
state." Weston concludes, "The incident just narrated does show what
strange effects can be produced sometimes by a mind terror-struck at
the consciousness of sin."[9] Weston's account here, his editor Philip Caraman writes, coincides with that in the official biography by Francisco de
Peralta, who relates Weston's own narration of the incident in 1605.[10]

Here Weston demystifies exorcism in a way undreamt of by Harsnett
and by those many who believe that *King Lear*, along with the rest of
early modern drama, substitutes theater for religious ritual. Ministering to
the sinner through the sacrament of penance, Weston does not perform
any part of the exorcism rite—the invocations, adjuration, laying on of
hands, sprinkling with holy water, or touching with relics. Instead he
curtly dismisses the report of demonic activity as hysterical fantasy, the
"strange effects" of a "mind terror-struck." Sounding curiously modern,
Weston actually anticipates by several centuries Sigmund Freud's famous
analysis of Christoph Haizmann, the seventeenth-century painter who
reputedly enjoyed a miraculous rescue from possession and a pact with
the devil. Concluding that Haizmann in reality suffered from frustrated
longing for his father, the doctor explained: "The states of possession
correspond to our neuroses. . . . We merely eliminate the projection of
these mental entities into the external world which the middle ages carried out; instead, we regard them as having arisen in the patient's internal
life, where they have their abode."[11]

The passing resemblance to Freud, of course, puts into sharp relief the more significant differences between the psychologist and the

priest. "Consciousness of sin," not repressed wish, causes the disturbance; confession, not psychoanalysis, is the cure. Weston's story is not really about exorcism at all but about the necessity of auricular confession and the power of the sacrament of penance, two flashpoints of early modern religious dispute. The man begins, in effect, as a Catholic who has succumbed to demonic discrediting of confession: "The devil convinced me that I had to seek pardon and help from God, not through confession, but by penance and austere living. Therefore I used either to make an insincere confession or no confession at all." This devil echoes the many Protestant thinkers who repudiated auricular confession and denied sacramental status to penance. John Calvin, for example, wrote: "We condemn that auricular confession as a thing pestilent in its nature and in many ways injurious to the church and desire to see it abolished." Priests, in his view, being neither vicars nor successors of the apostles, were irrelevant to the private motions of repentance and the divine mercy of forgiveness. Calvin concluded, "Their fiction of the sacrament of penance, therefore, was falsehood and imposture."[12]

Weston's narrative dramatically validates confession and penance against such charges. In his account, as in Peter Canisius's catechism, the sacrament is "excellent and full of comfort," able to purge "the filths of the soul," to transport a man "out of the whirlpool of mortal sin," though "loaden and pestered with many and those very heinous sins."[13] Weston enacts the special role of priests, recently ratified by the Council of Trent, as Christ's "own vicars, as presidents and judges," who "in accordance with the power of the keys . . . may pronounce the sentence of forgiveness or retention of sins."[14] Sinners find solace in auricular confession, just as an annotation to the 1582 Rheims New Testament, quoting St. Cyprian, claims: "[They] confess to God's priests sorrowfully and plainly, opening their conscience, uttering and discharging the burden of their mind, and seeking wholesome medicine for their wounds."[15]

The entire exorcism dispute finally recedes before the exigencies of present suffering and the need for penitential healing and sacramental reconciliation. Ministering patiently to a tormented sinner, Weston tolerates the demonic fantasy; he might well say with Edgar, "Why I do trifle thus with his despair / Is done to cure it" (4.6.33–34). I do not suggest that Weston is modern or postmodern, that he is a model for Edgar in some sort of abstrusely coded shadowplay, that Edgar is a figure of a priest, or even that he is unambivalently good. The story shows the inadequacy of received interpretive models, the limitations of the binary thinking that fuels most religious polemics (both sides). Early modern Catholics could be as shrewd and as skeptical as early modern Protestants. The story reveals also the prejudices of descendant criticism, challenging established views about the Protestant demystification of religion and its echoing in *King Lear*. Most important, it shows William Weston at work: the priest heals a corrosive despair by using the available models, beliefs, and energies of his cultural moment and by deploying the transhistorical power of the sacrament.

Another Jesuit whose reputation as a liar and a fraud has been established by his enemies is Weston's friend and successor as superior, Henry Garnet. Most believe with good reason that the Porter in Shakespeare's *Macbeth* welcomes to hell a Jesuit, probably Henry Garnet, S.J., author of *A Treatise of Equivocation*, who was executed in 1606 for complicity in the Gunpowder Plot: "Faith, here's an equivocator that could swear in both the scales against either scale, who committed treason enough for God's sake, yet could not equivocate to heaven. Oh, come in, equivocator" (2.3.8–11). The Porter may also allude to one of Garnet's aliases (Farmer) in his preceding comment: "Here's a farmer that hanged himself on th'expectation of plenty" (4–5). So saying, the Porter reflects the official contemporary view of Garnet and the Jesuits, and a prevalent modern one.

Once again let us look at the substance behind the shadow.[16] At the Roman College Garnet won praise from the mathematician Christopher Clavius and the theologian Robert Bellarmine. He lectured in Hebrew, metaphysics, and mathematics. In 1586 he went on the dangerous English Mission with his friend Robert Southwell. The arrest of William Weston less than a month after Garnet's arrival left the mission leaderless and Garnet reluctantly became the superior. He then assumed responsibility, in the words of the charter document given to Robert Persons and Edmund Campion in 1580, for preserving and advancing all in the Catholic faith ("conservandi, Christo propitio, et promovendi in fide et religione nostra Catholica omnes") and for reclaiming the lapsed ("reducendi . . . quicunque . . . aberrassent"). All Jesuits on the mission were strictly forbidden to mix themselves in matters of state ("Non se immisceant negotiis statuum"), even to speak against the queen, or to tolerate such speech in others.[17] For twenty years Garnet took all his charges seriously, ministering, writing, dispensing sacraments, evading the authorities, and conscientiously reporting on his troubles and triumphs in a remarkable series of letters, many to the general of the society in Rome, Claudio Aquaviva.

A run through Garnet's letters (many available in the Farm Street archives, Foley's *Records*, and Caraman's biography), published writings, and other extant documents presents quite a different picture of him from that of the damned traitor and equivocator. Regarding the complicated question of treason, I shall notice in passing only the curious choice of the Porter's phrase "treason enough for God's sake" (editors seem unanimous in the pointing). And of course I acknowledge the well-observed irregularities in the trial; Garnet's "threats, admonitions, and warnings" against rebellion in general and the plot in particular, including an attempt to get the pope to forbid Catholics to engage in sedition; and his obligation to keep silence about things revealed under *sigillum confessionis*, the seal of confession.[18] We might also hear the words of the condemned priest himself in a letter to Anne Vaux, April 3, 1606, to be published after his death by her to all the Jesuits: "I sought to hinder it (the plot) more than men can imagine as the pope will tell. It was not my part (as I thought) to disclose it. I have written this day a detestation of that action for the King to see. And I acknowledge myself not to die a victorious martyr but as a penitent thief." Garnet finally judged himself guilty of not revealing his general knowledge of some impending action but not of treason or lying. "For matter of the Pope's authority, of *sigillum confessionis*, of equivocation, I spoke as moderately as I could and as I thought I was bound. If any were scandalized thereat it was not my fault but their own."[19]

Historians continue to contradict the official verdict of treason, but few have examined, let alone questioned, the charge of equivocation and Garnet's claim that if any were scandalized it was their own fault. Equivocation is a verbal species of dissimulation notoriously comprising mental reservation, such that one can licitly, under certain circumstances, answer a question one way verbally and another way mentally. Condemnation of the practice and association of it with Jesuits has been loud and consistent through the centuries. Thomas Morton, who had a long-running debate with Robert Persons on the subject, declared, "This man we see (as if he would drive out Satan by Satan) teacheth by lying how a man may avoid a lie. Yet this is the general doctrine of their school more than heathenish, for among pagans this was a decree of conscience: craft in an oath doth not lessen but strengthen perjury."[20] In the government account of the trial, *A True and Perfect Relation* (London, 1606), the attorney general Edward Coke denounced "perfidious and perjurious equivocating, abetted, allowed, and justified by the Jesuits." He specifically mentioned *A Treatise of Equivocation* "seen and allowed by Garnet."[21] Contrasting Jesuits to those truth tellers who followed Christ to eternal life, Robert Abbot confidently predicted damnation for Garnet and all equivocators: "Atque ita sub Papatu factum est, ut quanquam partim, per crassam nimis inscitiam, partim per idololatrias, & sacrilega in Christum dogmata plerique nonnisi scoriis & paleis & cinere, nec alio quam aere putrido & lethali vescerentur; qui hausto ad profundam faecem Antichristi calice, certissima morte perierunt" (But whoever has served the papacy, as yet some through a dense and excessive ignorance, others through a love of idol worship and sacrilegious doctrine against Christ, for the most they were feeding only on slag, and chaff, and ashes, and on nothing but putrid and deadly air; having drained the cup of the Antichrist to its last dregs, they have died a most certain death).[22] Later Pascal's *Les provinciales* (1656–59), especially letter 9, set the stereotype of the equivocating Jesuit in brilliant satirical prose for all posterity. And David Jardine, who edited the *Treatise* in 1851, called it a "manual of contrivances for deception and justifications of falsehood"; its discovery converted "sympathy for the supposed victims of religious persecution" into "suspicion and dislike of the votaries of a system as inconsistent with morality as with civil government."[23]

This version of history, the Jesuits, and Henry Garnet has long shaped the reception and understanding of Shakespeare's *Macbeth*. In 1747 William Warburton glossed the Porter's equivocator as follows: "Meaning a Jesuit: an order so troublesome to the State in Queen Elizabeth and King James the First's times. The inventors of the execrable doctrine of equivocation." Henry N. Paul viewed the play as a compliment to King James, who triumphed over the Gunpowder Plot and the diabolical traitors, including the equivocator Henry Garnet. Garry Wills refocused Paul's argument in *Witches and Jesuits: Shakespeare's Macbeth* (1995): "The Gunpowder Plot would be suggested in two ways—its menace to the king in Macbeth's regicide, and its failure in the final disposal of traitorous Garnet (safely made the butt of scorn in the Porter scene). 'The equivocations [*sic*] of the fiend' are fearful but containable. The proof is the baffling of the Plot by Garnet's defeat." Wills here well reminds us of Macbeth's revealing declaration at the end of the play: "I pull in resolution, and begin / To doubt th' equivocation of the fiend / That lies like truth" (5.5.42–44). Accordingly, Garnet is a prototype for Macbeth, traitor, equivocator, trafficker with devils. Taking this approach to a kind of culmination, Frank L. Huntley used Coke's rhetoric against Garnet to analyze the structure of Shakespeare's play and to conclude that Macbeth becomes finally "a doctor of Jesuits":

> Early in the play he [Macbeth] is a brave, true, and loyal man. But in embracing the Jesuitical doctrine of equivocation he communes not with God but with the devil, and he violates all three rules for its application: truth, discretion, and justice. "Devilish Macbeth" out-Jesuits Father Garnett by becoming himself "a doctor of Jesuits" (in Sir Edward Coke's formula of arraignment), a doctor of five D's: of "dissimulation" (that is Act I); of "deposing of Princes" (in Act II); of "disposing of kingdoms" (he is crowned in Act III); of "daunting and deterring of subjects" (the murders at Fife in Act IV); and of "destruction" (Act V).[24]

The story of equivocation and the English Jesuits actually begins before Garnet's *Treatise* with Robert Southwell, who advised Anne Bellamy that if "upon her oath she were asked whether she had seen a priest or not, she might lawfully say not, though she had seen one, keeping this meaning in her mind, that she did not see any with intent to betray him." Southwell wrote a pamphlet, now lost, defending such equivocation from the writings of "the Doctors and Fathers of the Church, and agreeing to the policies and proceedings of all ages and in all Christian nations." Tortured and interrogated by Edward Coke in February 1595, he put the attorney general a case: suppose the French should invade and

Her Majesty be hid in a private house, known only to Mr. Attorney, "and that Mr. Attorney's refusal to swear, being hereunto urged, should be a confession of her being in the house." If Mr. Attorney should refuse to swear, he "were neither Her Majesty's good subject nor friend." The chief justice said he would refuse to swear; Coke said that the case was not like and called Southwell a "boy priest." The chief justice went on to declare that the doctrine of equivocation would "supplant all justice"; Southwell responded that in this case refusing to swear was a confession, that the oath needed to be administered by lawful authority, that every oath ought to contain judgment, justice, and truth (quoting Jerome), and that no man was bound to answer every man.[25] Shortly after the trial and Southwell's execution Garnet wrote the *Treatise*, in his words "to defend Father Southwell's assertion, which was much wondered at by Catholics and by heretics."[26]

In 1597 the Jesuit John Gerard suffered imprisonment and torture and during one of the interrogations had to defend Southwell's views on equivocation. "In general equivocation is unlawful save when a person is asked a question, either directly or indirectly, which the questioner has no right to put, and where a straight answer would injure the questioned party." Gerard, like Garnet, adduced the sayings of Christ as precedent, when he said he did not know the day of judgment (Mark 13:32) and when he said he was not going to Jerusalem for the feast of booths (John 7:8–10). Garnet fully expostulated the doctrine with reference to scripture, the church fathers, and English law. Equivocation needs to have "certain fit limitations" and "convenient moderation," he warned, "without the which neither God could be pleased, nor the link and conjunction of human societies, either civil or ecclesiastical and spiritual, could be duly maintained."[27]

Despite the line of righteous condemnation from Coke onward, I don't think many moderns would have a problem with the kind of equivocation the Jesuits defend. Do any of us who read the story of Anne Frank, for example, condemn the neighbors who concealed her in the annex and lied to the SS? My point is not to equate the Elizabethan government with the Third Reich but, *mutatis mutandis*, to identify the casuistic situation the Jesuits addressed. Dissimulation in certain cases, they argued, was justifiable because it observed the duty of self-preservation, the dictates of justice, and the larger law of charity. One might conceal the truth to save the innocent from persecution. In similar circumstances most of us would consider it our duty to lie outright and not even bother with the moral niceties of *oratio mixta* and mental reservation. Accordingly, we might rather accuse Robert Southwell, John Gerard, and Henry Garnet of scrupulosity than of mendacity.

But this would be another kind of anachronistic presumption. Why did these Jesuits, charged with caring for a persecuted flock, themselves hunted, imprisoned, tortured, executed, trouble to articulate a doctrine of equivocation at all?

First of all, they did so because they took seriously church traditions in moral theology, particularly the unconditional prohibition against lying in St. Augustine's *De mendacio* and *Contra mendacium*. As Augustine says, "Cum igitur mentiendo vita aeterna amittatur, nunquam pro cuiusdam temporali vita mentiendum est" (Since, therefore, eternal life is lost by lying, a lie may never be told for the preservation of the temporal life of another).[28] Both surviving manuscript copies of Garnet's treatise are in fact titled *A Treatise against Lying and Fraudulent Dissimulation*, the more familiar title, *A Treatise of Equivocation*, having been both times canceled.[29] Second, they developed a doctrine of equivocation because they had trained long and hard in casuistry, the study of cases, the application of general moral laws to specific circumstances and the determination of relative degrees of fault or sin assignable to transgressions. Now relegated to the limbo of pseudosciences like phrenology and alchemy, casuistry occupied some of the best minds from the later Middle Ages through the seventeenth century. Jesuits in seminary wrestled with questions that ranged from the mundane (Is Mass valid on a portable altar?) to those that took on particular urgency in the English Mission (Could a priest lawfully deny that he was a priest? Could a Catholic ever tell a lie under oath?).[30] Third, Ignatian discipline required a thrice-daily examination of conscience to ensure that one remained focused on salvation and God's will and did not get distracted by inconsequentials like earthly life, liberty, and happiness.[31] For those trained in this discipline, the wearing of disguise and the concealment of faith, the telling of a lie, posed greater potential perils to the soul than Coke, Topcliffe, and the government did to their bodies.

Now that we have reviewed the specific context we can better see the larger picture and make some corrective observations. The doctrine of equivocation (*pace* Warburton) did not originate with the Jesuits. Garnet's arguments draw upon those of Continental theologians, especially the Spanish Augustinian Martin Azpilcueta (Doctor Navarrus) and his discussion of a medieval text, *Commentarius in cap. Humanae Aures* (Rome, 1584). Seen properly, equivocation is a minor kind of religious dissimulation, a major topic at issue among Christians since Paul rebuked Peter in 2 Galatians 11:14 for Judaizing, that is, for obeying Jewish laws at Antioch and wanting Gentile converts to do likewise, thus dissembling their true convictions. Dissimulation is not even a specifically Catholic phenomenon: as Perez Zagorin has observed in a masterful study, *Ways of Lying* (1990), "Dissimulation appears as a central feature of practically all forms of religious dissidence in the early modern era."[32] Jews in Spain and Portugal "converted" to Catholicism but secretly maintained Jewish beliefs and practice; Catholics used the Inquisition to hunt them down, even proceeding against those who had died. Calvin wrote several treatises against the "Nicodemites," Protestant dissimulators in France, Flanders, and elsewhere who hid their faith and conformed outwardly to Catholic rites. Many English Protestants in the reign of Mary I did likewise, including Sir William Cecil, future Catholic persecutor and minister of Elizabeth I, and those many denounced by Wolfgang Musculus in *The Temporysour* (tr. 1555) and by Peter Martyr Vermigli in *A Treatise of the Cohabitation of the Faithful with the Unfaithful* (1555).

This larger perspective on equivocation as a species of religious dissimulation reveals pervasive historical distortion in the case of Henry Garnet. History has branded Garnet as an equivocator and traitor, a prime example of Jesuit perfidy and a corrupt Catholicism; it has extolled so-called reformers, who stood for simple truth against the pope, the Jesuits, and the religion of lies. But Martin Luther goes much further than any Jesuit by actually justifying the lie direct, the *locutio contra mentem*. He cites many of the same scriptural examples—Abraham's lie about Sarah being his sister (Gen. 12:11–13), Jacob's lie about being Esau (Gen. 27), Rahab's concealment of the spies (Josh. 2)—but simply disagrees with Augustine and wastes no time with any theory of equivocation. Luther flatly approves what he calls the "obliging lie," the lie that helps someone and prevents sin: "Therefore it is not proper to call it a lie; for it is rather a virtue and outstanding prudence, by which both the fury of Satan is hindered and the honor, life, and advantages of others are served. For this reason it can be called pious concern for the brethren, or in Paul's language, zeal for piety."[33] Christ himself, Luther claims, used this "obliging lie" when he pretended he would go farther, προσεποιήσατο πορρώτερον πορεύεσθαι (Luke 24:28).[34] And his incarnation, Luther goes on to say, dithyrambically, the clothing of the immortal God in the weak flesh, was itself a kind of lie, a wondrous deception of the devil, who thought "he would kill a man and was himself being killed after being decoyed by Him into a trick. But by God's wonderful counsel the same thing happened to him that is commonly said: 'That cunning might deceive cunning.'"[35]

Addressing the grand historical distortion that had denigrated Catholics as equivocating liars and extolled Protestants as tellers of the plain truth, John Henry Cardinal Newman noted that many English Protestant moralists—Jeremy Taylor, John Milton, William Paley, and Samuel Johnson—had also justified the lie, unequivocally:

> Taylor says: "To tell a lie for charity, to save a man's life, the life of a friend, of a husband, of a prince, of a useful and a public person, hath not only been done at all times, but commended by great and wise and good men. Who would not save his father's life, at the charge of a harmless lie, from persecutors or tyrants?" Again, Milton says: "What man in his senses would deny, that there are those whom we have the best grounds for considering that we ought to deceive— as boys, madmen, the sick, the intoxicated, enemies, men in error, thieves? I would ask, by which of the commandments is a lie forbidden? You will say, by the ninth. If then my lie does not injure my neighbor, certainly it is not forbidden by this commandment." Paley says: "There are falsehoods, which are not lies, that is, which are not criminal." Johnson: "The general rule is, that truth should never be violated; there must, however, be some exceptions. If, for instance, a murderer should ask you which way a man is gone."[36]

At this point we may well observe that the most important kind of dissimulation practiced by early modern Protestants, Jews, and Catholics was not equivocation, with its relatively specialized theory of mental reservation, but outward conformity to mandated religious practices. Church papistry, Catholic attendance at Church of England services, was a widespread phenomenon, as Alexandra Walsham has shown.[37] Since such attendance was enforced with increasingly strict penalties during Elizabeth's reign, many Catholics simply showed up once in a while at state services in order to keep their lands, their families, and their lives. Who could blame them? Thomas Bell, an influential priest in northern England, defended the practice, as did Alban Langdale, chaplain to the Montague, who wrote that "many parishes in England there be where neither the curate nor parishioners are open professors of Protestantism nor known Protestants but dissembling Catholics."[38] Martyrdom was a counsel of perfection, and, to a lesser extent, depending upon where one lived, so was recusancy.

Paris may have been worth a mass for Henry of Navarre but not for Henry Garnet. In his writings he spoke out clearly and consistently against the dissimulation of church papistry. In *An Apology against the Defence of Schism* (1593), Garnet maintained that among the principal virtues pertaining to Christian duty, the first was "an exterior confession of faith."[39] Presence at a service was a sign distinctive that signified conformity, and no Catholic could pretend otherwise. "It is much alike as if a man, hanging up an ivy garland at his door as though he had wine to sell, should answer such as offer to buy wine that, although there be a garland hanged up, yet he had no such meaning as to show that he had wine" (sig. E2). Because schism consisted largely in ceremony, one could not draw a distinction between the "inward act of religion" and the "exterior" (sig. E8v). "If schism be outwardly it must also be inwardly" (sig. G6v). "How odious the name of a prevaricator is . . . a straddler of whose legs you cannot know the right from the left, which helpeth the contrary part and betrayeth his own" (sig. N5). Garnet continued the argument in an appendix to his *A Treatise of Christian Renunciation* (1593). "Neither can that man follow him [Christ] which daily taketh not up his Cross." Every Christian needed to "carry a continual and rooted hatred even to his own life and soul," the one "despised for Christ," the other "afflicted, mortified, and denied from the filthy disorder of secular delights for the love of the same Christ." Going to church signified conformity in schism and false religion, and there could be no equivocation: "Now by a contrary protestation in words to seek to disanull the protestation of the fact, what is it else, but as if a man very expert in the art of lying should in telling two contrary tales with one breath desire to be fully believed in both. But howsoever these absurd protesters persuade themselves yet have they justly received the ordinary reward of liars, not to be believed at all."[40] To encourage Catholics, Garnet advocated prayer, specifically the rosary. He published *The Society of the Rosary* (1596) from his secret press, dedicated to Mary, "rainbow against heretics";[41] he founded rosary sodalities for men and women and translated Pinelli's life of the Virgin.

There is one final irony worth savoring: I have heard tell of a letter surfacing recently in Rome that accuses Garnet, despite his official and published condemnations, of leniency in practice toward church papists.[42] Inconsistency? I truly hope so. For such a letter shows us again Henry Garnet, like William Weston, responding to pastoral urgencies.

Attention to the substances of Catholic figures from the period can unsettle some prejudices and dispel some misconceptions, notably the pervasive English myths of Protestant "Reformation" and all the attendant corollaries. For too long these myths have unhistorically branded Catholicism as a religion of superstition, presided over by evil, equivocating Jesuits. Patient, clear-eyed research in the historical and cultural records abundantly available affords a clearer view. Such research, free from the special pleading that inflects the arguments of both sides, can situate Shakespeare's work more accurately and authentically in his turbulent times and provide a corrective to simplistic, anachronistic, and prejudiced readings. Finally, such research can reveal Jesuits like William Weston and Henry Garnet as they truly were: priests who ministered capably, flexibly, inconsistently, and compassionately to an erring and persecuted flock.

Notes

1. Philip Caraman, introduction to William Weston, *An Autobiography from the Jesuit Underground by William Weston*, ed. and trans. Philip Caraman (New York: Farrar, Straus and Cudahy, 1955), xvi. I draw the account of Weston's life in

this paragraph from Caraman's introduction and Theodor Harmsen, "Weston, William (1549/50–1615)," in *Oxford Dictionary of National Biography*, ed. H. C. G. Matthew and Brian Harrison (Oxford: Oxford University Press, 2004), www.oxforddnb.com. In the Farm Street archives, London, there is a copy of Stonyhurst MS, Anglia, i, no. 28, which contains Weston's handwritten Latin account of some exorcisms.

2. Weston, *Autobiography*, 55.

3. Christopher Bagshaw, *A true relation of the faction begun at Wisbich* (1601), sig. A3. On this controversy, see P. Renold, ed., *The Wisbech Stirs*, CRS 51 (London, 1958); Peter Milward, *Religious Controversies of the Elizabethan Age* (London: Scholar Press, 1977), 116–26. Harsnett's *Declaration* is reprinted in full as Part II of F. W. Brownlow's *Shakespeare, Harsnett, and the Devils of Denham* (Newark: University of Delaware Press, 1993). I quote Harsnett from this edition (259).

4. Lewis Theobald, ed., *The Works of Shakespeare*, 7 vols. (London, 1733), 5:163–64; Kenneth Muir, "Samuel Harsnett and *King Lear*," *Review of English Studies* 2 (1951): 11–21; Kenneth Muir, *Shakespeare's Sources*, vol. 1, *Comedies and Tragedies* (London: Methuen, 1957), 147–61; Kenneth Muir, *The Sources of Shakespeare's Plays* (New Haven: Yale University Press, 1977), 202–6; and Muir's Arden edition of *King Lear* (London: Methuen, 1955), Appendix 7, "Samuel Harsnett and *King Lear*," 253–56.

5. I cite Shakespeare from *The Complete Works*, ed. David Bevington, 5th ed. (New York: Longman, 2004).

6. Stephen Greenblatt, "Shakespeare and the Exorcists," in *Shakespearean Negotiations: The Circulation of Social Energy in Renaissance England* (Berkeley: University of California Press, 1988), 127; Brownlow, *Shakespeare, Harsnett*, 126, 128; Amy Wolf, "Shakespeare and Harsnett: 'Pregnant to Good Pity?'" *Studies in English Literature* 38 (1998): 259, 263; Richard Dutton, "Jonson, Shakespeare, and the Exorcists," *Shakespeare Survey* 58 (2005): 19, 22.

7. Martin Luther, "Of the Devil and His Works," in *The Table Talk of Martin Luther*, trans. William Hazlitt (London: H. G. Bohn, 1877), 247.

8. Quoted in Montague Summers, *The History of Witchcraft and Demonology* (1926; repr., London: Routledge and Kegan Paul, 1973), 230–31.

9. Weston, *Autobiography*, 142-45, 148.

10. Ibid., 147 n.

11. Sigmund Freud, "A Seventeenth-Century Demonological Neurosis," in *Articles on Witchcraft, Magic and Demonology*, ed. Brian P. Levack, vol. 9, *Possession and Exorcism* (New York: Garland, 1992), 28.

12. John Calvin, *Institutes of the Christian Religion*, trans. Henry Beveridge, 2 vols. in 1 (1989; repr., Grand Rapids, MI: William B. Eerdmans, 1994), 1:550, 2:635.

13. Peter Canisius, *A Sum of Christian Doctrine*, 1592, sigs. N3–N4.

14. *Canons and Decrees of the Sacred and Ecumenical Council of Trent*, trans. James Waterworth (London: Dalman, 1848), session 14, ch. 5.

15. New Testament (Rheims, 1582), annotation to John 20:23 (277).

16. I draw the account of Garnet's life here from Philip Caraman's *Henry Garnet, 1555–1606 and the Gunpowder Plot* (New York: Farrar, Straus, 1964), and his *A Study in Friendship: Saint Robert Southwell and Henry Garnet* (St. Louis, MO: Institute of Jesuit Sources, 1995), as well as Thomas M. McCoog, S.J., "Garnett, Henry (1555–1606)," in *Oxford Dictionary of National Biography* (2004). See also Henry Foley, *Records of the English Province of the Society of Jesus*, 7 vols. in 8 (London: Burns and Oates, 1877–83), 4:35–193.

17. Leo Hicks, ed., *Letters and Memorials of Father Robert Persons, S.J.*, CRS 39 (London: J. Whitehead and Son, 1942), 316, 318.

18. Quote from McCoog, "Garnett, Henry." Gratian's *Decretum* (1151) contains the injunction "Deponatur sacerdos qui peccata penitentis publicare praesumit" (secunda pars, dist. VI, c. II) [Let the priest who dares make known the sins of a penitent be deposed]. Canon 21 of the Fourth Lateran Council (1215) confirms the obligation of secrecy, as did medieval English councils, synods, and jurists (see "The Seal of Confession," in *The Catholic Encyclopedia*, www.newadvent.org/cathen/, accessed January 2007). On Garnet's possible involvement in the Gunpowder Plot and on his subsequent reputation, see Thomas M. McCoog, S.J., "Remembering Henry Garnet, S.J.," *Archivum Historicum Societatis Iesu* 75 (2006): 159–88.

19. Foley, *Records*, 4:104.

20. Thomas Morton, *An exact discovery of Romish doctrine* (London, 1605), sig. G2.

21. Edward Coke, *A True and Perfect Relation of the Whole Proceedings against the Late Most Barbarous Traitors* (London, 1606), sigs. H4v–I1.

22. Robert Abbot, *Antilogia adversus Apologium* (London, 1613), sig. K3v.

23. David Jardine, introduction to Henry Garnet, *A Treatise of Equivocation* (London: Longman, Brown, Green, and Longmans, 1851), xix–xx. Defenders of Garnet include Robert Persons, *A treatise tending toward mitigation* (St. Omer, 1607), and Andreas Eudaemon-Ioannes, *Apologia pro Henrico Garneto* (Cologne, 1610). See Peter Milward, *Religious Controversies of the Jacobean Age* (Lincoln: University of Nebraska Press, 1978), 82–89.

24. William Warburton, ed., *The Works of Shakespeare*, 8 vols. (London, 1747), 6:363; Henry N. Paul, *The Royal Play of Macbeth* (New York: Macmillan, 1950); Garry Wills, *Witches and Jesuits: Shakespeare's Macbeth* (New York: Oxford University Press, 1995), 105; Frank L. Huntley, "*Macbeth* and the Background of Jesuitical Equivocation," *PMLA* 79 (1964): 399. A. E. Malloch offered

corrections to Huntley in "Some Notes on Equivocation," *PMLA* 81 (1966): 145–46. Starting with the traditional assumptions, Arthur Kinney offers a more searching reading of equivocation in the play under the subheading "Catholic Lexias" in *Lies Like Truth: Shakespeare, Macbeth, and the Cultural Moment* (Detroit: Wayne State Press, 2001), 230–42. Some commentators have taken a different view of equivocation in *Macbeth*, arguing that it suggests the indeterminacy of language or the illegitimacy of all aspirations to power; see Steven Mullaney, "Lying Like Truth: Riddle, Representation, and Treason in Renaissance England," *English Literary History* 47 (1980): 32–47; William O. Scott, "Macbeth's—and Our—Self-Equivocations," *Shakespeare Quarterly* 37 (1986): 160–74. Richard C. McCoy defies the tradition by arguing that Malcolm's equivocations are a "force for good and a source of grace. Indeed, it is precisely because he equivocates that Malcolm is my hero." "'The Grace of Grace' and Double-Talk in *Macbeth*," *Shakespeare Survey* 57 (2004): 28.

    25. I quote from Pierre Janelle, *Robert Southwell the Writer: A Study in Religious Inspiration* (London: Sheed and Ward, 1935), 81–82. See also Christopher Devlin, *The Life of Robert Southwell, Poet and Martyr* (London: Longmans, 1956), Appendix C, "Equivocation," 333–35; Philip Caraman, ed., *John Gerard: The Autobiography of an Elizabethan* (London: Longmans, 1951), Appendix E, "Father Southwell's Defence of Equivocation," 269–70.

    26. Henry Garnet to Robert Persons, April 22, 1598, quoted in A. E. Malloch, "Father Henry Garnet's Treatise of Equivocation," *Recusant History* 15 (1979): 387.

    27. See Caraman, *John Gerard*, 126–27, 53–54. In the second edition of this work (1956, Appendix F, 281), Caraman published a contemporary account of Gerard's examination on equivocation from the Petyt manuscripts (38/f. 341) in the Inner Temple, dated May 13, 1597, the day after the hearing. The manuscript confirms the accuracy of Gerard's report.

    28. Augustine, *De mendacio* [On Lying], Patrologia Latina, ed. J.-P Migne (Paris, 1886), 40:495; *The Fathers of the Church: A New Translation*, ed. Roy J. Defferari, vol. 16, *Saint Augustine: Treatises on Various Subjects* (New York: Fathers of the Church, 1952) (translation on 67).

    29. Malloch, "Father Henry Garnet's Treatise," n. 22; on the authorship of this work, see A. F. Allison, "The Writings of Fr. Henry Garnet, S. J. (1555–1606)," *Biographical Studies* 1 (1951): 7–21.

    30. See P. J. Holmes, *Elizabethan Casuistry*, CRS 87 (London: CRS, 1981); Camille Wells Slights, *The Casuistical Tradition in Shakespeare, Donne, Herbert, and Milton* (Princeton: Princeton University Press, 1981); Perez Zagorin, *Ways of Lying: Dissimulation, Persecution, and Conformity in Early Modern Europe* (Cambridge, MA: Harvard University Press, 1990), 153–254. See also Jon R. Snyder,

Dissimulation and the Culture of Secrecy in Early Modern Europe (Berkeley: University of California Press, 2009).

31. See *The Spiritual Exercises of Saint Ignatius Loyola*, trans. Anthony Mottola (New York: Doubleday, 1989), 48–53.

32. Zagorin, *Ways of Lying,* 12.

33. Martin Luther, *Lectures on Genesis, Chapters 6–14*, vol. 2 of *Luther's Works*, ed. Jaroslav Pelikan et al. (St. Louis, MO: Fortress Press, 1960), 292.

34. Martin Luther, *Lectures on Genesis, Chapters 15–20*, vol. 3 of *Luther's Works*, ed. Jaroslav Pelikan et al. (St. Louis, MO: Fortress Press, 1968), 327.

35. Martin Luther, *Lectures on Genesis, Chapters 26–30*, vol. 5 of *Luther's Works*, ed. Jaroslav Pelikan et al. (St. Louis, MO: Fortress Press, 1967), 150-51.

36. John Cardinal Henry Newman, *Apologia Pro Vita Sua*, ed. Martin J. Svaglic (Oxford: Clarendon Press, 1967), 244–45.

37. Alexandra Walsham, *Church Papists: Catholicism, Conformity, and Confessional Polemic in Early Modern England* (Woodbridge: Boydell Press, 1993).

38. Alban Langdale, "Reasons Why Catholics May Go to Church" [1580], in *Early Modern Catholicism: An Anthology of Primary Sources*, ed. Robert S. Miola (Oxford: Oxford University Press, 2007), 75.

39. Henry Garnet, *Apology against the Defence of Schism* ([London], 1593), sig. E5; hereafter cited parenthetically in the text.

40. Henry Garnet, *A Treatise of Christian Renunciation* ([London], 1593), sig. A4, sig. K4v.

41. Henry Garnet, *The Society of the Rosary* ([London], 1596), sig. A3v.

42. Thomas McCoog, S.J., pers. comm., January 2007.

Chapter 2

Decorum and the Politics of Ceremony in Shakespeare's *Titus Andronicus*

GARY KUCHAR

Shakespeare's *Titus Andronicus* is an orgy of indecorum. The play unfolds through a series of speeches, actions, and rituals that systematically fail to accommodate rhetorical style to the ethos of speaker, the prejudices of the audience, and the circumstances of the occasion. As Jane Hiles has observed, these failures of decorum are conspicuously structural features of the play. The plot of *Titus Andronicus*, Hiles notes, "turns on a series of rhetorical failures . . . because characters mistake the context in which they are speaking, and it is axiomatic that discourse depends upon context."[1] Although individual characters are certainly responsible for many forms of indiscretion in the play, the causes of indecorum in *Titus* sometimes run deeper than individual oratorical failures; at crucial instances, indecorum is also a function of antagonisms within the contexts themselves. This is especially true in the repeated instances of ritual indecorum, those moments in the play where ceremonial actions break down as a result of, among other things, interruption and violence. To the extent that collective ritual actions articulate forms of social identity, such failures of ceremony appear as symptoms of larger cultural disorder. Such disorder, I would suggest, speaks not only to English perceptions of Rome (ancient or contemporary) but also to the play's own Elizabethan moment, particularly the state's concerns with the politically persuasive power of liturgy.

Viewed in the context of Tudor liturgical politics, the patterns of ceremonial indecorum in *Titus Andronicus* reveal their enormous theatrical power. Such power, at once dramatic, liturgical, and political, stems from the shared Elizabethan knowledge that religious "schism consisted largely in ceremony."[2] In other words, breakdowns in ceremonial coherence in *Titus* expose what is probably the most sensitive pressure point in the entire Elizabethan Settlement, namely the crown's effort to unify the nation through conformity to a state-sanctioned liturgy.

Despite various efforts to identify the play's confessional bias, *Titus*'s religious politics do not reduce to a partisan expression of either conformist, Puritan, or recusant sympathies.[3] Nicholas R. Moschovakis rightly resists such efforts when he contextualizes the play in the general terms of Christian and pagan cultures. According to Moschovakis, "Reflections of Christian culture in *Titus* facilitate an alienation effect, defamiliarizing early modern pieties," while conversely making "the vices of pagans appear all too familiar."[4] If Moschovakis explains how anachronism gets deployed in the play to evoke parallels between pagan and Christian "pieties" that justify violence, I will demonstrate how ceremonial indecorum works to generate a somewhat more subtle and in many respects more uncanny parallel between late Imperial Rome and late Elizabethan England. Through failures in ritual decorum Shakespeare's play discloses the point at which Roman culture is most radically different from itself, the point at which the story Rome tells about itself becomes most profoundly and dangerously incongruous. In this way, *Titus*'s Rome mirrors, albeit in a distortedly hyperbolic form, how Elizabethan liturgical policies threatened to reiterate the social antagonisms they were designed to mitigate. In other words, both Shakespeare's Rome and his England become legibly and self-destructively other to themselves in and around the question of ceremonies. Importantly, failures of ceremonial decorum in *Titus* lead us to read at the level of social antagonism rather than simply at the level of character. Through patterns of ceremonial indecorum, *Titus* encourages us to interpret Roman culture systemically. Such patterns provide us with nothing less than a way to think in genuinely political terms. This, it seems to me, is one of the play's real accomplishments.

To argue that *Titus* is about the politics of ceremony is to suggest, *inter alia*, that it is about how ceremony does or does not negotiate social tensions (between, for example, familial and civic roles) and how it succeeds or fails in establishing key modes of differentiation (most importantly that of Roman versus barbarian). Rather than being a static expression of an existing order, collective rituals, including those in *Titus*, are supposed to at least maintain, at best instantiate, social order.[5] This concern with the socially productive force of ritual renders *Titus* profoundly relevant to Elizabethan religious culture. The play's nightmare vision of a conflicted society whose rituals exacerbate, rather than mitigate, social tensions shows Elizabethan culture its own worst possible image. *Titus*'s Rome gives us a picture of what the Book of Common Prayer seeks to prevent. The play thus offers a distorted image of what might happen should the culture of common prayer again fail in unifying disparate religious and linguistic groups under one, English, rubric. As Sarah Beckwith suggests later in this volume, one of the fundamental goals of the Book of Common Prayer is to "instantiate rather than describe a preexistent 'we.'" But as she goes on to say, "The paths from the 'I' to the 'we' are constantly in the process of interruption and derangement."[6] What *Titus Andronicus* gives us, I am suggesting, is a nightmare vision in which this type of derangement gets, as it were, totally out of hand.

In more precise historical terms, the perverse rites that take place in *Titus* resonate against the backdrop of the Elizabethan state's dangerously fragile justification for liturgical reform prior to the more conceptually rigorous work of Richard Hooker—a justification enshrined most clearly in Cranmer's "Of Ceremonies," which appeared at the end of the 1549 Prayer Book and was placed as a preface to the 1559 version.[7] By viewing *Titus* as an image of the kind of nightmare the Book of Common Prayer sought to prevent, we can see the parallels between *Titus*'s Rome and Elizabeth's England as going beyond Moschovakis's interpretation, in which "Christian" violence is an unjust repetition of pagan tyranny, to something more perspicacious and uncanny: Reformation England is like *Titus*'s Rome to the extent that its ceremonies betray a point of radical self-difference generating pressure that erupts in two forms of violence: literal violence enacted on the body and symbolic violence intended to destroy the honor, identity, or, if you like, soul of the victim.

"Irreligious Piety": Act 1

Michael Neill observes how the opening ceremonies in *Titus* exacerbate social conflict when he remarks that the "rites performed at the [Andronici] tomb, the sacrifice of Alarbus, and the interment of Titus' sons amount both to a symbolic enactment of those traditional Roman values of piety and order for which Titus stands, and an intimation of the latent barbarity by which this civilization will be consumed."[8] What allows Neill to make this observation about the latent contradictions operative in the Andronici ritual is its indecorum of occasion, the fact that the ceremony is an uncomfortable mix of victory procession and funeral march. The indecorum of this ritual becomes a theme rather than an implicit structural feature when Tamora interrupts the Roman rite by identifying the sacrifice of her son Alarbus as an act of "irreligious piety," thereby instigating a pattern of disrupted ceremonies that runs until the play's final scene.

The dramatic power of this opening scene, perhaps testified to by the Peacham drawing, lies in the way it both stages and interrogates the question of ceremonial decorum. At first blush, this interruption of the Roman procession would seem to give us a non-Roman or outsider perspective on the sacrifice that is about to unfold. Yet what Tamora really does in this scene is expose the non-Roman nature of the ritual itself. As Jonathan Bate notes in his Arden edition of the play, ancient "Rome prided itself on not allowing human sacrifice."[9] By the time of the late republic, Romans often distinguished themselves from their barbarous neighbors on the grounds that they did not advocate human sacrifice. Tamora thus gives voice to Plutarch's view of Roman hypocrisy when he asked: "Did they think it impious to sacrifice human beings to the gods, but necessary to sacrifice them to the Spirits [Manes]?"[10] What is at stake in Plutarch's query is much more than simple hypocrisy, presuming hypocrisy is ever simple, for he is calling attention to a point where the articulated difference between Roman and barbarian cultures becomes an unarticulated difference within Roman culture itself. Like Plutarch, Tamora exposes the point where an "unrecurring wound" opens between the ideological image of Rome as the epitome of Western civilization and its lived reality as a brutal imperial power.

What becomes visible in Tamora's cry of "irreligious piety," then, is the point at which official Roman culture fails to recognize its rituals as instances of the very barbarity it defines as other to itself. The implications of this blindness come into view when we consider how Lucius's call for a sacrifice initiates the play's fascination with symbolic as well as literal forms of violence:

> Give us the proudest prisoner of the Goths,
> That we may hew his limbs and on a pile
> *Ad manes fratrum* sacrifice his flesh
> Before this earthly prison of their bones,
> That so the shadows be not unappeased,
> Nor we disturbed with prodigies on earth.
> (1.1.99–104)

Lucius's call to sacrifice is disturbing not just because of the literal violence it promises to do to the body of Alarbus but also because of the way it shockingly performs the very symbolic violence it is designed to prevent. Though Lucius seeks to appease the spirits of the dead as a way to ensure the smooth running of Roman life, his sacrifice has the exact opposite effect. This gap between the ritual's intentions and its actual results is immediately visible in the contradiction between the rite's violent form and its ostensibly unifying content. The irony of Lucius's call to sacrifice is that the disjunctions between the bloody medium of the rite and its pacifying message call attention to the disjunctions unfolding in act 1, such as the succession crisis between Bassanius and Saturninus, the generational conflict between Titus and his sons, and the personal conflict Titus experiences in his opposing roles of father and general. Although the act of killing Alarbus is ostensibly an expression of power and victory, it is implicitly legible as a sign of Rome's internal fractures. As a palpably indecorous ritual in which form contradicts content, the sacrifice of Alarbus is a symptom not just of Rome's moral and spiritual decline but of the fact that the Romans in power do not yet recognize themselves as being in a state of decline.

When Tamora identifies Lucius's call to sacrifice as an act of "irreligious piety," she identifies the place within Roman culture where it fails to render itself fully coherent to itself. This diagnostic gesture is both dramatically powerful and politically topical insofar as it echoes, even as it is distinct from, similar gestures in Elizabethan culture. One such example occurs in a passage from William Allen's 1582 work of Catholic apology *A Briefe Historie of the Glorious Martyrdom of XII Reverend Priests.* Decrying the English state's use of torture against missionary priests and their recusant supporters, Cardinal Allen responds to an Elizabethan official's motion that a group of "Priests last comitted to the Tower might be sent to *Bride-wel* to be whipt" with a vocative very similar to Tamora's: "ô prophane irreligious and malicious Athiest."[11] Allen's accusation that English authorities can torture priests because they are profanely absent of religious sentiment is similar to Tamora's cry of "irreligious piety." Yet there is a subtle and crucial difference here. While Allen accuses Protestant authorities of being areligious, Tamora accuses the Romans of false consciousness. In doing so, Tamora follows Plutarch in seeing human sacrifice as a misguided form of religious action. Allen, on the other hand, situates the torturers and executors of priests as utterly alien to the sacred sphere. So where Tamora's cry interprets Alarbus as a victim of contingent violence masquerading as religious ritual, Allen's lamentation interprets his Catholic brothers as victims of an atheistical state. The difference here is that Tamora sees Alarbus not as a martyr but as a victim of Rome's false consciousness about its own religious rites, whereas Allen, of course, is writing a martyrology. This ostensibly subtle difference is crucial because it is one example of how Shakespeare's play challenges viewers to follow Plutarch in demystifying such ritualized violence. Rather than interpreting some instances of religiously mediated violence as legitimate and others as illegitimate, the play challenges readers to recognize Lucius's actions as symptomatic of a broader social malaise—a challenge made all the more ambiguous, though by no means inoperative, given that it is initiated by the queen of the Goths.

What is crucial about the play's opening rituals is not just that they generate an alienation effect by getting an English audience to see its culture's violence as being like ancient or contemporary Roman violence, as Moschovakis argues; even more uncannily, these rituals disclose how religious violence is a symptomatic manifestation of unacknowledged self-difference and thus a sign of false consciousness. The parallels between Roman and English self-difference come into focus when we consider how the contradictions apparent in Alarbus's torture and sacrifice parallel the contradictions that Elizabeth Hanson has noted with regard to the use of torture by English authorities in "the relatively short period [of] the last half of the sixteenth century." According to Hanson, the use of torture was an "aberration in English juridical practice . . . a departure from a legal tradition that abhorred and ridiculed the highly organized practice of judicial torture on the Continent."[12] Thus just as the Romans practiced a form of ritualized violence that they identified as characteristic of the barbarian other, so Tudor authorities practiced a form of torture that English law had long identified with the inhuman practices of the Inquisition. The cultural contradictions rendered grotesquely visible in Alarbus's sacrifice would thus appear strangely familiar to an English audience, who, like the ancient Romans, differentiated themselves from others on the grounds that they did not use a form of violence that they, at that very moment, had begun using. Tamora's diagnosis of Lucius's call for ritual sacrifice exposes the point at which Rome is unknown to itself. By making this self-difference visible to an audience, Shakespeare allowed his viewers to turn the analysis onto themselves, recognizing how Elizabethan culture perpetuated religious violence through the same kind of false consciousness as their Roman forebears. What the play's opening allows us to see, then, is that the conditions for catastrophic, culture-extinguishing violence occur when articulated differences between us and them pass into unarticulated differences within us.

Decorum and the Prayer Book

As Tamora's cry of "O irreligious piety" suggests, the diagnosis of late Roman/Elizabethan culture unfolds in the opening act through competing notions of decorum. While Tamora's accusation of impiety indecorously interrupts a sacred rite, it simultaneously exposes the impropriety of such a ritual according to Roman conventions. Tamora thus commits an act of putative impropriety in the very process of exposing the more substantial indecorum of sacrificing Alarbus. What we are presented with in the first scene, then, is a conflict between competing notions of ceremonial decorum and the ethical implications attendant upon each. The question of ceremonial propriety that Tamora raises in the opening to *Titus* would be familiar to virtually all early modern playgoers from, if nothing else, Thomas Cranmer's "Of Ceremonies, Why Some Be Abolished and Some Retained" in the Prayer Book of the period. This well-crafted if conceptually and contextually fraught essay strives to instantiate exactly the liturgical order lacking in the Rome of *Titus Andronicus*. But as the so-called Prayer Book Rebellion in Devon and Cornwall during the reign of Edward VI (1549) would seem to suggest, such efforts inspired as well as quelled political resistance. Beginning one day after the 1549 Prayer Book services were put into use, the Devon rebellion saw an army of several thousand lay siege to Exeter for reasons seeming to do more with liturgy than economics.[13] Demanding the restoration of the old ways, the rebels compared the new Communion Service to a "Christmas Game."[14] Later in the period, in 1572, members occupying the opposite side of the religious spectrum published an attack on the more conservative Elizabethan Prayer Book. The *Admonition to the Parliament* became an immediate best seller, with its colorful critique of the Prayer Book as having been "culled and picked out of that popish dunghill, the portuise and mass-book, full of all abominations."[15] When considered in combination with the Prayer Book's own internal tensions, such events reveal how "Of Ceremonies" threatened to exacerbate the very conflicts it was designed to address. In part, this may be because the idea of the golden mean shaping "Of Ceremonies" and helping underpin the entire Elizabethan Settlement was, as even Richard Hooker would later admit, a very fragile, because potentially tautological, claim to discretion.[16]

Cranmer faced two key and, in the long run, apparently irresolvable problems in "Of Ceremonies."[17] The first was an essentially political dilemma: he had to negotiate between precisian and papist extremes that existed not just on the nonconforming margins of English culture but within the church itself. That ministers could secretly and sometimes even openly identify themselves with either of the two extremes remained true throughout Edward's and Elizabeth's reigns (to say nothing of Mary's), producing an ecclesiastical body that was always at risk of deformation.[18] The second problem was a more conceptual and less well-recognized dilemma arising from the intractable material Cranmer inherited: the archbishop had to instantiate a new model of liturgical order on the basis of a principle of decorum whose authority and clarity presupposed an agreed-upon preexisting order. In other words, Cranmer had to generate the edifying order to which his claim of decorum would appeal. To be sure, this required no small rhetorical feat and almost inevitably ran the risk of generating at least some opposition. In light of this highly fraught political and conceptual context, Cranmer offers what G. J. Cuming refers to as "the first tentative statement of the Anglican *via media*" and what Diarmaid MacCulloch surmises was a "rather hastily tacked on [addition to the 1549 Prayer Book] . . . probably reflecting last-minute jitters about what conclusions might be drawn from the liturgical possibilities still on offer."[19]

One of the ways Cranmer negotiates between religious extremes in the essay is through a careful finessing of the principle of adiaphora. The idea that some religious matters are indifferent to salvation allows Cranmer to defend against papist conservatism and precisian iconoclasm at one and the same time. One key formulation runs as follows: "Although the keeping or omitting of a ceremony in itself considered is but a small thing, yet the willful and contemptuous transgression and breaking of a common order and discipline is no small offense before God."[20] As Evelyn B. Tribble has observed, such formulations reveal "the fundamentally divided character of Tudor thinking about ceremonies" as "ceremonies simultaneously signify everything and nothing."[21] Because "Of Ceremonies" deals with rituals that are neither commanded nor forbidden by scripture, the question concerning them could begin a slide down the proverbial slippery slope toward relativism and liturgical incoherence. The chapter's opening salvo implicitly acknowledges the potentially corrosive effect of relativism implicit in all problems of adiaphora, even as it seeks to contain this threat by recourse to the concept of "discretion," perhaps the most important Elizabethan term for the capacity to express and discern decorum: "Of such ceremonies as be used in the Church and have had their beginning by the institution of man, some at the first were of godly intent and purpose devised and yet at length turned to vanity and superstition, some entered into the Church by undiscreet devotion and such a zeal as was without knowledge" (18).

Because indecorum and indiscretion are the causes of irreligion, decorum and discretion are the church's natural solutions to schism. Building on two of the thirteen articles composed in 1538, Cranmer suggests that the very thing occasioning the Book of Common Prayer is the indecorous "excess and multitude" of ceremonies that have "so increased in these latter days that the burden of them was intolerable" (19).[22] Decorum and discretion thus bear enormous conceptual weight in the essay, implying, at once, aesthetic, ethical, political, social, and spiritual meanings. The dense combination of meanings at work in these key Ciceronian words is bewilderingly complex. Hence John Donne's satirical remark in *The First Anniversary* that "Wicked is not much worse than indiscreet."[23] Whatever else Cranmer's essay is, it constitutes a careful attempt to make these conceptually packed and inherently elusive concepts do his bidding. By fashioning them to his own ends, he will instantiate the conditions of decorum upon which his appeal to discretion will rest, thereby redefining the very meaning of English worship and thus of England itself.

Cranmer does this by basing his case on scripture, specifically 1 Corinthians 14:40. Seeking to both contain and authorize the impulse to liturgical reformation, Cranmer alludes to what, in his hands, appears to be one of St. Paul's most Ciceronian moments: "Let all things be done among you, Saith Saint Paul, in a seemly and due order. The appointment of the which order pertaineth not to private men, therefore no man ought to take in hand nor presume to appoint or alter any public or common order in Christ's Church, except he be lawfully called and authorized thereunto" (18). The conspicuous shuffling in this passage between the desire to institute change and the need to contain the desire for change is characteristic of the essay as a whole. By characterizing their opponents as extremists, English Protestant authorities from Cranmer to Whitgift forged a via media in which the golden mean stood as a cure for the liturgical pathologies besetting the state. "Of Ceremonies" presents such pathologies as lying at the root of England's need for reformation:

> in this our time the minds of men are so diverse that some think it a great matter of conscience to depart from a piece of the least of their ceremonies, they be so addicted to their old customs, and again on the other side, some be so newfangled that they would innovate all thing, and so do despise the old, that nothing can like them but that is new, it was thought expedient not so much to have respect how to please and satisfy either of these parties, as how to please God and profit them both. And yet lest any man should be offended whom good reason might satisfy, here be certain causes why some of the accustomed ceremonies be put away and some retained and kept still. (19)

Rather than obscuring the mutually antagonistic audiences that his essay must confront, Cranmer rhetorically exploits the differences among those he is addressing. His strategy here is to delegitimize the extremes as consisting of essentially two unreasonable parties, both of which don't know what is good for them as far as liturgy is concerned. This is not an especially subtle form of coercion. If such a maneuver is designed to persuade those who might be inclined to disagree, it does so in a way that nonetheless risks hardening the positions of those who are more firmly committed to alternative traditions. Witness the Devon and Cornwall rebellion. Yet, given his aims, what choices did Cranmer have? Facing mutually antagonistic audiences, his claim to decorum provided as good a way as any of constructing an audience that was willing to identify with the forms of discretion being fashioned in the essay and in the Prayer Book as a whole. His wager, surely a pretty good one, was that enough English souls would conform to the models of discretion being outlined as to render nonconforming extremists perceptible as spiritually indecorous and thus politically abhorrent.

Although the Prayer Book strategy worked reasonably well for some time, in hindsight it is difficult to disagree with Timothy Rosendale's shrewd assessment of Cranmer's efforts: "The Book of Common Prayer proved, in its efforts to stabilize conflict into dialectical ambiguity, tragically unable fully to contain the conflicting energies it sought to synthesize."[24] According to Rosendale, the book mediates religious conflict through dialectical ambiguity, especially the ambiguity it generates between individual conscience and the prerogatives of state authority. The English Reformation, he argues, "was at once an unprecedented extension of state power over its subjects and an unprecedented validation of individual authority over against that power. . . . [The Book of Common Prayer] discursively constructs a Christian nation characterized centrally by order even as it elevates individual discretion over that order."[25] Therein lies the productive and yet potentially debilitating tension between state decorum and individual discretion fostered by the Prayer Book. The book's strategy is fragile precisely because it empowers resistance to the notions of decorum it seeks to instantiate. Insofar as early modern Christians appear to have not generally shared Sir Thomas Browne's self-professed capacity to adapt to alternative styles of devotion, such a strategy remains vulnerable to changing religio-political circumstances.[26] Thus the ire that radical Protestants expressed in the *Admonition to the Parliament*. For the writers of this widely read critique of the Prayer Book, Cranmer is guilty of indecorum in the very effort to instantiate the terms by which judgments about decorum can be made. The potential for circular arguments and attendant violence implicit here should be evident; after all, what is at issue is a complexly imbricated set of historical, theological, and aesthetic materials, judgments, and practices. Cranmer negotiated such intractable material by deftly deploying concepts he inherited and had little choice but to use in the pursuit of controlling national forms of worship. However you look at it, throughout the latter sixteenth century, the Elizabethan Settlement rested on the insecure foundation of Prayer Book decorum. It is from this perspective that I am suggesting we view the repeated instances of indecorum in *Titus*, for the theatrical power that such repetitions possess lies in the way they hit upon an especially vulnerable cultural pressure point.

Given the enormous weight borne by the concept of decorum in the Elizabethan Settlement, it is little wonder that Shakespeare was sensitive to it. As David Hillman has argued, Shakespeare was particularly alert to "the potential of the word 'discretion' to do little more than explain things away."[27] In early modern England, as in *Titus*, competing notions of decorum threatened to preclude meaningful dialogue, precipitating rather than mitigating conflict. The volatility of decorum and discretion as concepts becomes especially visible when rhetoricians try to define the precise relationship between decorum and ethical behavior, between discretion as a capacity for felicitous style and discretion as a capacity for graceful action. In *De officiis*, for example, Cicero risks circularity when he tries to theorize the moral dimensions of decorum: "Such is its essential nature, that it is inseparable from moral goodness; for what is proper is morally right, and what is morally right is proper. The nature of the difference between morality and propriety can be more easily felt than expressed. For whatever propriety may be, it is manifested only when there is a pre-existing moral rectitude."[28] George Puttenham re-states the crux of the problem when he observes, "But herein resteth the difficultie, to know what this good grace [decorum] is, and wherein it consisteth, for peraduenture it be easier to conceaue then to expresse."[29] There is something about the principle of decorum that makes it, para-doxically, rely upon both the absolute singularity of a particular speech act and the diffuse generality of agreed-upon rules of etiquette. As a result, you may know an instance of propriety when you see it but you can't define it in the abstract. Needless to say, it is inherently difficult (if virtually unavoidable) to compose laws and unify nations upon such elusive concepts.

The Elizabethan rhetorician John Hoskyns identifies the sheer gen-erality of the problem when he declares: "Let Discrecõn bee the great-est & generall figure of figures."[30] While the fuzziness of decorum as a concept leads to near-circular thinking in Cicero, it leads to stark and widely acknowledged imprecision in Puttenham.[31] "Of Ceremonies" both depends on and remains susceptible to the kinds of slippages inher-ent to decorum. On the one hand, ritual propriety rests upon a subjective human judgment and is thus indifferent to salvation; yet on the other hand it is said to be a way of expressing holiness through an imitation of the true order of God's will, thereby manifesting what in Ciceronian terms is an underlying moral structure. This tension between the subjec-tive and objective polarities of decorum as a concept helps ground Cran-mer's claim to ceremonial authority even as it risks making the problem of liturgical propriety intractable, as it appears to have been.

"Of Ceremonies" ultimately finesses the problem of decorum through Erastianism, specifically the principle that nations have the authority to define their own liturgical traditions: "In these our doings, we condemn no other nations, nor prescribe anything but to our own people only. For we think it convenient that every country should use such ceremonies as they shall think best to the setting forth of God's honor or glory and to the reducing of the people to a most perfect and godly living, without error or superstition. And that they should put away other things which from time to time they perceive to be most abused, as in men's ordinances it often chanceth diversely in diverse countries" (20–21). By containing the limits of contingency to national borders, Cranmer tries to overcome centuries of Catholic authority without playing into precisian hands. This highly fraught maneuver means that in the very gesture of limiting the play of contingency he calls attention to the arbitrary nature of the nation as the border separating realms of religious decorum—a nation, we must remember, that was still in the process of being meaningfully defined. In any case, Cranmer's essay more or less admits what Shakespeare's *Titus* corroborates: that the really sticky problem is not foreign states so much as the parties within the state who do not adhere to accepted rules of discretion.

The fragility of the Elizabethan Settlement is even more profound when we recall that the English Church was but one of many ecclesiastical bodies to lay claim to the authority of decorum through the application of the via media. Lutheran churches as well as nonconforming groups within England used the same rhetoric of the golden mean to authorize themselves throughout the late sixteenth and seventeenth centuries, producing a constant shifting of extremes.[32] The overall result of the religious application of the rhetoric of decorum was an entrenching of the very differences such rhetoric was employed to address.

As I have alluded, this entrenching of conflict through the rhetoric of decorum was evinced in precisian attacks on the church's liturgical reforms. Attacks from the more evangelical wing of the church and from nonconforming Protestants often exposed the fragility of its claims to authority on the grounds of decorum. John Field's 1572 manifesto "A View of Popish Abuses," for example, expresses disgust at the English Church's apparently tautological authorization of its reforms, asserting that the claim to decorum is an incoherent misuse of political power rather than an expression of genuine spiritual authority. Participating in the controversy over priestly vestments, Field complains that "as for the apparel, though we have been long borne in hand, and yet are, that it is for order and decency commanded, yet we know and have proved that there is neither order nor comeliness nor obedience in using it. There is no order in it, but confusion; no comeliness, but deformity; no obedience but disobedience, both against God and the Prince."[33] For Field, the Book of Common Prayer exacerbates rather than annuls the indecorous "excess" that the book claims for its own exigency. Earlier in the same treatise, Field makes a similar point, asserting, "In all their order of service there is no edification, according to the rule of the Apostle, but confusion. They toss the Psalms in most places like tennis balls."[34] Such charges of indecorum cut to the quick of the church's claim to authority and to its attempt to identify itself on the basis of a ceremonial middle ground between papist and precisian extremes. Thus when the author of the Marprelate tracts confesses that he "cannot keepe decorum personae" when responding to Bishop Bridges' defense of the church, he is implying that decorum cannot, in principle, be kept when responding to an indecorous text and an indecorous liturgical program.[35] The result is an orgy of religious invective in which Marprelate presents his text as having been infected or contaminated by the disorder of Bridges' text. Like Tamora, Marprelate must engage in an act of indecorum to expose what he sees as a worse form of it. What is finally revealed by such polemical exchanges is that religious conflicts in Elizabethan England, like the opening ceremonies of *Titus Andronicus*, are fought in the language of Ciceronian decorum—the language of discretion, edification, and order. By paying further attention to ceremonial indecorum in acts 1 and 5 of *Titus*, we can better grasp the play's theatrical force, its political topicality, and its anti-Ciceronian ethical vision.

Of Triumphs and Funerals: Act 1 Redux

The careful depiction of ceremonial indecorum in *Titus* is first staged through a martial triumph. On the face of it, the scene is designed to be a spectacular example of a military triumph *all'antica*, which Anthony Miller describes this way: "In ancient Rome, a triumph was the procession of a victorious consul from the Campus Martius, around one or more of the Circuses, through the Forum, where an encomiastic oration might be delivered, to the temple of Jupiter Capitolinus, where the consul offered [generally nonhuman] sacrifices."[36] Shakespeare appears to go out of his way to indicate that Titus's procession is not an *ovanti* or minor triumph, even though such a triumph would appear to be appropriate given the number of losses Titus says he has experienced. In an *ovanti*, which is usually celebrated after a battle where there have been a substantial number of Roman losses, the leader of the triumph wears a crown of myrtle and enters on foot.[37] Titus, however, refers to his laurel crown, suggesting (however an actor may have entered) that greater pomp is intended than in a traditional *ovanti*. Establishing the full triumphalist status of Titus's entry is important because such martial splendor conflicts with the funereal qualities of the procession. Titus enters as both victorious general and grief-stricken father. This awkward combination of roles is expressed ceremonially by having the Roman burial rites follow directly upon and even overlap with the martial triumph.

The incongruity of Titus's two roles is signaled in his opening salutation: "Hail, Rome, victorious in thy mourning weeds!" (1.1.73). The speech thus begins by calling attention to the contradictory nature of both occasion and speaker. The incongruity of Titus's roles as heroic public general and grief-stricken private patriarch is further suggested by an inadvertently indecorous mercantile analogy:

Lo, as the bark that hath discharged his freight
Returns with precious lading to the bay
From whence at first she weighed her anchorage,
Cometh Andronicus, bound with laurel boughs.
(1.1.74–77)

As Bate's note indicates, Titus's figure means that just as "the boat has picked up valuable fresh cargo in return for what was discharged, so Titus has gained a victor's headgear (*laurel* boughs . . .) in return for his deeds."[38] Yet the "precious lading" of Titus's figure also seems to inadvertently connect up with the bodies of his dead sons, which are the more visible "freight" on stage during the speech. In this way, the speech initiates a series of dramatic ironies in which there is an indecorous gap between what Titus intends to say and what we hear him as actually saying.

Such irony is audible, for example, when Titus compares himself to Priam, inadvertently opening up a proleptic dimension to the unfolding ritual: "Romans, of five-and-twenty valiant sons, / Half of the number that King Priam had, / Behold the poor remains, alive and dead" (1.1.82–84). This inadvertently proleptic allusion to a patriarch who suffered the destruction of his kingdom initiates the burial rites that are to follow, thereby shifting the martial triumph into something that would look to an English audience like a Rogationtide procession or an aristocratic funeral, or both at the same time. Thus just as Titus's role as speaker oscillates between victorious general and grieving father, both of which are mediated by his role as quasi-priest, so the occasion shifts from victory march to deferred funeral procession, thereby foreclosing any hope of a stable decorum of subject. This absence of decorum signals that the loss of social cohesion haunting Rome is implicit within and even exacerbated by the very ceremony that should signify its coherence. For example, where traditional rogation processions functioned as "rituals of demarcation, 'beating the bounds' of the community, defining its identity over against that of neighbouring parishes, and symbolizing its own unity in faith and charity," Titus's procession expresses the absence of boundaries in Rome as it mixes the living with the dead, Roman with barbarian, and pagan with Christian practices.[39] This uncouth mixing of the living and the dead in his address to his sons may have appeared to an Elizabethan audience as a grotesquely literal version of the dignified expression in the Anglican Order for the Burial of the Dead: "In the midst of life we be in death" (309). A feeling of strange familiarity might also have been inspired by the high Roman style of the scene in its resembling of post-Reformation aristocratic funerals that owed more "to the rituals of antiquarian feudalism than . . . those of Christianity."[40] Thus while Titus's pagan ostentation would simultaneously appear foreign and familiar, Roman and English, the overall effect of the scene would be exactly the kind of ceremonial confusion that Field accused the Book of Common Prayer as promulgating.

The mixing of Christian and pagan practices degenerates even further as the rite devolves into what Barbara L. Parker identifies as a parody of Catholic suffrages. Titus's allusion to the propitiatory nature of his ceremony creates an implied analogy between Styx and purgatory as he interrupts himself, asking: "Titus, unkind and careless of thine own, / Why suffer'st thou thy sons unburied yet / To hover on the dreadful shore of Styx?" (1.1.89–91).[41] I would add to Parker's analysis that the association between Catholic and pagan belief in the propitiatory function of prayers for the dead is further signaled by the way Titus echoes Deiphobe's warning to Aeneas in book 6 of *The Aeneid*:

> Slow, are you, in your vows and prayers?
> Trojan Aeneas, are you slow? Be quick,
> The great mouths of the god's house [to the underworld] . . .
> Will never open till you pray.[42]

Here again, allusion implies an element of dramatic irony, as Titus's identifications with Priam and Aeneas betray a degree of confusion about what role he is playing and where it is going. For while Aeneas must pray to open the gate to the underworld, Titus must pray to ensure that the grave into which his sons will be buried will remain shut. Yet his prayers, of course, ultimately fail as he descends into a psychological underworld when several more of his sons are committed to the grave.

It is Lucius, however, who announces the apotropaic dimension of Roman ceremony most clearly when he demands Alarbus's sacrifice "Ad manes fratrum" (1.101). As we have already seen, Lucius's call for a human sacrifice exemplifies how ceremonial rhetoric in the play is structured primarily by dramatic irony, as this sacrificial gesture will be the very cause of Roman disturbance. What is worth further consideration, though, is the way that the emergence of Latin at this crucial ceremonial moment reiterates the point at which Roman culture becomes most radically other to itself. The Latin tag *Ad manes fratrum* sticks out like a foreign body in the speech; it intrudes into the ritual at the very same time that it demarcates the most authentically Roman moment in the play thus far. In this respect, the shift from English to Latin works to demarcate the divisions internal to Roman society itself, rather than separating civilized

Roman from barbaric Goth. It is precisely this internal division *within* Roman culture that gets performed in the play's opening ceremonies and that occasions the ensuing violence.

The overall effect of this indecorum is that the ceremonies of act 1 not only exacerbate the absence of boundaries in Rome but also fail to express anything like a genuine feeling of loss. Indeed, one of the recurring themes of the play is that ceremony does more to repress than it does to alleviate grief. This feature of ceremony as a way of denying loss occurs in Titus's forced description of his tears as tears of joy: "[so] Cometh Andronicus, bound with laurel boughs, / To resalute his country with his tears, / Tears of true joy for his return to Rome" (1.1.77–79). Instead of clearly expressing grief, the ceremony aspires to the kind of triumphalist euphoria that psychoanalysts associate with the state of manic mourning. In a state of mania, the griever suffers a form of melancholia where the affect of grief is disavowed in favor of a temporary feeling of euphoria. Rome's ceremonially sanctioned denial of personal and collective grief helps create the psychological and sociopolitical conditions for catastrophic violence. Like many Elizabethan revenge tragedies, the play warns that repressed mourning breeds conflict. And insofar as Roman ceremony does more to further than to annul conflict, it appears uncannily similar to Elizabethan England, in which real tensions are openly legible within the very documents designed to annul conflict over ceremony.[43]

The failure of ceremony both to alleviate grief and to do the work of differentiation is further exacerbated by the role of interruption. When Titus interrupts himself by pausing to ask, "Titus, unkind and careless of thine own, / Why suffer'st thou thy sons unburied yet / To hover on the dreadful shore of Styx?" (1.1.89–91), he initiates a pattern of disrupted ceremonies that is repeated by Tamora and that continues until the final scene, where Young Lucius's mourning rites are disrupted by an unnamed Roman. Anxiety about ceremonial interruption was of serious concern for Elizabethan authorities, so much so that the 1559 Act of Uniformity stipulated a penalty of one hundred marks for a first offense (8).[44] While the interruption of a religious ceremony was a crime in Elizabethan England, civic ceremonies often incorporated interruption as part of their theatrical charm. As Ann Hurley has shown,

"Interruption as a feature of [Elizabethan] social ritual in both life and art is so common that it, paradoxically, needs to be pointed out."[45] Titus's self-interruption, or what Puttenham would call aposiopesis, thus has the effect of signaling a confusion between civic and sacred rites. While an Elizabethan audience would generally view interruption as consonant with the decorum of a civic ritual, as in the example of Richard II's interruption of the joust between Bolingbroke and Mowbray, they would almost certainly see it as an improper violation of religious ceremony. In this respect, Titus's aposiopesis does more than simply show that in ancient Rome distinctions between civic and religious ceremonies were not clearly defined; it reiterates the very confusion that Puritan-minded critics accused the Anglican Church of promulgating with regard to funeral ceremonies. Many critics, such as John Knox, insisted that funerals were a civic rather than an ecclesiastical office.[46] Such critics viewed the very tradition of funeral sermons as being "put in the place of trentalles, whereout spring many abuses."[47] Others, such as John Field, felt that the 1559 Anglican Burial Order remained too popish in its use of prayers and ministerial mediation. Field thus complains of the rite's "strange mourning . . . whereby prayer for the dead is maintained."[48] By behaving as though the ceremony were simultaneously civic and ecclesiastical, Titus expresses exactly the confusion such Puritan critics felt in the wake of the liturgical controversies raging in the period. So what Barbara L. Parker identifies as an unequivocal parody of Catholic suffrages in act 1 could just as easily have been seen by Puritan playgoers as a parody of the Elizabethan Prayer Book.

This confusion over the ritual status of funeral ceremonies is further expressed when Titus addresses the tomb. At this particular moment, Titus appears very much like a distorted version of a Catholic priest engaging in a funeral rite or an Anglican minister as viewed through the eyes of a precisian: "O sacred receptacle of my joys, / Sweet cell of virtue and nobility, / How many sons hast thou in store" (1.1.95–97). Rather than clearly delineating the symbolic relations between the living and the dead, as such ceremonies are traditionally designed to do, this prosopopoeia furthers their confusion. Such confusion is first intimated when Titus describes the tomb as his son's "latest home," meaning not only last but also, inadvertently, most recent. The same dramatic irony occurs during the burial rites, when Titus says: "Make this his latest farewell to their souls" (1.1.152). Even more provocatively, his description of the tomb encapsulates the impossibility of achieving a decorum of occasion in this context as Titus shifts his description from a sacred to a profane register, from a metaphor in which the tomb is like a monastic room or "sweet cell" to a storage space or "store."[49] The latter term furthers the double meaning of *latest*, as it implies "How many more sons are to arrive?" as well as "How many are there already?" This ostensibly innocent shift in metaphorical vehicles encapsulates the larger cultural shift from sacred to profane announced in act 5 by an unnamed Goth who finds Aaron's baby in a "ruinous monastery," "a wasted building" (5.1.21, 23). By alluding to Henry VIII's dissolution of the monasteries, this Goth identifies the confusion between sacred and profane orders of meaning that are haunting Rome and are unsettling Titus's speech. Notice, for example, that Titus identifies precisely this confusion between the sacred and the profane when his ostensibly innocent shift in metaphorical vehicles metonymically connects his family's tomb to the shift from sacred to secular forms of wealth associated with dissolved monasteries. Thus just as his mercantile analogy inadvertently refers to his son's coffins as well as his heroic deeds, so his description of the tomb attaches itself to the larger subtext of post-Reformation confusion over the boundaries between ecclesiastical and civic orders of meaning and authority. As a whole, the scene enacts a loss of the sacred, where the term *sacred* should be understood in relation to its etymological sense of separating, differentiating, and defining.

The post-Reformation context evoked by the unnamed Goth in act 5 helps explain why the breakdown in coherent borders between the living and the dead in Titus's funeral oration would have real force for an Elizabethan audience. As Peter Marshall explains, the Dissolution of the Monasteries resulted in the disinterment of bodies buried in sacred ground. At varying stages of Tudor reform, "Carcases were cast out of graves 'for gaine of their stone or lead coffins.'" Moreover, the dissolution of monasteries and chantries was defensible only on the grounds that purgatory and prayers for the dead were illegitimate papist fictions, since many sites were donated by patrons with the understanding that prayers would be said for them by their religious inhabitants.[50] The question of liturgical propriety at stake in Tudor England is thus complexly bound up with Protestant attacks on purgatory and the mourning practices associated with it, all of which are embodied by the monastic dissolution carried out under Henry VIII. Indeed, the Dissolution of the Monasteries functioned as a kind of synecdoche for the liturgical controversies raging in the period; it was a stark reminder of England's abandoning of purgatory and the modes of propitiatory prayer associated with it. In this respect, Titus's funeral speech and its retroactive contextualization through the prism of post-Reformation England reads not only as a parody of Catholic suffrages but also, and more primarily, as a symptom of the liturgical controversies besetting Tudor England.

As I have suggested, the dramatic irony at work in Titus's speech is made audible by the way the vehicles of his metaphors take on a life of their own, attaching themselves to material contexts that exceed his intention. This process works to reveal the incoherence of the social context in which Titus is operating. In the course of the rite, Titus oscillates between the roles of father, general, and priest, none of which is seamlessly continuous with the others; moreover, he speaks to Roman and Goth auditors on the stage itself as well as to a theater audience that is not significantly less incongruous than the audience to which the 1559 Prayer Book is addressed. Furthermore, he speaks in the context of a military triumph that is morphing into a funeral, in a "headless Rome" where the sacred blurs with the profane. From a Ciceronian vantage point, Titus faces a rhetorical situation in which there is no reasonable way to achieve a discreet harmony of speaker, occasion, and audience. The key thing to notice here is that our attention moves from the particularity of Titus's speech to the generality of Roman disorder through the operations of indecorum. Shakespeare leads us to read systemically—to read, that is, at the level of social antagonism rather than at the level of individual oratorical failure—by exposing the impossibility of sustaining anything like discretion.

Act 5 or Act 1 Redux Redux

By using the principle of ceremonial indecorum as a way of disclosing social antagonism at a systemic level, Shakespeare's tragedy puts on display the antagonisms at issue in the 1549 and 1559 Prayer Books. Just as

Titus's ceremony calls attention to Rome's difference from itself through his inability to bring the roles of father, general, and priest together in a coherent way, and just as his ceremony reiterates the tension between civic and ecclesiastical orders of meaning, so "Of Ceremonies" threatens to exacerbate the very tensions it seeks to resolve by defining true English worship over and against extremes that exist within the nation and the church itself. In a worst-case scenario, the Prayer Book threatens to be an instance of the indecorum against which it defines itself, thereby producing the kind of ceremonial incoherence staged in *Titus*.

By leading readers to recognize the disjunctions among Titus's various roles, the occasion on which he is speaking, and the contradictory audiences to which he is addressing himself, Shakespeare is asking us to listen with the kind of ear Cicero speaks of when he says that "we observe others and from a glance of the eyes, from a contracting or relaxing of the brows, from an air of sadness, from an outburst of joy, from a laugh, from speech, from silence . . . we shall easily judge which of our actions is proper, and which is out of accord with duty and nature."[51] The kind of Ciceronian reading demanded by Titus's triumph is similar to, even as it should be carefully distinguished from, readings found in anti-Catholic religious polemic in Elizabethan England. There is, for example, an obvious parallel between John Foxe's critique of Thomas More's defense of purgatory and the kind of response demanded by Titus's "indecorous" allusions to Styx/purgatory. Just as Foxe's *The Story of Simon Fish* exposes what he sees as various forms of indecorum in More's defense of Catholic tradition, so we are led to notice the indiscretion of Titus's propitiatory prayer for his sons. Foxe's critique of More's vision of purgatory rests on the claim that More is an indecorous poet, weaving medieval fictions that have no verisimilitude and thus no theological authority. According to Foxe, More's "Poetical booke" does not keep *"Decorum personae*, as a perfect Poet should have done."[52] Foxe exposes the radical incoherence of More's account of purgatory to demystify it as an absurd Catholic fiction, one belonging to a world that England has outgrown.

Titus Andronicus has been seen as voicing this kind of Foxian critique of Catholic superstition and ceremonialism, and not entirely without reason. Bate explains the Foxian view of the play when he claims that the "Goth's meditation upon Henry VIII's dissolution of the monasteries [in

5.1.20–21] . . . carries forward the *translatio imperii ad Teutonicos*"—the idea that there is an analogy between the destruction of Rome by the ancient Goths and the renewal of Catholic Rome by North European humanist reformers. From this Protestant perspective, the end of the play endorses a providentialist reading of Roman history, casting Lucius in the role of quasi-religious reformer.[53] While acknowledging the play's capacity for containing (if not endorsing) such a view, I would like to add my voice to those who see this reading as ultimately antithetical to the deeply unsettling nature of Lucius's actual role in the play's conclusion. By considering how ceremonial interruption works in this final scene to exacerbate social antagonism and to thereby defer any genuinely redemptive movement in the play's conclusion, I will offer further evidence for the view that Lucius is, as Anthony Brian Taylor puts it, "a severely flawed redeemer."[54]

Rather than bringing all conflict to a convincing end, the concluding sequence repeats—in the symptomatic sense of the word—the ceremonial indecorum of act 1. In the final analysis, Lucius reiterates the violence that his original "pious" action set in motion in the first place. At the close of the play, Lucius stands in the position of official mourner and leader that Titus played at the play's opening (5.3.145). The parallel position between Titus in act 1 and Lucius in act 5 is first signaled by the Romans' hailing of Lucius, which echoes Titus's hailing of Rome at the play's outset: "Lucius, all hail, Rome's gracious governor!" (5.3.145). The indecorum evinced through Titus's conflicting roles as grieving father and victorious general recurs in this scene as Lucius begins speaking as governor but quickly interrupts himself and begins speaking as grieving son:

> Thanks, gentle Romans. May I govern so
> To heal Rome's harms and wipe away her woe.
> *But, gentle people, give me aim awhile,*
> For nature puts me to a heavy task.
> Stand all aloof, but, uncle, draw you near
> To shed obsequious tears upon this trunk.
> (5.3.146–51, emphasis added)

This self-interruption is a crucial moment in the play because it betrays Lucius's failure to discern the link between failed mourning and "Rome's harms." In Lucius's mind, there is no connection between the filial role he plays through the funeral rites that are about to be observed and his political desire to "wipe away [Rome's] woe." Lucius, in other words, completely overlooks what the audience is being asked to observe, namely the connection between the inability to mourn through an authentic avowal of loss and the cycle of violence destroying Rome.

Like the various interruptions operating in act 1, Lucius's self-interruption expresses social antagonisms and leads to further violence. To begin with, it precipitates the last and perhaps the most disturbing act of ceremonial indecorum in the play, namely the interruption, by an unnamed Roman, of Young Lucius's mourning rites for Titus, an act that brings into focus the violent consequences of Lucius's own subtle, but crucial, act of self-interruption: "You sad Andronici, have done with woes, / Give sentence on this execrable wretch [Aaron]" (5.3.175–76). This last ceremonial disruption is uniquely irksome because it prevents Young Lucius from voicing what appears to be the most authentic expression of grief in the play as a whole. At this point in the play, Young Lucius is in the process of being interpellated into Roman society through mourning rites; he is learning how to be a Roman by learning how to display ostentatious and thus inauthentic acts of mourning. His father Lucius commands him, "Come hither, boy, come, come and learn of us / To melt in showers" (5.3.159–60). Marcus then provides Young Lucius with an example to follow:

> How many thousand times hath these poor lips,
> When they were living, warmed themselves on thine!
> O now, sweet boy, give them their latest kiss;
> Bid him farewell.
>
> (5.3.165–68)

Marcus repeats one of the central dramatic ironies of Titus's first speech, describing his final kiss as "latest." The effect here is to further undercut the differentiation of living and dead that is ostensibly being performed in the ritual. Moreover, Marcus's hyperbolic images suggest that this is an inauthentically public expression of a grief that is, nevertheless, genuinely felt. Indeed, what is troubling here is not that Marcus is faking his grief but that he is giving strange expression to what we must presume is a true feeling of loss. Public modes of expression still fail to mediate privately felt grief. Importantly, the formalized hyperbole of Marcus's and Lucius's mourning rites becomes more demonstrably inauthentic when Young Lucius resists it, opting instead for the inexpressibility topos: "O Lord, I cannot speak to him for weeping, / My tears will choke me if I ope my mouth" (5.3.173–74). This is a striking moment in the play because Young Lucius explicitly voices the limitations of Roman ceremony that have been repeatedly expressed in the course of events. By thematizing the limits of ritualized behavior in Rome, the boy makes visible the connection between ceremonial failure and the conflagration of violence unfolding in the play. He opens a space for the reader to recognize the connection between failed mourning and social violence that Lucius overlooked in the previous speech. What is crucial about the boy's use of the inexpressibility topos at this moment, then, is not that he looks like a Protestant reformer opting for an extempore lamentation rather than a set prayer. (Catholic literature, such as Robert Southwell's *Marie Magdalens Funerall Tears*, gives voice to the inexpressibility topos just as Protestant literature does.) On the contrary, what is crucial here is that he resists the overly formal ostentation of his father's and uncle's prayers, opting instead for something that sounds more like an expression than a disavowal of loss.

Such potentially redeeming moments in the play are fleeting, though, for the boy's seemingly authentic expression of grief is quickly disrupted: "You sad Andronici, have done with woes" (5.3.175). The interruption of this young boy's stark lamentation is the clearest disavowal of loss that occurs in the play. Like Lucius's use of Latin in act 1, this disruption denotes the "unrecuring wound" arising from the failure to authentically carry out the work of mourning. While this interruption provides Lucius with the opportunity to begin healing the collective wounds of Rome by rebuking the impropriety of such a gesture, thereby drawing attention to the authenticity of Young Lucius's grief, he does not. Instead, Lucius endorses this unnamed Roman's interpretation of the play's violence as a function of foreign influence rather than internal antagonism and failed mourning. As a result, the play ends with yet another disavowal of mourning. This time, though, the disavowal is totally explicit as Lucius denies Tamora any funeral rites:

> As for that ravenous tiger, Tamora,
> No funeral rite, nor man in mourning weed,
> No mournful bell shall ring her burial,
> But throw her forth to beasts and birds to prey.
> (5.3.194–97)

The play's final negation of ceremony has, it seems to me, the rather obvious effect of drawing Rome ever closer to the very enemy from whom
such a negation is designed to differentiate Rome. The play ends just as
it began: with an execution that signifies the very barbarity and radical
self-difference undercutting Rome's identity as a civilized political body
from the outset. Had Lucius done something other than what Tamora
had done throughout the course of the play, he might have successfully
differentiated civilized Rome from revenging Goths. Instead, he further
exacerbates Rome's otherness to itself around the question of human
sacrifice. The providentialist view of the play is thus undone by the way
Lucius becomes a mirror image of the inhuman executioner he thinks he
is killing off. It is not until *Cymbeline* that we see a character named Lucius
realize that "We should not, when the blood was cool, have threatened /
Our prisoners with the sword."[55]

IN ACT 5 AS IN ACT 1, CEREMONIES EXACERBATE ROME'S DIS-
avowal of its internal differences. What is more, self-difference continues to be made legible in act 5 through a patterning of indecorum. The
overall result of this pattern is that the play does more than ask us to
read according to principles of decorum; it asks us to interrogate the
connections between decorum and morality presupposed by the concept
itself. The two gestures we have seen that can qualify as ethical—namely
Tamora's plea for Alarbus and Young Lucius's anguished cry of grief for
Titus—are both, when viewed in their Roman contexts, indecorously out
of place. In turn, both gestures explicitly call attention to the inauthen-
ticity of Roman rituals, demarcating a limit point within the self-coherence
of Roman culture. By doing so, Shakespeare suggests that there is often
something indecorous about ethical acts. By dislocating the conventional
Ciceronian association of justice and decorum, Titus anticipates more

mature interrogations of ethical action, such as Kent and Cordelia in *King Lear* or Paulina in *The Winter's Tale*. In Shakespeare's plays, there is often something profoundly indecorous, unstylish, even weirdly disturbing or excessive, about a genuinely ethical act. Ethical actions in Shakespeare have the effect of rewriting the rules of decorum, of changing our perception of what counts as discretion or as demarcating a limit point of social and rhetorical coherence. For Shakespeare, genuine ethical action seems more in sympathy with St. Paul's conception of Christian life as a form of divine foolishness than with the ostensibly Ciceronian values of order and decency seen by Tudor authorities to be voiced in 1 Corinthians.[56] Think, for example, of Paulina's obstinate behavior before her king, or Cordelia's refusal to voice her love within the framework of epideictic decorum. In these scenes, we witness a more complete unraveling of the Ciceronian association between ethics and decorum than we do in Shakespeare's first revenge tragedy. Indeed, just as Shakespeare's great villains consistently put the lie to the humanist assumption that eloquence is inherently moral, that decorum is intrinsically a sign of ethical well-being, so his representations of moral actions tend to challenge the Ciceronian thesis that decorum is inherently just.[57]

To put this another way, *Titus* deconstructs the principle of decorum in ways that hyperbolize the kinds of conceptual breakdowns visible in theoretical treatises by Ciceronians such as Puttenham, as well as in official defenses of the church's liturgical policies, such as in "Of Ceremonies." In this way, the play's grotesquerie does much more than parody Roman Catholic ceremonialism; it exposes some of the key aporias at the heart of the Elizabethan Settlement. Such a deconstruction of Ciceronian values opens the space for alternative interrogations of ethics, including the kind James Knapp finds at work in *Measure for Measure* in chapter 10 of this volume. For Knapp, *Measure for Measure* eschews ethics as an application of general principles to particular situations, seeking, instead, for a more subtle way of thinking ethics in terms of the intertwining experience of time, embodiment, and the word. *Titus*'s demystification of decorum also consolidates the sort of genealogical interpretation of culture that Michel de Montaigne envisions when he relates that "once, having to justify one of our observances, which was received with steadfast authority far and wide around us, and preferring to establish it, not as is usually done, merely by force of laws and examples, but by tracking it to its origin, I there found its foundation so weak that I nearly became disgusted with it, I who was supposed to confirm it in others."[58] While religious ceremonies were officially viewed as reflecting and embodying edifying forms of decorum in Elizabethan culture, almost all forms of them were thought, by one group or another, to do exactly the opposite. The theatrical power and political force of Shakespeare's play lie in the way it stages the perceived indecorum of religious ceremony and the cultural violence arising from it. What *Titus* ultimately offers, then, is insight into how a culture's ceremonies embody its unarticulated differences from itself.

Notes

1. Jane Hiles, "A Margin for Error: Rhetorical Context in *Titus Andronicus*," *Style* 21 (Spring 1987): 62.

2. See chapter 1 of this volume.

3. Jonathan Bate, introduction to *Titus Andronicus*, Arden 3rd series (London: Routledge, 1995), 19–21, interprets *Titus* in terms of Protestant providentialism, contextualizing the play in relation to the *translatio imperii ad Teutonicos* or translation of empire to the German peoples. (All subsequent citations to the play and its notes are from this edition; those to the play are given parenthetically in the text by act, scene, and line.) Barbara L. Parker, *Plato's Republic and Shakespeare's Rome* (Newark: University of Delaware Press, 2004), ch. 6, develops Bate's contextualization by reading the play as an unambiguous, if rather incoherent, anti-Catholic allegory. Lukas Erne, "'Popish Tricks' and 'a Ruinous Monastery': *Titus Andronicus* and the Question of Shakespeare's Catholicism," in *The Limits of Textuality*, ed. Lukas Erne and Guillemette Bolens (Tübingen: Gunter Narr, 2000), 135–55, does the opposite, attempting to see the play as an expression of distinctly recusant sympathy.

4. Nicholas R. Moschovakis, "'Irreligious Piety' and Christian History: Persecution as Pagan Anachronism in *Titus Andronicus*," *Shakespeare Quarterly* 53 (2002): 461.

5. For an account of ritual as productive rather than merely reflective of social order, see Catherine Bell, *Ritual Theory, Ritual Practice* (New York: Oxford University Press, 1992).

6. See chapter 4 of this volume.

7. For a discussion of Hooker's critique and reformulation of Anglican ceremonialism, see Peter Lake, *Anglicans and Puritans: Presbyterianism and English Conformist Thought from Whitgift to Hooker* (London: Unwin Hyman, 1988), ch. 4.

8. Michael Neill, "'Exeunt with a Dead March': Funeral Pageantry on the Shakespearean Stage," in *Pageantry in the Shakespearean Theatre*, ed. David M. Bergeron (Athens: University of Georgia Press, 1985), 169. Eugene M. Waith discusses the importance of ceremony to *Titus* in "The Ceremonies of *Titus Andronicus*," in *Mirror up to Shakespeare: Essays in Honour of G. R. Hibbard*, ed. J. C. Gray (Toronto: University of Toronto Press, 1984), 159–70.

9. *Titus Andronicus*, 135 n. 127.

10. Plutarch, *Plutarch's Moralia*, vol. 4, trans. Frank Cole Babbitt, Loeb Classical Library (Cambridge, MA: Harvard University Press, 1962), 284A, "The Roman Questions," no. 83, p. 127.

11. William Allen, *A Briefe Historie of the Glorious Martyrdom of XII Reverend Priests* (1582), in *English Recusant Literature, 1558–1640*, vol. 55, ed. D. M. Rogers (Menston: Scolar Press, 1970), Biiiv.

12. Elizabeth Hanson, *Discovering the Subject in Renaissance England* (Cambridge: Cambridge University Press, 1998), 24.

13. I draw here on Timothy Rosendale, *Liturgy and Literature in the Making of Protestant England* (Cambridge: Cambridge University Press, 2007), 118–19.

14. G. J. Cuming, *A History of Anglican Liturgy* (London: Macmillan, 1969), 96.

15. Quoted in ibid., 133.

16. For a discussion of Hooker's critique and reformulation of the Anglican via media, see Lake, *Anglicans and Puritans*, ch. 4. Christopher Crosbie, "Fixing Moderation: *Titus Andronicus* and the Aristotelian Determination of Value," *Shakespeare Quarterly* 58 (2007): 147–73, attempts to read the play as a rigorous expression of Aristotle's ethics of equity and the golden mean. The thesis requires Crosbie to maintain that Titus's reaction to Lavinia's rape is more reciprocal and ethical than Marcus's, failing to mention, unsurprisingly, that this "reciprocity" leads Titus to kill his daughter. I would suggest that, rather than advocating an Aristotelian ethics, the play performs a *reductio ad absurdum* of it.

17. A historian of no less authority than James II apparently thought that "after all the frequent and pressing endeavours that were used [in the last four reigns] to reduce this kingdom to an exact conformity in religion, it is visible the success has not answered the design, and that the difficulty is invincible" (quoted in Rosendale, *Liturgy and Literature*, 201).

18. For discussions of incidents in which conforming parishioners were at loggerheads with nonconforming ministers, see Judith Maltby, *Prayer Book and People in Elizabethan and Early Stuart England* (Cambridge: Cambridge University Press, 1998), esp. 13–14.

19. Cuming, *History of Anglican Liturgy*, 92; Diarmaid MacCulloch, *Thomas Cranmer: A Life* (New Haven: Yale University Press, 1996), 41.

20. Subsequent citations to "Of Ceremonies" are given parenthetically in the text by page numbers and are from *The Book of Common Prayer 1559: The Elizabethan Prayer Book*, ed. John E Booty (Charlottesville: University Press of Virginia, 1976), 18.

21. Evelyn B. Tribble, "The Partial Sign: Spenser and the Sixteenth-Century Crisis of Semiotics," in *Ceremony and Text in the Renaissance*, ed. Douglas F. Rutledge (Newark: University of Delaware Press, 1996), 27.

22. For discussion of the connections between the thirteen articles and the development of the Book of Common Prayer, see Cuming, *History of Anglican Liturgy*, 92.

23. John Donne, "The First Anniversary," in *The Oxford Authors: John Donne*, ed. John Carey (Oxford: Oxford University Press, 1990), line 338.

24. Rosendale, *Liturgy and Literature*, 178.

25. Ibid., 13, 110.

26. See Sir Thomas Browne, "Religio Medici," in *The Major Works*, ed. C. A. Patrides (New York: Penguin Books, 1977), 57–162.

27. David Hillman, "Puttenham, Shakespeare, and the Abuse of Rhetoric," *Studies in English Literature, 1500–1900* 36 (Winter 1996): 83.

28. Cicero, *De officiis*, ed. T. E. Page, E. Capps, and W. H. D. Rouse, trans. Walter Miller, Loeb Classical Library (New York: G. P. Putnam's Sons, 1928), 1.27.94, p. 97.

29. George Puttenham, *The Arte of English Poesie* (Kent: Kent State University Press, 1970), 268.

30. Quoted in Hillman, "Puttenham," 76.

31. See, for example, the following definition of *decorum*: "euery thing which pleaseth the mind or sences, and the mind by the sences as by means instrumentall, doth it or some amiable point or qualitie that is in it, which draweth them to a good liking and contentment with their proper objects" (Puttenham, *Arte of English Poesie*, 76).

32. For a discussion of the via media and a larger bibliography on the topic, see Joshua Scodel, introduction to *Excess and the Mean in Early Modern English Literature* (Princeton: Princeton University Press, 2002), esp. 4–8.

33. John Field, "A View of Popish Abuses," in *Puritanism in Tudor England*, ed. H. C. Porter (London: Macmillan, 1970), 136.

34. Ibid., 130.

35. *The Marprelate Tracts, 1588–1589* (Menston: Scolar Press, 1967), 2.

36. Anthony Miller, *Roman Triumphs and Early Modern English Culture* (Basingstoke: Palgrave, 2001), 1.

37. See Sir William Segar, *Honor, Military, and Civill, Contained in Foure Books* (London, 1602), 140.

38. *Titus Andronicus*, 132 n.

39. Eamon Duffy, *The Stripping of the Altars: Traditional Religion in England, c. 1400–c. 1580* (New Haven: Yale University Press, 1992), 136. For a reading of the breakdown in distinctions occurring in Titus's Rome along the anthropological lines of Mary Douglas, see Linda Woodbridge, "Palisading the Body Politic," in *True Rites and Maimed Rites: Ritual and Anti-ritual in Shakespeare and His Age*, ed. Linda Woodbridge and Edward Berry (Urbana: University of Illinois Press, 1992), 270–98.

40. Lawrence Stone, *The Crisis of the Aristocracy, 1558–1641* (Oxford: Clarendon Press, 1965), 575. Neill makes a closely related point in "Exeunt with a Dead March," 154–55.

41. Parker, *Plato's Republic*, 117–18.

42. Virgil, *The Aeneid*, trans. Robert Fitzgerald (New York: Vintage Books, 1983), 6.84–87, p. 161.

43. For the classic account of manic mourning, see Sigmund Freud, "Mourning and Melancholia," in *The Standard Edition of the Complete Psychological Works of Sigmund Freud*, vol. 14, ed. James Strachey (London: Hogarth Press, 1981), 73–102.

44. For an analysis of Shakespeare's representations of disruptions in church, see Bruce Boehrer, "Disorder in the House of God: Disrupted Worship in Shakespeare and Others," *Comparative Drama* 38 (Spring 2004): 83–102.

45. Ann Hurley, "Interruption: The Transformation of a Critical Feature of Ritual from Revel to Lyric in John Donne's Inns of Court Poetry of the 1590s," in Rutledge, *Ceremony and Text*, 105.

46. See Stephen Greenblatt, *Hamlet in Purgatory* (Princeton: Princeton University Press, 2001), 311 n. 56.

47. Cited in Peter Marshall, *Beliefs and the Dead in Reformation England* (Oxford: Oxford University Press, 2002), 156.

48. Field, "View of Popish Abuses," 129.

49. See *Titus Andronicus*, 133 n.

50. See Marshall, *Beliefs and the Dead*, 104–5 and chs. 3 and 4.

51. Cicero, *De officiis*, 1.41.146, p. 149.

52. John Foxe, "The Story of Simon Fish," Appendix D in *The Complete Works of St. Thomas More*, vol. 7, ed. Frank Manley et al. (New Haven: Yale University Press), 443.

53. See Bate, introduction to *Titus Andronicus*, 19–21, and Parker, *Plato's Republic*, ch. 6.

54. For related views of Lucius, see Anthony Brian Taylor, "Lucius, the Severely Flawed Redeemer of *Titus Andronicus*," *Connotations* 6, no. 2 (1996–97):

138–57, and Moschovakis, "'Irreligious Piety,'" 466. Taylor ably and persuasively handles pro-Lucius responses to his article by Jonathan Bate in "'Lucius, the Severely Flawed Redeemer of *Titus Andronicus*': A Reply," *Connotations* 6, no. 3 (1996–97): 330–33; Maurice Hunt, "Exonerating Lucius in *Titus Andronicus:* A Response to Anthony Brian Taylor," *Connotations* 7, no. 1 (1997–98): 67–93; and Philip Kolin, "'Lucius, the Severely Flawed Redeemer of *Titus Andronicus*': A Reply," *Connotations* 7, no. 1 (1997–98): 94–96.

55. *Cymbeline* 5.6.77–78, *The Norton Shakespeare*, 2nd ed., ed. Stephen Greenblatt (New York: W. W. Norton, 2008), 3044.

56. See 1 Cor. 3:18–23 and 4:10–13.

57. For this argument, see Brian Vickers, "'The Power of Persuasion': Images of the Orator, Elyot to Shakespeare," in *Renaissance Eloquence: Studies in the Theory and Practice of Renaissance Rhetoric*, ed. James J. Murphy (Berkeley: University of California Press, 1983), 411–36.

58. Michel de Montaigne, "Of Custom, and Not Easily Changing an Accepted Law," in *The Complete Essays*, trans. Donald M. Frame (Stanford: Stanford University Press, 1965), 84.

Chapter 3

Miracles and Mysteries in
The Comedy of Errors

RICHARD MCCOY

Near the end of *As You Like It*, Rosalind tells her many admirers, "I am a magician" and commands the audience as well as the other characters to "Believe then if you please that I can do strange things."[1] What does it mean to believe if you please, to believe *As You Like It*, or to believe in any of Shakespeare's plays? Samuel Taylor Coleridge's famous concept of "that willing suspension of disbelief for the moment, which constitutes poetic faith," presents a seemingly simple answer to these questions.[2] Poetic license temporarily allows us to believe manifestly preposterous fantasies too good to be true. Elsewhere Coleridge describes this experience as "a sort of temporary Half-Faith, which the Spectator encourages in himself & supports by a voluntary contribution on his own part, because he knows that it is at all times in his power to see the thing as it really is."[3] Drama thus presents not reality but illusion. In one of his many lectures on Shakespeare, Coleridge explains that all the "excellencies of the drama, as unity of interest, appropriateness of style . . . and the charm of language and sentiment . . . as far as they tend to increase the inward excitement, are all means to this chief end, that of producing and supporting this willing illusion."[4] Nevertheless, he insists that illusions are not delusions. Indeed, in his approach to drama, Coleridge seeks a mean between "two extremes in critical decision—The French, which evidently presupposes that a perfect Delusion is to be aimed at . . . [and] [t]he opposite, supported by Dr Johnson," who flatly refuses to believe dramatic fictions at all; it thus represents "an intermediate State, which we distinguish by the term, Illusion."[5] For Coleridge, illusions can be a means of access to a higher truth.

I want to suggest that Coleridge's search for an "intermediate State" has intriguing parallels with the Reformation quest for a via media on the vexed issue of Christ's "real presence" in the Eucharist. Coleridge had a strong interest in theology as well as philosophy, and his poetics often link religious faith with poetic faith, amplifying our sense of the meaning of belief in Shakespeare.[6] Indeed, he uses one of the most loaded terms of Reformation controversy to describe the powers of the imagination. By "incorporating the Reason in Images of the Sense, and organizing (as it were) the flux of the Senses by the permanence and self-circling energies of the Reason," imagination "gives birth to a system of symbols, harmonious in themselves, and consubstantial with the truths, of which they are the *conductors*."[7] *Consubstantial* was the term applied to Martin Luther's alternative to the Catholic doctrine of transubstantiation. Coleridge also took a firm Protestant stance toward that doctrine, for he too objected to a Catholic conception of the sacrament having a power *ex opere operato* as well as traditional notions of Christ's "real presence" in the Eucharist.[8] Yet even though he appropriated the term associated with Lutheranism to amplify his explanation of the power of symbols, he actually rejected Luther's Eucharistic doctrine as too Catholic. As Nicholas Halmi explains, Coleridge "lamented that Luther would never 'have had to seek a murky Hiding-hole in the figment of Consubstantiation' precisely if [he] had understood 'the true definition of a Symbol as distinguished from the Thing on one hand, and from a mere metaphor or conventional exponent of a Thing on the other.'"[9]

This distinction between the symbol and the thing it represents is a recurrent and crucial concern for Coleridge, and it is closely linked to his insistent distinction between an imitation and a copy. In one of his general lectures on poetry he considered "whether poetry ought to be a *copy* or only an *imitation* of what is true nature? According to every effect he had been able to trace, he was of opinion that the pleasure we receive arose, not from its being a *copy*, but from its being an imitation, & the word imitation itself means always a combination of a certain degree of dissimilitude with a certain degree of similitude."[10] In his view, few grasped this elusive distinction more firmly than Shakespeare, for while some might find it "hard to express that sense of the analogy or likeness of a Thing which enables a Symbol to represent it, so that we think of the Thing itself—& yet knowing that the Thing is not present to us," Shakespeare's plays hold the mirror up to nature and show its form without pretending to be the thing itself: "Surely, on this universal fact of words & images depends by more or less mediations the *imitation* instead of *copy* which is illustrated in very nature *shakespearianized*—that Proteus Essence that could assume the very form, but yet known & felt not to be the Thing."[11] For Coleridge, an analogy or likeness can and must suffice because it allows us to "think of the Thing itself," even while "knowing that the Thing is not present to us."

Here too, Coleridge grapples with a subject comparable to controversies over the real presence. In their understanding of the Eucharist, many reformers also found it "hard to express that sense of the analogy or likeness of a Thing which enables a Symbol to represent it, so that we think of the Thing itself—& yet knowing that the Thing is not present to us." Martin Luther and Ulrich Zwingli debated these issues at a Reformation summit conference at Marburg in 1529, but they parted confirmed in their differences.[12] Afterward, John Calvin criticized Luther for positing "the sort of local presence that the papists dream about" and objected to Zwingli for denying "the reality and efficacy" of the sacraments by reducing them to symbols, allegories, and parables.[13] He and his followers wanted to move beyond what Calvin's successor, Theodore Beza, called the false dichotomy of "transubstantiation or a trope."[14]

Calvin and his disciples found their via media between these extremes in what Kilian McDonnell describes as the "doctrine of the efficacy of the sacramental signs."[15] For many reformers, the sacraments had the power that Coleridge attributes to symbols precisely because their efficacy allowed believers to "think of the Thing itself" while "knowing that the Thing is not present to us." Calvin describes the words of the consecration as a form of "living preaching which edifies its hearers, penetrates into their very minds, impresses itself upon their hearts and settles there, and reveals its effectiveness in the fulfillment of what it promises."[16] Gradually, the Calvinist view shaped the liturgical and theological consensus in the English Church. In his preface to the Book of Common Prayer, Thomas Cranmer acknowledges that religious ceremonies "had their beginning by the institution of man," but he affirms their value as a reminder of our "duty to God by some notable and special signification."[17] Peter Martyr describes the Eucharist as a "sacramental conjunction" that sustains "the most effectual signification."[18] Richard Hooker calls it "a *presence of force and efficacie* through all generations."[19] Even Puritan theologians affirm the efficacy of sacramental signs. William Perkins allows that liturgical language is a human invention whose words cannot "cause a real worke, much less to produce a wonder."[20] While warning that we must observe "many cautions concerning sacred tropes," Perkins says that such "tropes are emphaticall," providing not only "delight and ornament" but also "matter for the nourishment of faith."[21] Anne Kibby points out that despite his reputation for austerity, "Perkins was quite willing to worship a rhetorical deity who communicated through tropes and figures."[22]

The Reformers' belief in the moral and sacramental efficacy of figurative language marks a point where religious faith and poetic faith begin to converge in the early modern period. Sir Philip Sidney, in his high-minded *Apology for Poetry*, describes the Psalms as "heavenly poesy" and treasures their "notable *prosopopoeias* . . . [which] maketh you, as it were, see God coming in His majesty."[23] Like Calvin, he valued the capacity of scriptural language to edify and penetrate hearts and minds and "strike, pierce, . . . and posses the sight of the soul" (107), and, like Perkins, he praises tropes and figures for what he calls their "forcibleness or *energia*" (138). This energy is the source of poetry's "moving" power that inspires its readers to "well-doing" (112), working on their emotions and their will. For Sidney, poetry's *energia* has a moving power akin to the efficacy attributed to the sacraments by Reformation theologians.[24] And in both instances, the impact is personal and psychological. Thomas Cranmer contends that sacramental change does not occur in the elements; instead, "the real conversion is in him that receiveth the sacraments; which real conversion is inward, visible, and spiritual."[25] As

Christopher Cocksworth explains, for Cranmer, "the effective potential of the Sacrament was a product of its affective force."[26] This affective emphasis increasingly reinforced the Protestant notion of the Eucharist as a form of emotional and social communion rather than metaphysical sacrifice. Robert Hill promulgates this view in a section entitled "A Communicant Instructed" that is included in his treatise *The Path-way to Pietie* (1606), defining the sacrament as a "coniunction [that] appeares in the *unitie of Spirite*" and that "is neither a *commixtion* of *persons* nor an vnion of *substances*, but a *confederation* of our *affections*, and *concatenation* of our *wils*" that "shall appear in the *consociation* of our *persons*."[27]

Recent work on Shakespeare has suggested that a comparable "*confederation* of our *affections*, and . . . *consociation* of our *persons*" transpires in many of his plays. Jeffrey Knapp, among others, describes *Henry V* as a kind of "theatrical sacrament" sustained "not only with the inward participation of the audience but also with the sense of charity and communal endeavor that such participation is supposed to inspire."[28] Indeed, many of Shakespeare's plays can still inspire feelings akin to communion in audiences today as well as in his own time. I find that the seemingly miraculous reunion and rebirth in *The Comedy of Errors*, whose climax delivers "After so long grief, such nativity!" (5.1.407), also sustain a sense of comparable communion. I would add that, while this harmonious effect may have failed at one of its early performances, it has only increased over time.

One particular early performance of *The Comedy of Errors* during the winter revels at Gray's Inn in 1594 seems to have gone rather badly.[29] The record of these revels, entitled the *Gesta Grayorum*, reports that it was staged on one of many "grand Nights" when the "great Presence of Lords, Ladies, and worshipful Personages, that did expect some notable Performance" filled the Great Hall to capacity.[30] Because "there was no convenient room for those that were Actors" (29), "there arose such a disordered Tumult and Crowd upon the Stage, that there was no Opportunity to effect that which was intended" (29). The actors referred to are not the members of Shakespeare's company but rather members of Gray's Inn, and the latter apparently had a much grander show that was thwarted by overcrowding. Guests from the Inner Temple, the fraternal rival of Gray's Inn, had been invited for this illustrious performance, but the "Lord Ambassador" from the Inner Temple and his entourage were annoyed by the crowds, decided "they were not so kindly entertained, as was before expected," and departed in a huff, "discontented and displeased" (31). As a result, it was "thought good not to offer any thing of account, save Dancing and Reveling with Gentlewomen; and after such Sports, a Comedy of Errors (like to *Plautus* his *Menechmus*) was played by the Players. So that Night was begun, and continued to the end, in nothing but Confusion and Errors, whereupon it was ever afterwards called, *The Night of Errors*" (31–32).

This slighting reference constitutes our first recorded review of a Shakespeare play and it is surprisingly bad. *The Comedy of Errors* is derided as a feeble, improvised substitute for some truly "notable Performance," and the "Players" from his company as replacements for more illustrious "Actors" and members of Gray's Inn for whom "there was no convenient room." The next day an official inquiry by "a Commission of *Oyer* and *Terminer*" (32) was launched to assign blame for the Night of Errors, and Shakespeare's company was further insulted by the arraignment of a "Sorcerer or Conjurer" (32) for having "foisted a Company of base and common Fellows, to make up our Disorders with a Play of Errors and Confusions" (32). This mock-trial concluded with all charges of "Sorceries and Enchantments and . . . great Witchcraft" (32) blithely dismissed: the "Prisoner was freed and pardoned" (32), the prosecutors were sent to jail, "And this was the End of our Law-sports, concerning the Night of Errors" (34). The indignities suffered by Gray's Inn were partially dissipated by "mocking thus at our own follies" (34).

But the theatrical ambitions of the gentlemen of Gray's Inn could not leave it at that. After "a great Consultation . . . for the Recovery of our lost Honour," they decided to stage even grander "Plots and Devices" the next week. On January 3, an audience of many "Great and Noble Personages" assembled, including the "Earls of *Shrewsbury, Cumberland, Northumberland, Southampton,* and *Essex,* the Lords *Buckhurst, Windsor, Mountjoy, Sheffield, Compton, Rich, Burleygh, Mounteagle,* and the Lord *Thomas Howard;* Sir *Thomas Henneage,* Sir *Robert Cecill,*" and many other dignitaries (35). This time, they "all had convenient Places, and very good Entertainment, to their good Liking and Contentment" (35). As soon as this distinguished audience was "setled in very good Order," the revels prince and his entourage were joined by "the Ambassador of Templaria, with his Train likewise," and this time they too "had Places reserved for them" (35). A masque in honor of the Goddess of Amity followed. It featured an altar erected to the goddess; a priest or "Arch-Flamen, ready to attend the Sacrifice and Incense" to be offered to her; "Nymphs and Fairies" forming a chorus and orchestra; and a procession of famous "pair[s] of Friends," including Theseus and Perithous, Achilles and Patroclus, and others. The performance prompted some slight suspense at first, but the priest or "Arch-Flamen" quickly allayed it. Initially, two actors representing *Graius* and *Templarius* "came lovingly, Arm in Arm, to the Altar, and offered their Incense as the rest, but the Goddess did not accept of their Service; which appeared by the troubled Smoak, and dark Vapour . . . the Arch-Flamen, willing to pacifie the angry Goddess, preferred certain mystical Ceremonies and Invocations, and commanded the Nymphs to sing some Hymns of Pacification to her Deity, and caused them to make proffer of their Devotion again; which they did, and then the Flame burnt more clear than at any time before" (36). The priest's success in placating the goddess enabled him formally to pronounce "Grayus and Templarius to be as true and perfect Friends . . . and linked with the Bond and League of sincere Friendship and Amity as ever were *Theseus* and *Perithous*," and other famous comrades, and he "denounced an heavy Curse on them that shall any way go about to break or weaken the same" (36). Finally, after all these prayers and pronouncements, "the Curtain was drawn" and the "Shew ended," and the "Night of Errors, and the uncivil Behaviour wherewith they were entertained . . . was now clean rooted out and forgotten" (37).

The Masque of Amity must have been a grand spectacle. Its orderly processional and hieratic rites presumably compensated for the failure of the earlier "notable Performance" (29), thwarted by the "Tumult and Crowd" (31) the week before. Its "mystical Ceremonies and Invocations" (36) and smoke and incense probably gave the rituals a solemn aura. Perhaps they even reinforced the assurance that "Friendship and Amity" were happily restored and "that this love should be perpetual" (36). At the same time, it seems unlikely that anyone believed these ceremonial sacrifices had any real efficacy, even if the flame smoked and flared. The Arch-Flamen sounds a bit like the Wizard of Oz, and his special effects seem stronger on production values than credibility. As in the mock-trial of the "Sorcerer or Conjurer," the tone is hard to assess, but it seems doubtful that these solemn and extravagant proceedings would elicit even the "temporary Half-Faith" that Coleridge attributes to most dramatic performances. The "mystical Ceremonies and Invocations" are grandiose but also slightly ridiculous. Like many revels performances, the Masque of Amity is an odd blend of solemnity, extravagance, and possible mockery, and evaluating its dramatic impact is difficult.

By contrast, *The Comedy of Errors* sustains an aura of genuine miracle and mystery as well as restoring amity with less effort and more credibility. A willing suspension of disbelief comes more easily, and poetic faith aligns itself with religious faith. The play's religious undertone is reinforced from the start by its setting in Ephesus, a city visited and evangelized by St. Paul. In his fifth epistle to the Ephesians, Paul proclaims husband and wife "one flesh," a doctrine ardently embraced by Adriana, the wife of the Ephesian Antipholus. We also learn in Acts 19 that "God wrought no small miracles by the hands of Paul" (11), since he not only healed the sick but also cast out evil spirits by invoking the name of Jesus.[31] Yet even in this scriptural source, the lines between miracles, magic tricks, and con games are blurred. Not to be outdone, Paul's adversaries try to emulate his miracles, but they summon spirits beyond their control. "Then certain of the vagabond Jews, exorcists, took in hand to name over them which had evil spirits, the Name of the Lord Jesus, saying, We adjure you by Jesus, whom Paul preacheth. . . . And the evil spirit answered, and said, Jesus I acknowledge, and Paul I know, but who are ye? And the man in whom the evil spirit was, ran on them, and overcame them, and prevailed against them, so that they fled out of that house, naked and wounded" (12–16). Further disorders ensue when local craftsmen who sell their wares to visitors to the famous temple of Diana are antagonized by Paul's preaching that "they be not gods that are made with hands" (26), go after him and his companions, and plunge the city into turmoil: "Some therefore cried one thing, and some another, for the assembly was out of order, and the more part knew not wherefore they were come together" (32).

In *The Comedy of Errors*, the disorders are no less chaotic. In Shakespeare's Ephesus, everyone finds it hard to distinguish between fraudulent wonder-workers and genuine healers, and both visitors and residents find themselves strangers in a strange land. Shortly after his arrival there, Antipholus of Syracuse warns us:

> They say this town is full of cozenage,
> As nimble jugglers that deceive the eye,
> Dark-working sorcerers that change the mind,
> Soul-killing witches that deform the body,
> Disguised cheaters, prating mountebanks,
> And many suchlike libertines of sin.
>
> (1.2.97–102)

Plautus set his play in Epidamnum and made it a solidly grounded farce of mistaken or stolen identities. Shakespeare makes the errors in his play more mysterious and unsettling, and his characters cannot tell whether they are victims of tricks or supernatural forces or both.[32] The servant, Dromio of Syracuse, is so unnerved by these errors that he relapses into Catholic superstitions and folk magic: "O, for my beads! I cross me for a sinner. / This is the fairy land. O spite of spites, / We talk with goblins, owls, and elves, and sprites" (2.2.188–90). His master succumbs to similar fears, certain that "There's none but witches do inhabit here" (3.2.154). When he encounters the courtesan, he shouts, "Thou art, as you are all, a sorceress. / I conjure you to leave me and be gone" (4.3.61–62). As his bafflement grows, he can only pray for a deliverance beyond his powers: "The fellow is distraught, and so am I, / And here we wander in illusions. / Some blessed power deliver us from hence" (4.3.38–40).

Deliverance will eventually come in the form of a blessed maternal power, but before that happy ending a false religious power arrives in the form of Doctor Pinch. Desperate to reclaim her husband's alienated affections, Adriana seeks help from this supposedly higher source: "Good Doctor Pinch, you are a conjurer" (4.4.42). A conjurer supposedly has the power to summon and command spirits. It is a highly loaded term, used repeatedly in this play, six times in all. According to Keith Thomas, *conjurer* became a synonym for and slur against Catholic priests during the Reformation.[33] Their once sacramental powers were now derided as a perverse combination of superstition, delusional enchantments, black magic, and sorceries. The sacred words of the host's consecration in the Eucharist—*hoc est corpus meum*—were mocked accordingly as "hocus pocus." Conjuration was also associated with both necromancy (or the ability to raise the dead) and exorcism (or the ability to cast out the devils supposedly conjured up). The latter is Pinch's specialty, and he thus thunders at Antipholus of Ephesus:

> I charge thee, Satan, housed within this man,
> To yield possession to my holy prayers
> And to thy state of darkness hie thee straight:
> I conjure thee by all the saints in heaven.
>
> (4.4.49–52)

When Antipholus tells him to shut up, Pinch concludes that "both man and master is possessed" and says, "They must be bound and laid in some dark room" (4.4.87–89). Pinch gets a bitter dose of his own medicine when the "master and his man are both broke loose" and bind "the Doctor / Whose beard they have singed off with brands of fire" (5.1.170–73). The failed exorcist becomes the play's scapegoat, and he is tortured and humiliated by a tormentor who denounces him as "a mountebank, / [and] A threadbare juggler" (5.1.239–40).

In her introduction to *The Comedy of Errors*, Ros King finds in all these errors and insults oblique references to Richard Edwards's mid-Tudor Protestant satire *Jack Juggler*.[34] Edwards's play is an earlier comedy of errors and tricks adapted for a schoolboy audience from another Plautine comedy about twins. In *Jack Juggler*, the title character is a vice figure who frightens and mocks Jenkin Careaway, a hapless servant, by making him "bylive if I can / That he is not him selfe, but an other man" in order to drive him "starke staryng mad."[35] The tricks work, and the poor servant suffers a fate similar to the two Dromios, enduring confusion, fear, and beatings. Jenkin cannot figure out "How may it then bee that he should bee I / Or I not my selfe?" (518–19). Other characters also ask how "on[e] man may have too bodies and two faces? / And that one man at on time may be in two placys?" (786–87). Yet even though he cannot comprehend how it's done, Jenkin still realizes that all these tricks are "a shamfull lye" (519) rather than a miracle or magic. Marie Axton points out in her introduction to *Jack Juggler* that all the play's otherwise frivolous tricks and gratuitous errors are inspired by contemporary Protestant propaganda. *Juggler*, like *conjuror*, is a synonym for a priest, and in *Jack Juggler* beliefs in bilocation and transubstantiation are both simply duplicitous delusions. The Black Rubric, the controversial note added to the Communion Service of the 1552 Book of Common Prayer, drives this point home by insisting that "it is against the truth of Christ's true natural body to be in more places than in one at one time."[36] Axton notes that Nicholas Udall makes that same point in his translation of Peter Martyr's *Discours . . . Concernynge the Sacrament of the Lordes Supper*. There he denounces Catholic doctrine as "the iuglyng sleyghtes of the Romish Babylon" and says, "Christ is no iugler neither doth he mocke or daly with our senses . . . as the adversaries would have here in this matier of the sacrament" because "the Solle & live of man, nor also the Aungels or spirites, cannot be in diverse or soondrie places at one same selfe tyme for creatures they be."[37]

From the perspective of Protestant propaganda, Doctor Pinch is no less a fraud than Jack Juggler, and he is no less preposterous than the exorcists and conjurers denounced by Samuel Harsnett in his *Declaration of Popish Impostures*. In his discussion of Harsnett's influence on *King Lear*, Stephen Greenblatt argues that this attack on Catholic beliefs and practices aims "to demolish the experience of wonder; he seeks to shine the sharp, clear light of ridicule on the exorcist's mysteries and thus to expose them as shabby tricks." From this perspective, "performance kills belief; or rather acknowledging theatricality kills the credibility of the supernatural."[38] Greenblatt sees *The Comedy of Errors* coming to similar conclusions, and he contends that the "comedy's decorum rests upon the strict absence of supernatural agency."[39] In this view, disenchantment is inevitable, and all traces of the supernatural are completely dissipated. More recently, Richard Strier advances a similar argument in "Shakespeare and the Skeptics," maintaining that most of the plays project "a thoroughly secular world" in which "the working of miracles is ceased."[40] In his analysis of *The Comedy of Errors*, Strier says that the play's happy ending requires no belief in miracles because "the one event that is described in the play as 'past thought of human reason' and as a 'miracle' is clearly and evidently neither."[41] Yet this leap to skepticism and disenchantment strikes me as too abrupt and conclusive. It too readily discounts that quality that another great Romantic critic, John Keats, attributes to Shakespeare, namely "negative capability," which allows the mind to entertain "uncertainties, Mysteries, doubts, without any irritable reaching after fact & reason."

Keats's enthusiasm for uncertainties and mysteries seems more apt as a response to the conclusion of *The Comedy of Errors* than skeptical certitudes. Among other things, Emilia's last-minute arrival and speeches create a powerful religious aura. As an abbess, she enters in a nun's habit and offers the protection of an older ecclesiastical realm, imperiled by the Reformation but not wholly suppressed: "He took this place for sanctuary, / And it shall privilege him from your hands" (5.1.95–96).[42] She promises healing ministrations both medical and spiritual, consisting of "wholesome syrups, drugs and holy prayers," and she calls them a "charitable duty of my order" (5.1.105, 108). In doing so, she takes on the role of a *dea ex machina*, imparting a sense of what Kent Cartwright calls "immanent Providential design rather beyond the chance and fortune that typically govern comedy and farce."[43] At the same time, unlike Doctor Pinch, she claims no supernatural powers to cast out devils or to "conjure . . . by all the saints in heaven" (4.4.53), and she refuses to bind anyone. Rebuking Adriana's possessive jealousy, she opposes threats of bondage with the festive liberty:

Thou sayst his sports were hindered by thy brawls.
Sweet recreation barred, what doth ensue
But moody and dull melancholy, . . .
. . . .
In food, in sport, and life-preserving rest
To be disturbed would mad or man or beast.

(5.1.78–85)

When reunited with her own long-lost husband, Emilia practices what she preaches, saying, "whoever bound him, I will loose his bonds / And gain a husband by his liberty" (5.1.340–41). Most significantly, her long ordeal of loss and separation is assigned the Christological length of "thirty-three years" and reconceived as a "travail" (5.1.402) or labor that results in the delivery of her sons and the reunion of her family, and the play ends with a celebration of a "nativity" (5.1.406); amid the Christmas revels of Gray's Inn, the play's allusion to Christ's birth would only enhance the sense of some sort of higher "blessed power" at work in its resolution.

The positive view of the abbess as "a virtuous and a reverend lady" (5.1.135) suggests that *The Comedy of Errors* does not aim to inspire the harsh skepticism and disenchantment encouraged by conventional Protestant propaganda. Here and elsewhere, Shakespeare goes beyond what Greenblatt describes as Reformation attempts "to dismantle a corrupt and inadequate therapy without effecting a new and successful cure."[44] Conjurers are mocked and punished, but Doctor Pinch resembles Jack Juggler less than the foolish charlatan, Doctor Brundyche, of *The Croxton Play of the Sacrament*. In that late medieval play, Jonathan the Jew desecrates the host by crucifying it on a pillar but ends up losing his arm. Doctor Brundyche boasts that he can heal Jonathan's injuries, but Jonathan denounces him as a quack and throws him out. Jonathan then throws his arm and the host into a boiling cauldron, and Christ appears with his wounds bleeding in a dramatic Eucharistic miracle. That spectacle is intended to move all who see it, characters and audience, to compassion and remorse: "I show yow the streyteness of my greuaunce, / And all to meue yow to my mercy."[45] Jonathan and his companions respond accordingly, giving and receiving mercy, and go to present themselves to the bishop, who bears the restored host away to the church in a Corpus Christi procession. The play concludes with the Jews' conversion, absolution, and baptism. The audience is then enjoined to continue this "conversacion of all thes fayre men / With hartys stedfastly knett in one," and the play presents itself and its "conversacion" as a kind of theatrical communion.[46]

The Comedy of Errors extends a comparable invitation to everyone on stage and in the audience to a "gossips' feast" (5.1.405) or christening party sponsored by the godparents as a celebration of the twins' quasi-miraculous rebirth. While hardly a full-fledged miracle play on the order of *The Croxton Play of the Sacrament*, the play's reunion and rebirth still give hints of a Eucharistic miracle. Rather than mocking bilocation as a "shamfull lye," as *Jack Juggler* does, Shakespeare here and elsewhere enhances its mysterious and miraculous aspects. When the twins finally do appear together, almost everyone reacts as if they have seen a ghost. The duke says, "One of these men is *genius* to the other. / And so of these, which is the natural man / And which the spirit?" (5.1.333–35). The spookiness spreads as Antipholus of Syracuse asks his dumbstruck father, "Egeon art thou not? Or else his ghost" (5.1.338). Their questions indicate what Brian Gibbons calls feelings not only of "Astonishment . . . but also a powerful undertow of awe and fear."[47] That these two characters seem to be one but in two places at once—"Even now we hous'd him in the abbey here, / And now he's there"—strikes others as a mystery "past thought of human reason" (5.1.189–90) and a "miracle" (5.1.265). The conclusion of *Twelfth Night* assigns this sense of ubiquity a divine force when all look upon another twin with a "strange regard" (5.1.204), and he replies, "Nor can there be that deity in my nature, / Of here and everywhere" (5.1.221–22). This double vision affords, as Orsino says, "a natural perspective, that is and is not" (5.1.209), making the natural look supernatural. Hamlet describes this phenomenon in more learned terms when he describes his father's ghost as "*hic et ubique*" (1.5.158), and, though he may mock this as a mere stage trick with jokes about devils in the cellarage, the ghost remains a frightening power who haunts both Hamlet and the play.

In *The Comedy of Errors*, the mysteries are less sinister and the miracles are natural. The characters may be confused, as Jonathan Crewe notes, but the play lets the audience see "the benign and healing theatricality that is shaping their ends."[48] Still, the poetic faith sustained by Shakespeare's theatricality sustains a communion that partakes of religious faith. *The Comedy of Errors* may have been derided as nothing of any account at one of its earliest performances at Gray's Inn, and some of the members may have sneered at its performers as "base and common fellows." Shakespeare and his fellows did not present anything like the spectacular "mystical ceremonies and Invocations" of the Masque of Amity. Nevertheless, *The Comedy of Errors* creates more genuine feelings of goodwill and harmony than any performance at Gray's Inn. Fittingly, the play's last words are given to the humble twin servants whose efforts to sort out precedence are elegantly and kindly resolved: "We came into the world like brother and brother, / And now let's go hand in hand, not one before another" (5.2.426–27). No less fittingly, these words prove more efficacious and enduring than any speech recorded in *The Gesta Grayorum*—and they get the last laugh.

Notes

1. *As You Like It*, in *The Norton Shakespeare*, ed. Stephen Greenblatt (New York: W. W. Norton, 1997), 1.5.63, p. 54. All further citations of Shakespeare's plays are from this edition and are given parenthetically in the text.

2. Samuel Taylor Coleridge, *Biographia Literaria*, ed. James Engell and W. Jackson Bate (Princeton: Princeton University Press, 1983), 2:6.

3. Samuel Taylor Coleridge, "Desultory Remarks on the Stage, & the Present State of the Higher Drama," in *Lectures, 1808–1819: On Literature*, ed. R. A. Foakes (Princeton: Princeton University Press, 1987), 2:134.

4. Ibid., 2:267.

5. Ibid., 2:265.

6. See Mary Anne Perkins, "Religious Thinker," in *The Cambridge Companion to Coleridge*, ed. Lucy Newlyn (Cambridge: Cambridge University Press, 2002), 187–99.

7. Samuel Taylor Coleridge, *Statesman's Manual*, in *Lay Sermons*, ed. R. J. White (Princeton: Princeton University Press, 1972), 6.29.

8. J. Robert Barth, S.J., *Coleridge and Christian Doctrine* (New York: Fordham University Press, 1987), 171.

9. Nicholas Halmi, "Coleridge on Allegory and Symbol," in *Oxford Handbook of Samuel Taylor Coleridge*, ed. Frederick Burwick (New York: Oxford University Press, 2009), 345–58, 356. See also Nicholas Halmi, *The Genealogy of the Romantic Symbol* (Oxford: Oxford University Press, 2007), 110–19 and 127–32, for a subtle explanation of Coleridge's ambiguous views of the Eucharist. The passage Halmi cites comes from Coleridge's commentary on the sermons of John Donne; he applauds Donne for recognizing the sacrament as an epiphany but regrets that neither he nor "Luther before him, had carried this just conception to its legitimate consequents!" Samuel Taylor Coleridge, *Marginalia*, ed. George Whalley (Princeton: Princeton University Press, 1984), 2:280.

10. Coleridge, *Lectures*, 1:223–24.

11. Samuel Taylor Coleridge, *The Notebooks of Samuel Taylor Coleridge*, ed. Kathleen Coburn, 5 vols. (London: Routledge, 1957–2002), 2:2274.

12. Diarmaid MacCulloch, *The Reformation* (London: Penguin, 2004), 248–53.

13. Quoted in Jaroslav Pelikan, *The Christian Tradition: A History of the Development of Doctrine; Reformation of Church and Dogma, 1300–1700*, 5 vols. (Chicago:

University of Chicago Press, 1984), 4:186 and 192–93. See also Kilian Mc-Donnell, *John Calvin, the Church, and the Eucharist* (Princeton: Princeton University Press, 1967), 224–25, and Brian Gerrish, *Grace and Gratitude: The Eucharistic Theology of John Calvin* (Minneapolis: Fortress Press, 1993), 104–6 and 140–45. Resolving these disputes was not easy, nor was finding the middle path; as Gerrish says, Calvin sometimes "seemed to stumble between the rival opinions of Luther and Zwingli rather than to harmonize them" (10).

14. Quoted in Pelikan, *Christian Tradition*, 4:201.

15. McDonnell, *John Calvin*, 243.

16. John Calvin, *The Institutes of the Christian Religion*, ed. John T. McNeill, trans. Ford Lewis Battles (Philadelphia: Westminster Press, 1960), 4.17.39, vol. 2., p. 1416.

17. *The boke of common praier, and [ad]ministracion of the sacramentes, and other rites and ceremonies in the Churche of Englande* (London, 1552), Aiii^{r-v}.

18. Quoted in Joseph C. McLelland, *The Visible Words of God: An Exposition of the Sacramental Theology of Peter Martyr Vermigli, 1500–1562* (Grand Rapids, MI: Eerdmans, 1957), 20. See also Peter Martyr Vermigli, *The Oxford Treatise and Disputation on the Eucharist, 1549*, ed. and trans. Joseph C. McLelland (Kirksville, MO: Truman State University Press, 2000), 7:284.

19. Richard Hooker, *Of the Law of Ecclesiastical Polity*, 5.57.5, ed. W. Speed Hill, 7 vols. (Cambridge, MA: Belknap Press, 1977), 2:234.

20. William Perkins, *A Discourse of the Damned Art of Witchcraft*, in *Works* (Cambridge, 1618), 630.

21. Perkins, *The Art of Prophecying*, in *Works* (Cambridge, 1608), 2:742 and 745.

22. Anne Kibby, *The Interpretation of Material Shapes in Puritanism: A Study of Rhetoric, Prejudice, and Violence* (Cambridge: Cambridge University Press, 1986), 67.

23. Sir Philip Sidney, *An Apology for Poetry*, ed. Geoffrey Shepherd (1965; repr., Manchester: Manchester University Press, 1973), 99; hereafter cited parenthetically in the text.

24. As Shepherd points out in his notes, *energia* is Sidney's term for what his source, Julius Scaliger, calls "efficacy," the term used repeatedly by contemporary theologians (226).

25. Thomas Cranmer, *Writings and Disputations Relative to the Sacrament of the Lord's Supper* in *Works of Thomas Cranmer*, vol. 15, ed. Edmund Cox (Cambridge: Parker Society, 1846–48), 271.

26. Christopher J. Cocksworth, *Evangelical Eucharistic Thought in the Church of England* (Cambridge: Cambridge University Press, 1993), 29.

27. Robert Hill, "A Communicant Instructed," in *The Path-way to Pietie* (1606; repr., London, 1629), 230, 236.

28. Jeffrey Knapp, *Shakespeare's Tribe: Church, Nation, and Theater in Renaissance England* (Chicago: University of Chicago Press, 2002), 138. Anthony Dawson also discusses parallels between Hooker's reception theory of the Eucharist and audience participation in "Performance and Participation," in *The Culture of Playgoing in Shakespeare's England: A Collaborative Debate*, ed. Anthony B. Dawson and Paul Yachnin (Cambridge: Cambridge University Press, 2001), 45, 37–38, and both he and Knapp acknowledge their debts to Joel Altman's discussion of audience participation as a kind of political and poetic sacrament in "'Vile Participation': The Amplification of Violence in the Theater of *Henry V*," *Shakespeare Quarterly* 42 (1991): 6, 24.

29. *The Comedy of Errors* is generally considered an early play, dating from 1589–93; see the introduction by R. A. Foakes to his edition of the play (London: Arden, 1962), xvi–xxiii. Charles Whitworth argues in his edition (Oxford: Oxford University Press, 2002) that *The Comedy of Errors* "was composed expressly" for performance at Gray's Inn (2–5), as does Sidney Thomas, "The Date of *The Comedy of Errors*," *Shakespeare Quarterly* 7 (1956): 377–84.

30. *Gesta Grayorum or the History of the High and Mighty prince Henry Prince of Purpoole, Anno Domini 1594*, ed. Desmond Bland (Liverpool: Liverpool University Press, 1968), 29; hereafter cited parenthetically in the text.

31. All citations are from the Geneva Bible (1599).

32. Shakespeare's transformation of his Plautine source from straightforward farce to something more mysterious and religious is discussed by Barbara Freedman, "Egeon's Debt: Self Division and Self-Redemption in *The Comedy of Errors*," *English Literary Renaissance* 10 (1980): 360–83; Lorna Hutson, *The Usurer's Daughter: Male Friendship and Fictions of Women in Sixteenth-Century England* (London: Routledge, 1994), 222; Arthur Kinney, "Shakespeare's *Comedy of Errors* and the Nature of Kinds," in *The Comedy of Errors: Critical Essays*, ed. Robert S. Miola (New York: Routledge, 1997), 157–58; and Alexander Leggatt, *Shakespeare's Comedy of Love* (London: Methuen, 1974), 2–3.

33. Keith Thomas, *Religion and the Decline of Magic* (New York: Scribners, 1971), 54–55.

34. Ros King, introduction to *The Comedy of Errors*, ed. T. S. Dorsch, revised with a new introduction by Ros King (Cambridge: Cambridge University Press, 2004), 9.

35. *Jacke Jugeler* (lines 178–81), in *Three Tudor Classical Interludes: Thersites, Jacke Jugeler, Horestes*, ed. Marie Axton (Cambridge: D. S. Brewer, 1982), 69; hereafter cited parenthetically in the text by line number.

36. David Cressy and Lori Anne Ferrell, eds., *Religion and Society in Early Modern England: A Sourcebook* (London: Routledge, 1996), 48.

37. Marie Axton, introduction, 19–20. Axton also notes that Thomas Cranmer cites Plautus's comedy *Amphitruo* in his refutation of Stephen Gardiner's defense of transubstantiation (20).

38. Stephen Greenblatt, *Shakespearean Negotiations: The Circulation of Social Energy in Renaissance England* (Berkeley: University of California Press, 1988), 104, 109.

39. Stephen Greenblatt, "Shakespeare Bewitched," in *Shakespeare and Cultural Traditions*, ed. Tetsuo Kishi, Roger Pringle, and Stanley Wells (Newark: University of Delaware Press, 1994), 29.

40. Richard Strier, "Shakespeare and the Skeptics," *Religion and Literature* 32 (2000): 189, 177. The quotation is from Reginald Scott's *The Discoverie of Witchcraft* (1584). Strier says that the belief that the age of miracles is passed is the normative Protestant position.

41. Strier, "Shakespeare and the Skeptics," 175, and "Sanctifying the Bourgeoisie: The Cultural Work of *The Comedy of Errors*," in *Shakespeare and Religious Change*, ed. Kenneth J. E. Graham and Philip D. Collington (Houndmills: Palgrave Macmillan, 2009), 27.

42. John L. McMullan, "Criminal Organization in Sixteenth and Seventeenth Century London," *Social Problems* 29 (1982): 313–14. For sanctuary's surprising durability in the face of efforts to suppress it, see Isobel D. Thornley, "The Destruction of Sanctuary," in *Tudor Studies Presented to Albert Frederick Pollard*, ed. Robert William Seton Watson (1924; repr., Freeport, NY: Books for Libraries, 1969), 182–207.

43. Kent Cartwright, "Surprising the Audience in *The Comedy of Errors*," in *Re-visions of Shakespeare: Essays in Honor of Robert Ornstein*, ed. Evelyn Gajowski (Newark: University of Delaware Press, 2004), 216.

44. Greenblatt, *Shakespearean Negotiations*, 99.

45. Croxton, *The Play of the Sacrament*, in *Medieval Drama*, ed. Greg Walker (Oxford: Blackwell, 2000), lines 659-60, p. 228.

46. Ibid., lines 904–5, p. 261.

47. Brian Gibbons, "Erring and Straying Like Lost Sheep: *The Winter's Tale* and *The Comedy of Errors*," *Shakespeare Survey* 50 (1997): 120.

48. Jonathan Crewe, "God or the Good Physician: The Rational Playwright in *The Comedy of Errors*," *Genre* 15 (1982): 208.

Chapter 4

Acknowledgment and Confession
in *Cymbeline*

SARAH BECKWITH

Confession is a speech act that seeks its completion in the acknowledgment of another.

—James Wetzel

What is it I can confess? I can confess that I envy this man's art and that man's scope, the anger I failed to suppress at the last faculty meeting, that I have been wasting my time. To whom am I confessing this? If I have been unfaithful I can confess this to my husband; if I am Bill Clinton, I must apparently confess this to the nation. Who will then forgive me or him? Can I confess that my very existence here and now takes up far more than my fair share of the world's resources, and so I harm others, specific others, every day just by living the life I live? I can confess all the things—but only the things—for which I am accountable. I can hardly confess your sins, though I might, at times, in certain moods, be tempted to accuse you of them.

And what is it I can forgive? Can I forgive, say, my uncle's alcoholism, my rapist, my boyfriend's infidelity? Will my uncle, my rapist, my boyfriend be forgiven because of my forgiveness? Who is to say? Who can say?

Confessing is a speech act and so it is more closely akin to declaring, revealing, admitting, avowing, allowing, telling, than it is to lamenting, sorrowing, regretting.[1] The latter was encompassed in an older theological language of attrition and contrition, but the difference between contrition and feeling sorrow for something lies in the fact that contrition keeps the reality of the harm I have done before me, whereas I can be sorry for a million and one different things that do not involve my own responsibility in hurting. We have all been at the other end of: "I am sorry you feel that way." Perhaps we have even said it. Contrition keeps the reality of someone else's pain, a pain connected to my actions, before me, and it is this sense of the harm of the other that keeps me from the many possible corruptions (and consolations) of remorse as a private language, including a fascination with the cleanliness of my conscience or the complexity of my own mind. Confession in short must be performed; it is not something that takes place inside the mind.[2] And the kinship, the family resemblance of confessing to admitting, avowing, revealing, acknowledging shows why it is hard to do.[3] In confessing I have not only revealed something about myself but committed myself to a different future.

The recognition scene in *Cymbeline* is predicated on the fact or act of speaking and the new community that comes into being as a result of these acts of speech. As with *The Winter's Tale*, a self-involving remorse is overcome publicly: however spectacular and histrionic the divine intervention is, remorse is addressed through the overwhelming response to human others. The last extraordinary scene of *Cymbeline* links the languages of confession, acknowledgment, and recognition to create the unprecedented peace that is the "mark of wonder" in this play, the play that harmonizes Britain with ancient and contemporary Rome. Is it a Pax Romana or a Pax Britannia? Pardon, in any case, is the word to all.[4] In this pointed Christianization of Aristotle's "anagnorisis," in the multiple recognitions that come so thick and so fast in this bravura scene (twenty-four in all), in the crescendo of self-disclosures and the infection of truth telling that overcomes the protagonists, in the narrow path between the ludicrous and the wondrous, and between delight and dangerous risk,

Shakespeare parses out an astonishing exploration of the grammar of remorse, acknowledgment, and the re-creation of a community through forgiveness. We might see this as a Eucharistic community because it embodies forgiveness, and because it imagines the restoration of each person to himself or herself as inseparable from, intimate with, the restoration of that community. In the multiple confessions that end the play, the expression of each person's remorse engenders further truths, and these truths are seen to be part of a shared story that makes sense only when told together, a story of which each individual part turns out to be part of the same whole, a whole not visible until each individual part of those stories is told. It is, in short, a re-membrance.

Posthumus's Keys: The Penitent Lock

Posthumus speaks the inherited languages of sin and repentance and begins to show us the contours of remorse, a remorse that is vital to the acknowledgments of the last scene. The linking of remorse and acknowledgment here is key. I am depending on a particular understanding of remorse—as an awakening to the reality of an other.[5] That is why confession too is not the revelation of a past belonging to me but a recognition of the reality and effects of my speech and action in the lives of others. As James Wetzel has said in a passage I use for the epigraph to this essay, confession is a speech act that seeks its completion in the acknowledgment of another.[6] It is not an inward language at all, though of course it must be voiced in the language of acknowledgment.[7]

   It is Posthumus who asks the question: "Is't enough I am sorry?" (5.5.105), and his question might be said to sum up a few centuries of penitential discourse in one highly economical question.[8] For the question of sufficiency haunts penitential discourse. Early medieval contritionist understandings, such as the foundational work of Peter Lombard, the master of the *Sentences* on which every scholastic commentator cut his teeth, held that contrition was sufficient for God's forgiveness; for others it was priestly absolution that constituted the "matter" of the sacrament of penance, a penance that could be administered only through the church's officers.[9] For Luther nothing could ever be enough; there could, therefore, be no language of sufficiency or accounting, no earning or calculating, meriting or measuring to limit or usurp God's one-sided, utterly gratuitous preemptive and prevenient gift of grace. Posthumus's own language in the prison scene is shot through with the language of accounting and with a vocabulary straight from the medieval confessional. I quote at length:

> My conscience, thou art fettered
> More than my shanks and wrists. You good gods give me
> The penitent instrument to pick that bolt,
> Then free for ever. Is't enough I am sorry?
> So children temporal fathers do appease;
> Gods are more full of mercy. Must I repent,
> I cannot do it better than in gyves
> Desired more than constrained. To satisfy,
> If of my freedom 'tis the main part, take
> No stricter render of me than my all.
> I know you are more clement than vile men
> Who of their broken debtors take a third,
> A sixth, a tenth, letting them thrive again
> On their abatement. That's not my desire.
> For Innogen's dear life take mine, and though
> Tis not so dear, yet 'tis a life; you coined it.
> 'Tween man and man they weigh not every stamp;
> Though light, take pieces for the figure's sake;
> You rather mine, being yours. And so, great powers,
> If you will make this audit, take this life
> And cancel these cold bonds.
>
> (5.5.102–22)

I count: *bonds, coins, audit, render, debtors, worth, repent, clement, satisfy,* and a jumble of possessive pronouns trying to work out what belongs to whom. This is the logic of penance as counting and accounting, and it has an old and scandalous history, the history that prompted Luther's liberation from the impossibly exacting cost of sinning and its ruthless, insatiable demands. Here this penitential logic is rendered aporetic through the image of a life that is "coin'd." The very most Posthumus can render for Innogen's life is his own. But he ends up caught in a kind of dilemma that is also a discovery: how can he pay in a coin (his life) that it is not in his power to give even though that is the most he could ever tender or render: "For Innogen's dear life, take mine, and though / Tis not so dear, yet 'tis a life; you coined it" (5.5.116–17). The image of the sovereign's coin hovers between an understanding of himself as a creature, made in the image of God, therefore gifted, gift and recipient at once, to one of despair.[10] He can't pay, because nothing will be enough and the coin he might wish to pay in is not his to give. So he can only say: "great powers / If you will make this audit, take this life / And cancel these cold bonds" (5.5.120–22). How could even his life pay for his taking of Innogen's? Neither Innogen nor Posthumus owns his or her own life. The language of payment is useless, incommensurable. So the prayer to the "great powers" ends by turning to Innogen. His remorse leads him again and again to his sense of the utter particularity of the woman he imagines he has murdered, and his soliloquy ends with an address to her: "O Innogen / I'll speak to thee in silence" (5.5.122–23). Here he is like Leontes: "Whilst I remember / Her and her virtues I cannot forget / My blemishes in them and so still think of / the wrong I did myself."[11] Here is the perspective in which the meanings of what one has done, what one has become through doing it, and what victims have suffered are inseparable.

The "cold bonds," as both Martin Butler and Roger Warren note, stand for prisoner's fetters, the bond of life itself, and the bonds of old legal agreements.[12] In the penitential context of this speech they also stand for the chains of sin. What, then, is the penitent instrument? The language of the keys, of binding and loosing, and its theological and doctrinal fortunes tend to be traced around a series of scriptural passages: Luke 24:47–48, Mark 16:15–16, Matthew 28:18–20, John 20:21–23, and especially Matthew 18:18–19: "and I say unto thee, that thou art Peter, and upon this rocke I will build my congregation: and the gates of hel shal not prevaile against it. And I will give unto thee the keyes of the kingdome of heaven: and whatsoever thou shalt binde in earth, shal be loosed in heaven."[13] These keys are defined by medieval theologians as the apostolic authority granted to the church to confess and absolve. But the authority "of binding and loosing" is redefined by Reformers (for whom sinners are always already forgiven) in a range of ways: for Tyndale, the Gospel is the key; for Becon, the key is preaching; for John Jewell, the keys are not of confession but of "instruction" and "correction," and so on.[14] The point here is not to locate what particular doctrine of the keys is held by Shakespeare, a pointless, perhaps impossible endeavor. It is rather to show how the language of imprisonment and release is displaced from the physical fetters to the pinching, excoriating dilemma of a conscience in chains; to see how such language is inextricably bound up with questions of the relationship between human effort and divine will, of despair, and of the felt anguish of acknowledgment without grace; and finally to see how deeply engaged such a predicament might be to the most central and agonizing questions around guilt, responsibility, and salvation in his culture.[15] The scene poses the questions of the keys as a felt, existential question for a haunted soul confronting the results of his own murderous rage, for whom there appears to be no recourse but death.

The medieval theology of the keys would have stressed the tripartite nature of the sacrament of penance in contrition, confession, and satisfaction. The penitent lock would have consisted in the contrite sinner's confessing to a priest, and the sacrament of penance encompassed both his speech act and the speech act of the priest in absolving him. Sins, says Aquinas, are like bonds that must be loosened or dissolved; the priest's words "I absolve you" "derive from Christ's own words to Peter: *Whatsoever you shall loose on earth . . . and is the form used in sacramental absolution.*"[16] Calvin too consistently imaged sin itself as bondage.[17] The longevity and purchase of this figure are apparent in the fact that sin as bondage is used by Lancelot Andrewes in "A Sermon Preached at Whitehall upon the Sunday after Easter, being the Thirteenth of March, AD MDC." Linking the texts from Luke 4:18 and Isaiah 61:1, Andrewes comments on the word *captive:*

> The mind of the Holy Ghost then, as in other places by divers other resemblances, so in this here, is to compare the sinner's case to the estate of the person imprisoned. . . . The very term of "the keys" wherein it was promised, and wherein it is most usually delivered—the

terms of opening and shutting, seem to have relation as it were to the prison gate. The terms of binding and loosing, as it were, to fetters or bands. And these here letting forth or detaining, all and every of them to have an evident relation to the prisoner's estate, as if sin were a prison and the case of sinners like theirs that are shut up.[18]

Andrewes's sermon defends the work of the ministry in the act of ab-solution. In a long gloss on the grammar of John 20:23 he says that *remiseratis* stands first, and *remittuntur* second. Thus "it begins on earth and heaven follows hereafter." It is important, states Andrewes, that the scriptures set this down in two words. The apostle's part is delivered in the active and his own part in the passive, and thus "it is so delivered by Christ as if he were content it should be counted as the Apostles' agency in the act of the remission of sins." This is Andrewes's avant-garde con-formity and defense of the central office of priesthood in the act of reconciliation. But Posthumus has no priest to confess to, no friend, no human other. So he calls first to the gods and then to his dead lady: "O Innogen, I'll speak to thee in silence."

The Incorporate Past: Confession in the Book of Common Prayer

In the massive reevaluation of the ritual language of Catholicism, the Book of Common Prayer may be understood both to extend the peni-tential reach of the liturgy and to contract it. How is it possible to make both of these claims at once? Annual auricular confession had been in-augurated as a legal requirement for all Christians at the Fourth Lateran Council of 1215.[19] This practice was associated with the rites of Easter. To imagine it as some hole-in-the corner affair, some "ear-shrift," as Tyndale put it, would be to accept the polemical description of its most ardent en-emies.[20] Confession as practiced by the vast majority of parishioners was a preparation for the Easter Eucharist, and as such a part of the Mass, and, with the Eucharist, one of the only other repeated sacraments incorpo-rated into the liturgical year. It was never, for such parishioners, a particu-larly private event, since it was done mostly on Maundy Thursday, Good Friday, or Easter Sunday, when parishioners queued up in a crowded line to kneel before the parish priest. This kind of mandatory annual auricular confession associated with the Rites of Easter was abolished, but in the revised rites of the Book of Common Prayer parishioners were repeatedly sought to consult their minister if, after examining their consciences, they felt themselves to be out of charity with their neighbor and so not ready worthily to receive the sacrament. There was still a form of private and auricular confession and absolution in the "Order for the Visitation of the Sick," but as far as able-bodied people were concerned, it was only those who found that they could "not quiet their consciences," the ones who "requireth further comfort of counsel," who were encouraged to "come to me or some other discrete and learned minister of Gods woorde and open his griefe, that he may receive ghostly counsaile, advice, and comfort, as his conscience may be relieved."[21] The rite was thus exceptional rather than routine. The difference here was that the onus of examining their consciences was on the sinners and consultation of the minister was at their discretion. As Patrick Collinson has memorably said: "It was as if the great unwashed public had said to the clergy, "don't call us, we'll call you.""[22]

Nevertheless, the Book of Common Prayer allowed considerable scope for the minister to decide whether his parishioners were in a position to participate in the Eucharist, and it is clear that the extraliturgical practices of the ministry of reconciliation continued almost unbroken from the Middle Ages. The Morning and Evening Prayer, adapted from the medieval breviary, begins with a patchwork of scriptural quotations, all of which concern amendment of life and one of which the minister is to read. These readings (from Ezekiel 18, Psalm 51, Joel 2, Daniel 9, Jerome 10, Matthew 3, Luke 15, Psalm 143, and 1 John 1) form a patchwork of petitions for mercy, acknowledgments of sin, and desires for amendment, and weave together the penitential psalms and the central parables of forgiveness in the New Testament. Even more important, they are immediately succeeded by a general exhortation of the minister: "And although we ought at all times, humbly to acknowledge our sins before God: yet ought we most chiefly so to do, when we assemble and meet together."[23] John Booty, the editor of the Elizabethan Book of Common Prayer, has said that the penitential introductions to morning and evening prayer (which resembled the Order of Communion of 1548) "changed their spirit, if not their nature."[24] What follows is a general confession, a speech act made together in which the whole congregation kneels and is generally confessed and generally absolved.[25] That is, they are confessed and absolved all together and of all that they have done and left undone: "We have left undone those things which we ought to have done, and we have done those things which we ought not to have done."[26] "Forgive us," says the general confession in the "Order for the Administration of the Lord's Supper, or Holy Communion," "all that is past."[27]

The ostensible desire of the reforms was of course to realize the communal aspects of Eucharist as a prayer of thanksgiving, rather than to see it confected by a sacrificial clergy: the reforms worked both against the notion of a secret ear-shrift to a priest and the notion that a priest could, for example, celebrate a mass on his own.[28] But there has been a quiet revolution in the nature of speech acts of both confession and absolution. In the rubrics that specify the preparations for Holy Communion, each parishioner is called upon to examine his or her own conscience (rather than with an interlocutor), to think where he or she might have offended, and to "confess yourselves to Almighty God." What is the consequence of making confession a private utterance to the Deity rather than a speech act to an individual? Does it not have the effect of weakening the awareness that an offense against one's neighbor is an offense against God and vice versa, and thus the guiding concept of the simultaneity of sin against God, self, and neighbor? Might the effect not be to render sin more abstract, as it were, a private thought?[29]

"I confess to God, not to Tutu," declared General Tienie Groenewald as he chafed against the protocols of the Truth and Reconciliation Commission in South Africa. But here was Tutu's reply: "Jong, if you've had a fight with your wife, it is no use you only ask forgiveness of God. You will have to say to your wife you are sorry. The past has not only contaminated our relationship with God, but the relationship between people as well. And you will have to ask forgiveness of the representatives of those communities that you've hurt."[30] There was no separation for Tutu between the actions committed by this man and the actions committed against God; their separation was a corruption of Christian justice.

In the abolition of auricular confession, the vast, subtle, and capacious literature of classification of the sins and their remedies in the manuals for confessors, and penitential literature, a literature that was at once theological and psychological, was simply dispensed with, for the abolition of auricular confession and the new theology regarded the enumeration of sins as both intolerable and superfluous.[31]

I am reminded of George Eliot's brilliant depiction of Bulstrode's downfall in *Middlemarch*. Bulstrode committed a great sin in his youth when he hid the existence of a daughter who was likely to inherit the wealth of the widow he had married. A man who found the daughter and then concealed her identity had been blackmailing him on the strength of it ever since. Later that man chanced to be in Bulstrode's medical care, a care he neglected in such a way as indirectly to lead to the man's convenient death. Eliot makes it clear how comforting to his sense of holiness, how sweet to his nonconformist heart, is the confession of general sinfulness and unholiness that he makes regularly in the quiet of his own conscience in the face of his Maker. How different this is from the kinds of hard particularity he must face when his misdeed becomes public. Before that point, "his struggle had been securely private, and . . . had ended with a sense that his secret misdeeds were pardoned and his services accepted."[32] Eliot continues: "Sin seemed to be a question of doctrine and inward penitence, humiliation an exercise of the closet, the bearing of his deeds a matter of private vision adjusted solely by spiritual relations and conceptions of the divine purposes. And now, as if by some hideous magic, this loud red figure had risen before him in unmanageable solidity—an incorporate past which had not entered into his imagination of chastisements."[33] This is a brilliant description of the difference between the ruminations of a private conscience, no matter how demanding it might appear in its own best lights, and the confrontation with that "incorporate past" when it is confronted by the effects of that past in the actual lives of others. I mention this extraordinary passage from *Middlemarch* to point to the difference between a confession that is a speech act, one that says something to someone about something, and one that speaks of a general and ubiquitous sinfulness and therefore confesses nothing in particular—or everything all at once: "forgive us all that is past."

Patrick Collinson says: "Nothing can have made a greater negative impact than the lapse of the universal obligation to confess to a priest as the condition both of receiving the sacrament and of remaining an acceptable part of what was still a compulsory Christian society."[34] For the abolition of the so-called internal forum of confession in the pastoral office of confession meant that it was to the external forum, in the punitive and juridical context of the ecclesiastical courts with all their problems, that the peacemaking function fell.[35] Yet what was, in Collinson's terms, a "negative impact" for the parish and for the roles and rites of peacemaking might have presented an opportunity for Shakespearean theater.[36]

Debates over confession remained central to doctrinal, liturgical, and disciplinary concerns in the first three decades of Elizabeth's reign because of the concerted, but ultimately failed, attempt to reform the structure of the ecclesiastical courts into a classis structure. Something of this understanding of a mutual proclamation and mutual absolution is understood in some of the proposals for "church discipline" put forward in the "Admonitions" and constantly sought after by Thomas Cartwright (and others) in his arguments with Whitgift. Excommunication was a sanction that Cartwright saw as grossly abused by the ecclesiastical courts, and taken therefore so lightly as to be useless. Excommunication should be left to elders in the classis structure of a proper consistory, enacting a discipline that was one of the marks of a true church. Confession should therefore be "to the church," and penitential discipline, from first to last, a public performance, not a private contract between priest and penitent. Shakespeare had of course brilliantly examined what it might mean to make this a state policy in *Measure for Measure*, a searing indictment of the enactment of the presbytery. But in the later plays the search for forgiveness is a search for community, and the language of forgiveness, of confession and absolution, is made available for passionate utterance.

Passionate Utterance

It is time to parse out what I mean by *passionate utterance*. The language and the crucial vision here belong to Stanley Cavell's recent work on the legacy of J. L. Austin and Wittgenstein. In a richly suggestive recent essay Cavell revisits some of the key distinctions by which Austin anatomized performative utterances. Austin (famously) attempted to isolate some features of language in which something is done in the saying of the words, and he further divided performative utterances into the illocutionary, in which something is done in virtue of saying something, and the perlocutionary, in which something is done by virtue of saying something. Cavell notes that whereas Austin lovingly and lavishly and minutely parsed out the forms of illocutionary verbs, he was both vague and parsimonious when it came to discussing perlocutionary verbs: "Clearly, any, or almost any, perlocutionary act is liable to be brought off, in sufficiently special circumstances, by the issuing, with or without calculation, of an utterance whatsoever."[37] *"Any, Almost? Liable?"* responds Cavell, "Why is that roughly the end of a story rather than the (new) beginning of one?"[38] Cavell starts over again with Austin's distinctions to begin to map out a realm of speech about which Austin was skittish: the expression of desire.[39] He calls this "passionate utterance" and notes that it may include illocutionary and perlocutionary verbs in equal measure. It is striking that Austin did not name perlocutionary effects. Moreover, it is characteristic of perlocutionary verbs that their effects are not named in the saying, as for illocutionary utterances.[40] The perlocutionary act is "not, as it were, built into the perlocutionary verb." And this is because the second person essentially comes into the picture. I do not, suggests Cavell, generally wonder how I might make a promise or, if I am a judge, render a verdict or, if I am a minister, declare this man and woman man and wife, whereas I might well give considerable ingenuity and attention to how I might persuade you or console you or seduce you, and as I do so the possible parameters of your response are constantly before me. If I am a priest I do not generally wonder how I absolve you, but I may well wonder how I confess to you if you are not a priest. And how then will you hear my confession if you cannot absolve me? Absolution is an office, but confession, even if to an absolving priest, is not. Perlocutionary acts "make room for and reward virtuosity—and passionate expression makes demands upon the singular body in the way illocutionary force forgoes."[41] Austin described six necessary conditions for the felicity of performative utterance, and Cavell shows how these may be extended or overturned in the case of passionate utterance. If in performative utterance there is a conventional procedure, in passionate utterance there is none. If I confess my sins to my parish priest in the Middle Ages, I will enumerate my sins according a particular schema, the "forma confitendi."[42] I will be asked how I have sinned against the Ten Commandments, whether I have committed the seven sins, how I have not performed the seven corporal works of mercy, and so on.[43] But if I am confessing something to you, there will be no set form to follow. I am at the mercy of my own conviction, my own eloquence and honesty, and your ability to bear my words, and so I am also at the mercy of your response. If, in performative utterance, the particular persons and circumstances must be appropriate for the invocation of the procedure, now who has the authority, or the standing, is precisely what is at issue. Auricular confession, of course, *must* be to a priest. But I might have to dare to confess something to you, and you may well think I have completely overstepped the mark and transgressed an unspoken rule of our relations and so refuse my right to speak to you in this way. My confession will involve a claim to a particular standing with you, and it will risk refusal and rebuff. So, "establishing standing" and "singling out" are now the second conditions of passionate utterance. If in performative utterance the procedure must be executed correctly and concretely, such requirements are utterly moot in the case of passionate utterance, for there is no agreed-upon procedure.[44] For example, a condition of auricular confession is that it must be complete, a particularly troubling, demanding, even impossible requirement for the scrupulous such as Luther. Now in the medieval practice of the sacrament of penance, confession had been intrinsically linked with absolution. The sacrament of penance was begun when the penitent was moved to confess and was completed when the words of absolution had been said over the penitent. But if there is no such procedure, we will have to improvise, make it up as we go along. You may forgive me, but you will not absolve me. Austin's fifth and sixth conditions—where the requirement demands certain thoughts and conditions, the parties must have those thoughts and feelings—is also applicable to passionate utterance: the one declaring passion must be moved to declare it. The sixth condition—a requirement of subsequent conduct—is, in passionate utterance, a requirement for response in kind and now. "Unlike the performative case, it is open to the one addressed to resist the demand" such that "what is at stake is the question whether a 'we' is or is not in effect now."[45] Now, the "we" in the

Book of Common Prayer is meant to instantiate rather than describe a preexistent "we." But I am suggesting that the paths from the "I" to the "we" are constantly in the process of interruption and derangement. The ejection, isolation, and estrangement, not to say madness, withdrawal, resentment, and frustration, of the Renaissance protagonists who strut and fret their way across the stage point to the immense dissatisfactions, to the premature coercions, of a preemptive "we." *Cymbeline* tries a different pathway from the "I" to the "we," one enacting a fantasy of communal truth telling that is itself an exploration about the conditions under which truth telling might be possible.

Absolution still exists, of course, in the practices of the Reformed English Church. It exists not merely in the general absolution to which I have already alluded but also in the service for the Visitation of the Sick. But in general it tends now to be associated with the discredited (at least to some) church courts, therefore sometimes administered by lay people, and notoriously subject to financial commutation. In the Sarum Use, the word *absolvo* is used of God and the minister: "Deus . . . absolvat: ego te absolvo." But in the Book of Common Prayer, God *forgives* and the minister *absolves*.

We can parse out the grammar of forgiveness by saying that a king pardons, a priest absolves, but only humans and God forgive. And the Christian God and the ministers who must administer the Book of Common Prayer have been banished from the stage. The Shakespearean grammar of forgiveness is up to humans. But perhaps the theater, or at least Shakespearean theater, can teach the church a thing or two about forgiveness.

Scenes of Confession

Before I return to the last act of *Cymbeline* and its multiple confessions, I want to examine some scenes of confession both in medieval drama and in Shakespearean tragedy. In medieval drama Confession is a personification who offers shrift and absolution. Two onstage confessions are worth mentioning here, one in *The Castle of Perseverance* and one in the late medieval morality play *Mankind*. It is worth exploring these to show the consequences of a drama that no longer has such figures. In medieval drama, confession is more likely to happen offstage, and the work of the drama is often to bring its audience to an appreciation of the rite of penance.[46] Yet in *The Castle of Perseverance* we get an onstage confession from Humanum Genus to Confession. Confession seeks out Humanum Genus after he has sinned and begs him to confess:

> If he wyl be aknowe hys wronge
> And noþynge hale, but telle it me,
> And don penaunce sone a-monge
> I schal hym stere to gamyn and gle.
> (1328–31)[47]

The logic of the play is that mercy is available for the man who asks for it: "Whanne Mankynde cryeth," says, Confession, "I am redy" (1430). In *The Castle*, Humanum Genus confesses according to the schema of the Ten Commandments, the five wits, and so on, and he is absolved by Confession:

> If þou wylt be aknowe here
> Only al þi trespass
> I schal þee schelde from helle fere
> And putte þee fro peyne, unto precyouse place.
> (1455–58)

The Castle stages the repeated necessity of confession in the context of mankind's indefatigable perseverance in sin. In the morality play *Mankind*, the speech act of confession itself is given a more specific focus in a play that thematizes accountability for speech. Indeed mankind is reciprocally understood when the nature of mercy is understood. Mankind is a creature in need of mercy; he will know himself only when he calls upon mercy. Both these plays, then, centrally stage acts of confession. The personifications are not priests (though they *may* of course be dressed in the costume of priests), but part of the point of these penitential plays is to show the efficacy of penitential ritual. Both plays may be understood in the context of the polemical status of penance as a sacrament and the office of forgiveness in the judgment of confession. Wycliffite attacks on the necessity of confession and the sacrament of penance had contested the authority of the priest in the act of confession and absolution, for Wyclif had argued that true penance exists in the mind alone. Such a view had been ridiculed by his opponent, Thomas Netter, who had profoundly grasped the theological and epistemological as well as ecclesiological and political implications of such a statement, but Wyclif's view was widespread among Lollard communities.

When Mercy explains to Mankind that for "every idyll worde we must ȝrlde a reson" (173), he is invoking Matthew 12:36–37 ("But I say unto you that every idle word that men shall speak, they shall give account thereof in the Day of Judgement. For by thy words thou shalt be justified, and by thy words thou shalt be condemned").[48] The play explores the horrors, challenges, and difficulties of this terrifying judgment, in languages that move from the scatological to the sublime. In exploring the extent to which we are creatures who express or evade our cares and commitments in words, the play exposes us to the difficulty of saying certain words and to the necessity of our implication in what we say and do.

It is worth paying close attention to the play's acts of naming, since this is where the chief work of the play is located—in the move from naming to calling. The dramatis personae, Mercy and Mankind, announce who they are; they name themselves to the audience offstage and on (17, 113–15, 194–95, 219, 221–25), but the work of the play is to get the audience to see that they can be understood only reciprocally, through their mutual relationship and recognition. As Mankind is suborned by the vice characters (Titivillus, Mischief, New-Guise, Now-adays, and Nought), he comes to ask their mercy for the beating he has originally given them (650, 658). Seeking mercy from a place where it cannot be granted, where it is negated, he is brought to despair. Such despair was always considered one of the most troubling and vitiating sins because it obscures the mercy of God and so imperils the salvation of one's immortal soul. "Abouen alle synnes thanne is this synne most displesant to Crist, and moost adversarie," as Chaucer's *Parson's Tale* has it. In despair mercy is unavailable; it can no longer be a felt presence, so it cannot be called upon. Such is the vicious and intensifying hold of despair that it renders impossible the very thing it is most in need of. It thus obviates its own cure, and this is not quite true of any of the other sins. When Mankind seeks mercy from this confederacy of thieves and murderers—"I crye yow mercy of all that I dide amisse" (658)—he is "noughted" and a few lines later is tempted to kill himself at Mischief's suggestion.

Mercy reenters and in the formal language of confession asks him to "aske mercy":

> Dyspose yowrsylff meekly to aske mercy, and I wyll assent.
> 3elde me neythr golde nor tresure, but yowr humbyll obeysance
> The voluntary subjeccyon of yowr hert, and I am content.
>
> (816–19)

Mankind cannot bring himself to utter the words: it is a "wyle pety-cyun," a "puerilite," to ask for mercy again and again. But Mercy wants him to articulate words that seem a long way from his sanguine and per-functory, superficial invocation of mercy at their first encounter. Now the words will be sheerly difficult to say, but it is part of the discourse of confession that they must be spoken. Mercy exhorts Mankind time and time again to articulate the words that must come from his mouth to mean anything at all: "3et for my lofe, ope thy lyppes and sey, 'Miserere mei, Deus!'" (830). Finally Mankind, who has been unkind, is brought back to his own kind, to his own nature, and utters these words: "þan Mercy, good Mercy! What is a man wythowte mercy? / Lytyll ys oure parte of paradyse, where mercy ne were" (835–36). He acknowledges his specific relation to the character Mercy (that he is direly in need of him), to himself (that *he* is in need), and to God (this is what it means to be one of his creatures, mankind) at one and the same time. Mercy and Mankind are coincidently understood because mankind is a creature in need of mercy.

This is a crucial moment in the play to which the careful patterning of Mankind and Mercy's address has been leading all along. Mankind recognizes Mercy only at the same time as he knows himself; but he can bear knowing himself only under Mercy's loving gaze. It is not simply an identification of mercy but one that is utterable and conceivable only as a self-recognition—a self-recognition, moreover, that comes not through introspection but through mercy received at the hands of another. The play thus brilliantly charts what Wittgenstein calls "the dawning of aspects," in which something is read as an instance of something else. To know yourself as a member of the species mankind in the Christian anthropology of this play is to know yourself as a creature in need of mercy. It is in this way that the recognition of Mercy depends on the self-awareness of Mankind. The recognition of Mercy is not so much a naming *of* him as a call *to* him. This means that there is a history of theatrical recognition, of acknowledgment, in the morality play tradition, and that it almost invariably involves the sacrament of penance.[49] This history has been submerged because critics have substituted naming for calling and, in so doing, underestimated both the difficulties of learning and the seriousness of speaking. But in successfully banishing the particularity of voice they fail to see that the point of uttering words and the circumstances in which they get uttered are an intrinsic, indispensable part of the significance of those words.[50] When we are tempted to speak outside language games in this way, we lose not what the words mean in being said but what we mean in saying them.

I have been suggesting that the work of the play is to bring Mankind to contrition so that he might confess his need for Mercy. So confession and the recognition of mercy are coterminous. I have also been insisting that our analysis of *Mankind* must work at the level of the utterance, which is irreducibly social and circumstantial, and not at the grammatical abstraction of the sentence, suggesting that this is the burden of the ordinary language philosophy of Wittgenstein and Austin as well as the insight and idiom of the play itself.[51]

Now *Mankind* and *The Castle* can confidently allude to a penitential ritual that is still available, though it might be under heretical attack. Confession is still a component part of the sacrament of penance, and there are authorized agents who can hear confession and make absolution for individual sins. That is what these plays stake themselves on: they insist on the efficacy of that sacramental act and seek to bring their spectators to the centrality of confession and the need for its utterance.

After *Measure for Measure*, which annexes the confessional either to ducal/monarchical surveillance or to a purely juridical function, there are no more priests or friars to hear confessions on the Shakespearean stage.

"Let my trial be mine own confession," says Angelo, thereby substituting a judgment descending on him from on high for the humbling, contrite acknowledgment of need and humility that is central to any confessional act of speech. He thereby obviates the requirement that confession be acknowledged in the response of another, an understanding central to the play *Mankind*. It is beyond my scope here to give a full theatrical history of confession, but it is worth revisiting another crucial scene, one from Shakespeare's own work, because the tragedies seem intent on exploring a world where confession is unavailable and that absence informs the ethical world of these plays.

Shakespeare gives us an instance of "tragic" confession in Othello's deathbed confession of Desdemona. In the last act of *Othello*, Othello seeks to confess Desdemona. Acting as a demonic agency of justice, he believes that it is Desdemona's acknowledgment of guilt in confession that will make his killing an act of sacrifice and not murder. Confession is what links truth to reconciliation, yet here we are given a scene in which it is impossible for Othello to hear any truth because he has convicted Desdemona in his mind. Only her admittance of guilt will count as a confession for him, so Desdemona is rendered dumb. There is nothing she can say that might count as a confession except that which would be a lie. So the scene appears as a hideous quasi-blasphemous travesty of confession in which Othello is a usurper of the role of priest. If you confess to someone you must grant them authority in their own speech act—that is the whole point of confession, and it is why confession is seen to be so necessary in the travesties of justice we call show trials and also why we feel the terrible injustice in such attempts. Othello will accept as confession only what we already know is blatantly untrue. There is simply nothing Desdemona can say: her words are rendered utterly impotent because she has been granted no authority in their saying. And before she is stifled, her speech is. Desdemona might here say with Hermione, "My life stands in the level of your dreams" (*Winters Tale*, 3.2.78), as Othello might say with Leontes, "I have said. She's an adulteress" (2.1.89–90). Both have turned language itself into a private possession.[52] Embedded within this confession scene is another one: Desdemona imagines that Cassio's confession will speak the truth and show her innocence, but Othello stifles this avenue of escape too. "Cassio has confess'd that he has us'd thee."

Infectious Confessions: The Gift of Speech

So let me now turn finally to the last scene of *Cymbeline*. The people collected together in the last scene are unknown to each other in a variety of ways. Some are in a literal disguise: Posthumus as a Briton peasant, Innogen as Fidele, Belarius as Morgan. Some do not know their own identity and in this sense are unknown to themselves. This is true for Guiderius and Arviragus, but it is also true for Posthumus, who thinks he is a murderer though he is not one. All, in any case, have mistaken or confused views of each other. It is a situation ripe for exposure and discovery. And it reworks some of the most romancelike forms of recognition where the "fair unknowns" of medieval romance turn out to be gentle after all, where the creation by kingly knighting is confirmation, not creation, of prior identities that reconcile virtue with honorific status. All these delights inform part of the sense of playful recognition on the part of the audience, as Shakespeare revives his "mouldy old tales." Yet what informs the sense of fragility and wonder in this last scene and its extraordinary investigation of response and responsibility is that this particular community is restored through the speech act of confession. The scene is structured by means of five confessions: the deathbed confession of the queen; the long, cluttered, self-interrupting confession of Giacomo; the confession of Pisanio, completed by the outburst of Guiderius; and the confession of Belarius.

Now, the reported confession of the queen is central to begin to unpoison the speech of the community, and the fact that it is a deathbed confession means that there can be no question at all of its veracity. "She alone knew this," says Cymbeline, "And but she spoke it dying, I would not / Believe her lips in opening it" (5.6.40–42). This confession, whose truthfulness is guaranteed only by virtue of the fact that there is nothing at all to be gained for the queen by virtue of it, begins the unpoisoning of the court through further truthful speech.

It is the ring that motivates the second confession, the one by Giacomo. The ring, metonymy of Innogen, is just one of the complex signs in the play; it is embedded in the central narrative turn of the plot because it is the ring that is transformed from a token of fidelity to the marketplace of Giacomo's and Posthumus's fantasies. The ring is not only the pledge of Innogen's fidelity but the sign and pledge of their clandestine marriage, a marriage that is the only instance of truth and value in the entire corrupt court, where all have to mimic the displeasure of the king in her choice of husband. But the ring is also "the jewel," made the subject of a hideous barter with Giacomo in act 1, scene 4. The suddenness of this overturning is precisely an indication of the extreme fragility of even the deepest human bonds, bonds that rest alone on mutual intelligibility and trust, both of which, can, alarmingly, turn on a dime.[53] The ring, like the bloody cloth, changes its meaning. The bloody cloth, like a relic, is first of all the (spurious) sign of Pisanio's murder of Innogen at Posthumus's request. It is therefore also the sign of Pisanio's fidelity. It is certainly not what it seems to Posthumus, for whom it becomes first of all the sign of his desired revenge, then the very sign of his repentance. It is not until the end of the play, with the revelations by truthful speech, that the real meaning of the bloody cloth can be established (the signs need to be placed in a community of trust for the true significations to become clear). For Innogen has been understood by Posthumus up to this point as the gift of the gods. When Innogen gave him the ring, she said: "Take it heart, / But keep it till you woo another wife, / When Innogen is dead" (1.1.113–15). And his response to this was:

> . . . How, how? Another?
> You gentle gods, give me but this I have
> And cere up my embracements from a next
> In bonds of death.
>
> (1.1.115–18)

This same language of gift is repeated when he at first perceives that Giacomo has made his wife and his jewel equivalent: "The one may be sold or given, or if there were wealth enough for the purchase or merit for the gift. The other is not a thing for sale, and only the gift of the gods" (1.4.71–74). Giacomo's scornful response—"Which the gods have given you?" (1.4.75)—points to Giacomo's shrewd perception of Posthumus's sense of his lack of desert. Gifts may be hard to receive. Giacomo has no difficulty with the next devilish plant: Innogen may be his only in title. It is in the doubt about his desert, not the doubt about Innogen's merits, that Giacomo finds rich material for his new covenant. Innogen is reduced from gift to title, and then even that title is shown to be unstable, perhaps ill founded. As soon as Posthumus's anxieties get to work in this direction, he, and Innogen, are lost. I mean by this the following: if one sees life as a gift, that is not because one *first* sees life as a gift and then speaks in accents of gratitude. Rather, "a sense of life as a gift comes from speech and action which are in the key of a certain kind of gratitude."[54] The value of gift and gratitude are seen only in the way they deepen the lives of the people who live in this idiom, in this accent. Indeed, as Lewis Hyde has said, "True gifts only constrain us as long as we do not pass them along—only, I mean, if we fail to respond to them with an act or an expression of gratitude."[55] The suddenness of Posthumus's reversal is a terrifying instance of how easily and subtly that spirit may be debased, how seemingly casual yet utterly destructive that degradation is. The new covenant, the new wager, is a hideous parody. The reversal of the first exchange of tokens, and the sacred bond between Posthumus and Innogen, posited on the giving of their words to each other, has "turned" swiftly to this. Each will find cause bitterly to renounce not only the other but the whole of femininity, or the whole of masculinity, for which each has stood in. When the bonds, the troths of their exchanged vows, have been traduced, betrayed in this way, it is as if language itself were lost. The dense pun on *bonds* in Posthumus's penitent declamation in prison now opens out to another use of the term *bond.* Our word is our bond: to speak at all is to commit ourselves to our words. That is why linguistic competence is essentially an ethical matter.[56] To redeem language itself: this is the burden of confession in the last scene.

Giacomo's confession is in every sense what a confession should be in the medieval confessional manuals: bitter, self-accusing, complete, particular.[57] Though Cymbeline compels his confession and thus enacts one of the incoherences of coerced confession—confess freely or else—he is "glad to be constrained to utter that / Torments me to conceal" (5.6.141–42). He leaves out nothing. He gives the occasion, the circumstances, the motivation of his actions. He is so self-accusing that it is hard to understand the grammar of his speech at times. The consequent revelation to Posthumus of Innogen's innocence prompts Posthumus's own bitter outburst and self-accusation, which in turn outs Fidelio as Innogen. Then, in the absence of the fear released by the queen's confession, Pisanio can speak truthfully about the whereabouts of Cloten. "Let me end the story," says Guiderius and confesses his killing of Cloten. This is itself a confession that in putting him under threat of execution prompts the confession of Belarius's true identity and thus the restoration of the kingdom's heirs and the reuniting of the family. But Guiderius's words, "Let me end the story," are testimony to the fact that their individual confessions are part of a shared story, a story that can be told only together. No individual confession in itself makes sense, but all in all, and all prompting all, the participants tell a story in which each understands his or her individual role. Guiderius's mole, like Odysseus's scar, as the "donation of nature," but the stock mark of romance recognition, is gently and delightfully superfluous, for the "donation" has been the speech of each to each.

And speech as donation is exactly how Augustine defines confession. Confession, for Augustine, is the exact opposite of a lie. A liar seeks to own language as a possession, but confession is speech that in abjuring and disowning itself returns itself to the giver, who is God. So confession instantiates language as gift, according to Augustine, because it is only in saying what confession says that one is rightly related to God.[58] Or one might say, as Cymbeline does:

> . . . See,
> Posthumus anchors on Innogen
> And she, like harmless lightening, throws her eye
> On him, her brothers, me, her master, hitting
> Each object with a joy. The counterchange
> Is severally in all.
>
> (5.6.393–98)

It is this shared joy that frees "all those in bonds" as all the prisoners are released and "pardon" becomes the word to all (5.6.423). This counterchange, this reciprocation, is the new economy: it is gift, not wager. For Posthumus once saw Innogen as "the gift of the gods" but was deeply susceptible to Giacomo's piercingly scornful question: "Which the gods have given you?" So language returns as gift through the offerings of truthful speech, speech animated by the realizations, the making real, of each to each in remorse. This is Shakespeare's real presence, his remembrance that finds its own complex fidelity and its own peace with a discarded and vilified past, a past whose rejection has seemed structural to the thought of so many of his contemporaries.

Notes

1. This is important in Aquinas's unfinished treatment of penance in the *Summa theologiae*. Aquinas tells us that repentance is a virtue that he has previously defined as "a disposition to make choices according to right reason" (*ST* 3.85.1); translation from *Summa Theologica*, Complete English Edition, 5 vols, ed. and trans. English Dominican Province (Notre Dame, IN: Ave Maria Press, 1984). He explains that penitence grieves when there is good reason to grieve in proportion to the magnitude of the sins and with the full intention to get rid of them. He further argues that it is "a virtue or a virtuous act, not just an emotion." He has previously explained that the *actions* pertaining to penance are "performed by both the penitent sinner and the absolving priest that signify something holy" (3.85.1.ad. 1). He goes on to give a description of penance in terms of the familiar scholastic vocabulary of form and matter. What the penitent says gives material for the sacrament, and what the priest says gives it form. In fact, "The matter of penance is not God but human acts" (3.85.2.ad. 2).

2. See Timothy Gould, *Hearing Things: Voice and Method in the Writing of Stanley Cavell* (Chicago: University of Chicago Press, 1998), 70: "An unexpressed confession (which is not the same as a tacit, or unspoken, confession) is not a confession. The act of *making* a confession is indispensable to the existence of the confession." That confession must be performed might well strike one as being obvious, but the commitments secured through the act of confession are obscured by a long and still tenacious history by which thoughts are depicted as mental objects accessible only to the one whose mind they are in. The history of confession is then treated as part of the history and growth of an interiority. In the *Trialogus*, for example, John Wyclif declares that true penance exists in the mind, an assertion whose implications are well understood by Thomas Netter in his refutation of the epistemological implications of such a view. See Thomas Netter, *Doctrinale antiquitatum fidei Catholicae Ecclesiae*, 2.766–72, and the discussion in Alistair Minnis, *Fallible Authors: Chaucer's Pardoner and Wife of Bath* (Philadelphia: University of Pennsylvania Press, 2008), 274ff. Wittgenstein contends with confession in relation to the "hidden internal" in the *Philosophical*

Investigations, 2.11; see Ludwig Wittgenstein, *Philosophical Investigations*, trans. G. E. M. Anscombe (1953; repr., Oxford: Blackwell, 1999), 222. The criterion for the truthfulness of a confession as understood by Wittgenstein is not that it describes inner events but that it is taken up by others; see Richard Eldridge, *Leading a Human Life: Wittgenstein, Intentionality, and Romanticism* (Chicago: University of Chicago Press, 1997), 131.

3. Wittgenstein, *Philosophical Investigations*, remark 546: "And words can be wrung from us—like a cry. Words can be *hard* to say: such for example, as can be used to effect a renunciation, or to confess a weakness: Words are also deeds."

4. Though it is important, as I will go on to show, that the king's pardon comes after the spontaneous confessions of the community created through their acts of speech.

5. Raimond Gaita defines *remorse* beautifully as "a recognition of the reality of another person through the shock of wronging her, just as grief is the recognition of another through the grief of losing her." See his *Good and Evil: An Absolute Conception* (London: Routledge, 2004), 52.

6. James Wetzel, "Wittgenstein's Augustine: The Inauguration of the Later Philosophy," *Polygraph* 19/20 (2008): 129–47. This excellent essay addresses the whole question of the secularization of confession in fascinating ways.

7. See Augustine's *Confessions*, trans. Henry Chadwick (Oxford: Oxford University Press, 1991); 10.3, where Augustine contemplates the audience for confession, is highly relevant here, and see below.

8. All quotations from the plays are from *The Norton Shakespeare*, based on the Oxford text, ed. Stephen Greenblatt (New York: W. W. Norton, 1997).

9. Peter Lombard, *Sentences* 4.171.13; Duns Scotus, *Oxford Commentary on the Sentences* 4.16.1.7.

10. It is fascinating to see that this image of the soul likened to a coin with the king's stamp on it itself has an important history in accounts of human and divine agency. David Aers has recently argued that it is a central image for Ockham's thoroughly extrinsicist account of the workings of divine grace. Ockham's image for the grace at work in the sacraments is a leaden denarius bestowed by a sovereign will. He contrasts this with Aquinas's model of grace modeled on the human voice, for him an indication that spiritual powers can be in a body instrumentally (*ST* 3.62.4ad.1). For Ockham's image, see William of Ockham, *Scriptum super IV libros sententiarum magistri Petri Lombardi* (his commentary on the fourth book of Peter Lombard's *Sentences*) 6.6. See David Aers, *Salvation and Sin: Augustine, Langland and Fourteenth-Century Theology* (Notre Dame, IN: University of Notre Dame Press, 2009), 51. Aers's illuminating commentary on different models of human and divine agency as competitive or cooperative is highly relevant to Shakespeare's late work. The highly theatrical forms of intervention in

the late plays—oracle, heavenly music, Jupiter on his eagle—are the frame for what I have termed Shakespeare's miracles of the ordinary.

11. *The Winter's Tale*, 5.1.7–10.

12. Martin Butler, ed., *Cymbeline* (Cambridge: Cambridge University Press, 2005), notes to 5.3.122, p. 216; Roger Warren, ed., *Cymbeline* (Oxford: Oxford University Press, 1998), 232 n. The Norton does not mention sin but glosses "bonds" as "these old legal agreements; these cruel links with life; these harsh fetters" (3029 n. 5). The language of bonds is also invoked in the exchange of tokens that precedes Posthumus's banishment from Cymbeline's court. The bracelet that Posthumus gives Innogen is "a manacle of love," and with it Innogen becomes his "fairest prisoner" (1.1.123–24). I return to this idea later on in this essay.

13. Bishop's Bible, in *The New Testament Octapla: Early English Versions of the New Testament in the Tyndale-King James Tradition* (Edinburgh: Thomas Nelson and Sons, 1946), 97.

14. Thomas Becon, *The Castle of Comfort*, in *Works,* ed. John Ayre (Cambridge: University Press, 1845–50), 3:556; John Jewell, *Defence of the Apology*, in *The Works of John Jewell*, ed. John Ayre, (Cambridge: University Press, 1845–47), 3:369. Richard Hooker explores the issue in *Of the Lawes of Ecclesiastical Polity*, ed. P. G. Stanwood (Cambridge, MA: Harvard University Press, 1981), bk. 6, 3:14: "Our lord and Saviour in the 16th of St. Matthewes Ghospell giveth his Apostles regiment in generall, over God's Church. For they that have the keyes of the Kingdome of heaven are thereby signified to be stewards of the house of god, under whom they guide, command, judge and correct the family."

15. I don't have time in this essay to explore the way the providential plot of *Cymbeline* ("the more delayed delighted") negates every effort made by Posthumus to run his own fate and the questions of grace and agency this raises.

16. On the keys, see ch. 2 of Sarah Beckwith, *Shakespeare and the Grammar of Forgiveness* (Ithaca: Cornell University Press, 2011).

17. John Calvin, *Institutes*, 3.3.10.

18. Lancelot Andrewes, "A Sermon preached at Whitehall upon the Sunday after Easter, being the Thirteenth of March, AD MDC," in *Ninety Six Sermons by the Right Honourable and Reverend Father in God, Lancelot Andrewes, sometime Bishop of Winchester*, 5 vols. (Oxford: John Henry Parker, 1843; repr., New York: AMS Press, 1967), vol. 5.

19. H. J. Schroeder, ed., *Disciplinary Decrees of the General Councils: Text, Translation and Commentary* (St. Louis, MO: Herder, 1937), 259–60.

20. William Tyndale, *The Obedience of a Christian Man*, ed. David Daniell (London: Penguin, 2000), 117: "Shrift in the ear is verily a work of Satan." Repentance obviates confession for Tyndale: "When a man feeleth that his hert

consenteth to the law of God, and feeleth himself meek, patient, courteous and merciful to his neighbour, altered and fashioned like to Christ, why should he doubt but that God hath forgiven him and chosen him and put his spirit in him, though he never cram his sin into the priest's ear?" (118). Tyndale's question—"Why should he doubt?"—is not met with the same blithe confidence that he expresses here by the many thousands for whom it would become the key pastoral problem, the central question of practical divinity, and the main cause of a rash of suicides in the early seventeenth century. This is the territory explored in John Stachniewski, *The Persecutory Imagination: English Puritanism and the Literature of Religious Despair* (Oxford: Clarendon Press, 1991).

21. *The Book of Common Prayer 1559: The Elizabethan Prayer Book*, ed. John Booty (Charlottesville: University of Virginia Press, 1976), 257; all further citations are taken from this edition.

22. Thomas Becon, *The Potation of Lent*, in *The Early Works of Thomas Becon*, ed. John Ayre (Cambridge: University Press, 1843), 99. In the section on confession, Becon begins by glossing confession as (1) the confession of our faith—where we confess unfeignedly what the scriptures teach about God; (2) confession to God, whom we have offended with our sins; (3) confession to the person we've offended; and (4) open and public confession to the congregation, as in the primitive church. The fifth category is auricular confession, which needs to be separated from the abuses of it and as such "retained, maintained, and used."

23. Morning Prayer, in *Book of Common Prayer 1559*, 50.

24. Ibid., 357.

25. The "commonality" of common prayer is a central point in Ramie Targoff, *Common Prayer: The Language of Public Devotion in Early Modern England* (Chicago: University of Chicago Press, 2001), 28–35.

26. Morning Prayer, *Book of Common Prayer 1559*, 50.

27. Ibid., 259.

28. "And there shall be no celebration of the Lord's Supper except there be a good number to communicate with the priest, according to his discretion" (267).

29. The impossibility of separating out abuses from ceremony is addressed in the preface to the *Book of Common Prayer 1559*, "Of Ceremonies, Why some be abolished and Some retained" (20).

30. Quoted in Antjie Krog, *Country of My Skull: Guilt, Sorrow, and the Limits of Forgiveness in the New South Africa* (New York: Random House, 1998), 23.

31. It is fascinating to see how Richard Greenham addressed the question of a sense of generalized depravity, as opposed to the (more humbling) specifications of particular sins: "He told me . . . when any came with a troubled conscience for syn, wisely to discern whither they bee meanly greeved, with a general and roving sight of ther sins, or whither they bee extreamly throughn

down, with the burden of particular sins; if so they bee, then it is good at the first to shew that noe syn is so great, but in christ it is pardonable, and that ther is mercy with god that hee might bee feared. Soe on the one side shewing mercy to come from god, but soe as they are nothing fit to receiv mercy, unless they feel ther particular and prockt sins. But if ther sorrow bee more confused in general things, then it is good to humble them more and more, to give them a terror of gods justice, for particular sins. For experience doth teach us, that this is the best way to see sin and to bee humbled to see sin, because often men wil acknowledge greater sins they have been in, then that little (sin) they presently ly in" (*"Practical Divinity": The Works and Life of Revd Richard Greenham*, ed. Kenneth L. Parker and Eric J. Carlson (Aldershot: Ashgate, 1998), 161.

32. George Eliot, *Middlemarch* (Oxford: Oxford University Press, 1996), 493.

33. Ibid., 492.

34. Patrick Collinson, "Shepherds, Sheepdogs, and Hirelings: The Pastoral Ministry in Post-Reformation England," in *The Ministry: Clerical and Lay*, ed. W. J. Sheils and Diana Wood, Studies in Church History (Oxford: Blackwell, 1989), 216.

35. I explore this at length in Beckwith, *Shakespeare and the Grammar of Forgiveness*.

36. See Collinson, "Shepherds, Sheepdogs." I am grateful for Michael Neill for giving me a copy of his essay "'The Language of the Heart': Confession, Metaphor, and Grace in J. M. Coetzee's *Age of Iron*" in advance of publication; it is now published in *J. M. Coetzee's Austerities*, ed. Graham Bradshaw and Michael Neill (Burlington: Ashgate, 2010). Here he explores the nature of secular confession as a preoccupation in the writings of Coetzee. See here also Coetzee's essay, "Confession and Double Thoughts: Tolstoy, Dostoyevsky and Rousseau," *Comparative Literature* 37 (1985): 193–232.

37. J. L. Austin, *How to Do Things with Words*, 2nd ed., ed. J. O. Urmson and Marina Sbisa (Cambridge, MA: Harvard University Press, 1975), 110.

38. Stanley Cavell, "Performative and Passionate Utterance," in *Philosophy the Day after Tomorrow* (Cambridge, MA: Harvard University Press, 2005), 172–73.

39. The reasons for that skittishness are spelt out with extraordinary acumen in Cavell's essential companion essay to "Performative and Passionate Utterance," "Counter-philosophy and the Pawn of Voice," in *A Pitch of Philosophy: Autobiographical Exercises* (Cambridge, MA: Harvard University Press, 1994).

40. "Perlocutionary verbs not only do not name what they do (as to say the illocutionary "I promise, beseech, order, banish . . . you" *is* to promise, beseech, order, banish you), they can not . . . unprotectedly be said at all: to utter, "I seduce, alarm, amuse . . . you," is not only not to do anything, it is in an obvious sense not so much as to *say* anything (yet)" (Cavell, "Performative and Passionate Utterance," 171). Cavell here notes that Austin contrasts the illocutionary verb

with the perlocutionary on the grounds that it is conventional—presumably that the first four rules of the performative here apply. Cavell prefers to say, "The illocutionary act is, we might say, built into the verb that names it" (172).

41. Ibid., 173.

42. Such as the one in *Monumenta ritualia Ecclesiae Anglicanae*, ed. William Maskell, 3 vols. (Oxford: Clarendon Press, 1882), 3:293–303.

43. See, for example, John Mirk, *Instructions for Parish Priests*, lines 923ff.

44. On the completeness of confession, see the illuminating words of David Myers, *"Poor Sinning Folk": Confession and Conscience in Counter-Reformation Germany* (Ithaca: Cornell University Press, 1996), 165.

45. From the succinct summary in Stanley Cavell, "The Incessance and the Absence of the Political," in *The Claim to Community: Essays on Stanley Cavell and Political Philosophy*, ed. Andrew Norris (Stanford: Stanford University Press, 2006), 272.

46. See Julie Paulson, "A Theater of the Soul's Interior: Contemplative Literature and Penitential Education in the Morality Play *Wisdom,*" *Journal of Medieval and Early Modern Studies* 38, no. 2 (2008): 253–84.

47. *The Castle of Perseverance*, in *The Macro Plays*, ed. Marc Eccles, EETS 262 (Oxford: Oxford University Press, 1969). All citations are to line numbers from this edition.

48. *Mankind*, in Eccles, *The Macro Plays*; citations are to line numbers.

49. Much of the criticism of the morality play tradition confuses naming and calling. It understands the dramatis personae as abstractions, not people, and tends to confuse examples with generalizations. The difference here, as Toril Moi has taught us, is that it is possible to generalize from a particular case without putting one's subjectivity on the line. But it is impossible to see one's own experience as an instance of a more general cause without staking oneself in one's claims. Essential here is Stanley Cavell's "Must We Mean What We Say?" in *Must We Mean What We Say?* (Cambridge: Cambridge University Press, 2002), 19; see also Toril Moi's admirably lucid explication in *What Is a Woman? and Other Essays* (Oxford: Oxford University Press, 1999).

50. Stanley Cavell, *The Claim of Reason: Wittgenstein, Skepticism, Morality and Tragedy* (Oxford: Oxford University Press, 1982), 206ff.

51. David Schalkwyck, "Shakespeare's Speech," *Journal of Medieval and Early Modern Studies* 40, no. 2 (2010): 373–400.

52. See Beckwith, "Shakespeare's Resurrections," ch. 6 of *Shakespeare and the Grammar of Forgiveness*, and also Cavell, "Counter-philosophy," 115.

53. Wittgenstein, *Philosophical Investigations*, remark 432: "Every sign *by itself* seems dead. *What* gives it life?—In use it is alive. Is life breathed into it there?—Or is the *use* its life?"

54. Raimond Gaita, *A Common Humanity: Thinking about Love and Truth and Justice* (London: Routledge, 1998), 221.

55. Lewis Hyde, *The Gift: How the Creative Spirit Transforms the World* (1979; repr., Edinburgh: Canongate, 2006). He goes on to say: "It is true that when a gift enhances our life, or even saves it, gratitude will bind us to the donor. Until it is expressed, that is. Gratitude, acted upon or simply spoken, releases the gift and lightens the obligations of affection between lovers, family, and comrades. . . . It is not for a theory of gift exchange to explain why we so often enter and maintain relationships that have in them no life to offer" (73). One might also here think of the many commentaries that draw attention to the "as" in "Forgive us as we forgive" in the Lord's Prayer.

56. I am indebted to both Nancy Bauer and Richard Fleming for their comments and readings of Austin and Wittgenstein in a series of workshops held at Duke University on ordinary language philosophy in 2007–9. See Stanley Cavell's fascinating and important comments on J. L. Austin's idea of "our word is our bond" in "Counter-philosophy," 101, 120.

57. A remark of Cavell's is also relevant here: "And confession, unlike dogma, is not to be believed but tested, and accepted or rejected. Nor is it the occasion for accusation, except of yourself, and by implication those who find themselves in you" ("The Availability of Wittgenstein's Later Philosophy," in *Must We Mean What We Say?* 71). The distinction between this understanding of confession and the new sense of confession as a (dogmatic) declaration of faith as in the Augsburg Confession, etc., should now be apparent. Indeed, this sense of confession determines the historiographical paradigm of confessionalization as it is developed from the work of Heniz Schilling and Wolfgang Reinhard. In this paradigm, confession is the declaration of an allegiance, an allegiance closely connected with the articulation of dogmatic or doctrinal difference.

58. This is explored most profoundly in book 10 of Augustine's *Confessions*. I owe this formulation and this analysis to Paul Griffiths in his excellent book *Lying: An Augustinian Theology of Duplicity* (Grand Rapids, MI: Brazos Press, 2004), 92–93. Griffiths's book is an exploration of Augustine's exceptionless ban on the lie. A lie "grasps the gift, owning it in imagination, and, so, sinning." For Augustine, according to Griffiths, it is therefore performatively incoherent because "speech is a gift given, and a condition of its use is that it is received as such" (93).

Chapter 5

The Patience of Lear

HANNIBAL HAMLIN

One human experience that is universal and not historically determined is pain. In 1637, William Prynne was publicly mutilated for seditious writings, specifically for his critique of stage plays, *Histriomastix*. On a London scaffold, his nose was slit, his ears were cut off, and the initials "S. L." (for "Seditious Libeller") were burnt into his cheeks with a red-hot iron.[1] Prynne recorded his mutilation in detail: "The bloody Executioner performed the Execution with extraordinary cruelty, heating the Iron very hot, and burning one Cheek twice: After which he cut one of his Eares so close, that he cut off a piece of his Cheek too, and cut him deep into the neck, neare the jugular veine, to the great danger of his life. And then hacking the other Eare almost off, he left it hanging, and went down the Scaffold, till the Surgeon called him up againe, and made him cut it off quite."[2] There is much about this that a twentieth-first-century American or European finds difficult to comprehend. What we understand perfectly, however, is that Prynne's experience was excruciating. Cutting off an ear surely felt the same for Prynne as it would for us today. Few of us, on the other hand, would be likely to respond to maiming as Prynne did, when (at least by his own account) he raised his eyes to heaven and stated, "The more I am beat down, the more am I lift up."[3] Prynne's religious conviction enabled him to transform his experience from de-grading criminal punishment to heroic martyrdom.

Another, equally religious, but more common response to suffer-ing is to ask, "Why me? What have I done to deserve this?" A Christian believer, or any person of faith who believes in a good and just God by whose providence all things are governed, may well expect an answer. For such a person there is in fact someone—God—who ought to know why anyone suffers. The question "Why me?" demands an answer in a way it need not for the nonbeliever. If God is indeed good and just, and if indeed he governs all things, then everything happens for a reason. And even if we can make no sense of our suffering, it must be a part of God's inscrutable plan that we simply cannot comprehend. To think otherwise is to call into question some aspect of God: his goodness, his justice, his power, or his very existence. This is why innocent suffering (and its converse, the prosperity of the wicked) is one of the critical theo-logical problems.

Shakespeare's *King Lear* represents this problem in dramatic form. Samuel Johnson found the play disturbing for just this reason: "A play in which the wicked prosper, and the virtuous miscarry, may doubtless be good, because it is a just representation of the common events of human life; but, since all reasonable beings naturally love justice, I cannot easily be persuaded that the observation of justice makes a play worse; or that, if other excellencies are equal, the audience will not always rise better pleased from the final triumph of persecuted virtue."[4] Johnson's eighteenth-century contemporaries clearly agreed, since they preferred Nahum Tate's happy-ending *King Lear* to Shakespeare's original. But Tate's version and Johnson's ideal "pleasant" tragedy avoid the essential questions about God's justice posed by *King Lear*, which even Johnson recognized was a "just representation of the common events in human life." As Lear asks after Cordelia, the most innocent of the play's suffer-ers, dies, "Why should a dog, a horse, a rat have life / And thou no breath at all?" (5.3.305–6).

Shakespeare's unpleasant ending was a deliberate choice, since he departed in this from his major sources. The anonymous play *The True Chronicle History of King Leir*, Shakespeare's most direct source for the Lear plot, ends differently: the wicked daughters and their husbands are defeated and driven off by the king of Gallia, and he and Cordella have the rule of England bestowed upon them by a grateful, loving (and living) Leir. Cordeilla (her name, like Lear's, has various spellings) does die in Geoffrey of Monmouth's account, but only years after the events recounted in the plays. As in the chronicle play, she and the king of Gaul defeat her sisters and brothers-in-law, and they return to England with Leir. He has three happy years before dying of old age, and Cordeilla continues to reign in peace. She does die badly, but only in a later episode, when she is taken prisoner by her sisters' sons and hangs herself in prison (an act of stoic heroism, quite different from her enforced and pointless hanging in Shakespeare). Holinshed tells essentially the same story, as do *The Mirror for Magistrates* and Spenser's *Faerie Queene*. Why then does Shakespeare reject all the historical accounts in favor of an ending so much more bleak? An audience familiar with one of the other accounts of the story might well have wondered with Kent: "Is this the promised end?" (5.3.261).

To explore this question, it is useful to turn to another of Shakespeare's sources—not one canonized by Geoffrey Bullough's *Narrative and Dramatic Sources*, but a book whose reading nevertheless deeply and pervasively informed his play—the book of Job. The comparison of Shakespeare's *King Lear* and the biblical book of Job has become a critical commonplace. As early as 1949, G. Wilson Knight wrote that *"King Lear* is analogous to the Book of Job" but left the details of the analogy to be sketched out a decade later by John Holloway.[5] After remarking that the parallel between the two works "has seldom received much attention," Holloway notes a number of verbal points of contact and then concludes that the resemblance lies in the theme of patience in adversity: the protracted suffering of Lear derives from the prolonged suffering of Job and his discussion of it with his friends.[6] By 1990, Arthur Kirsch could write that "the depiction of suffering in the play has often been compared to that in the Book of Job."[7] As well as Holloway, Kirsch cites Rosalie Colie, but he might have added others: W. R. Elton, for instance, and Kenneth Muir, who in 1984 went so far as to argue that "there is no doubt that Job was much in his mind while Shakespeare was writing *King Lear.*"[8] More recent and extended discussions of Lear and Job include those by Steven Marx, Kenneth Gross, and Robert Pack. Many of the play's allusions to the biblical book are listed in Naseeb Shaheen's *Biblical References in Shakespeare's Plays.*[9] Although it has developed considerably since World War II, the history of this idea may in fact predate the twentieth century. Charles Lamb wrote of Nahum Tate, author of the famous "Hollywood ending" revision of *King Lear* (Stanley Cavell's term), that he had "put his hook into the nostrils of this Leviathan, for Garrick and his followers, the showmen of the scene, to draw the mighty beast about more easily."[10] The metaphor alludes to Job (in which God boasts that he can draw Leviathan with a hook).

Whenever it was first noted, however, the relationship between Job and *King Lear* is by now a familiar one. Yet the basic knowledge of *Lear*'s link to Job has been relatively undeveloped. For instance, Colie analyzes perceptively a number of important biblical allusions but doesn't go beyond a few key passages, Gross restricts his discussion to the matter of cursing, and Marx, whose treatment is in some ways the most extensive, largely eschews critical analysis, reading the two books "in tandem" in a rather peculiar effort to produce a kind of contemporary midrash.[11] Pack's treatment (from the perspective of a practicing poet), though intriguing, is entirely thematic.[12] As a result, a number of questions remain unasked and unanswered: Why did Shakespeare turn to the book of Job when writing *King Lear*? What were his sources for the Job story and its interpretation? What place did Job have in Shakespeare's culture in the early years of the seventeenth century? And finally, how does an awareness of *King Lear*'s relationship to Job affect our understanding of the play?

Job and Lear: Previous Performances

Despite the lack of conclusive evidence (we cannot ask Shakespeare himself), it is possible to suggest how he might have arrived at the idea of drawing together the stories of Lear and Job. Theater history is often conjectural, for there is so much that scholars cannot know: when particular plays were written and performed, who performed them, certainly who saw them. Such conjecture must not be substituted for fact, but in the absence of facts it can still sometimes be useful and suggestive. Although they still disagree on particular points, scholars generally accept that Shakespeare knew the anonymous *True Chronicle History of King Leir* and that it was his principal source for the story. The play, whose title is nearly identical to that of Shakespeare's 1608 Quarto, was printed in 1605, so it may have been read by Shakespeare before he wrote his own play; but it is possible that he already knew the anonymous play from performance.[13] When *King Leir* was played by the Queen's Men at the Rose in 1594, Shakespeare was active in the London theater, and it is reasonable to think he saw the play. This supposition is made more likely by arguments that Shakespeare had himself been a Queen's Man sometime during his mysterious "missing years," 1584 to 1592.[14]

Yet Shakespeare's is the only version of the Lear story that alludes to Job. Although there were numerous Job plays in France, Germany, Spain, and Italy throughout the Middle Ages and Renaissance, his story seems not to have caught on similarly in England, though there were plenty of other biblical dramas.[15] Nevertheless, there was apparently one Job play staged in sixteenth-century London: Robert Greene's *The History or Tragedy of Job*. The play has not survived, but it was entered in the Stationers' Register in 1594, the same year in which *King Leir* was played at the Rose.[16] It has been suggested that Greene's Job might have been played by the Admiral's Men, who were staging another biblical drama, George Peele's *David and Bethsabe*, and that Ned Alleyn might have played both leading parts, Job and David.[17] It is also possible, however, that *Job* was a Queen's Men's play, since they presented other plays by Greene, including his *Friar Bacon and Friar Bungay* in 1594. If Greene wrote *Job* for the Queen's Men, and it was staged in 1594, then the same company was playing both *Job* and *King Leir*, and it is possible, moreover, that the two leading roles were played by the same actor. Even if this was not the case, Greene's *Job* and *King Leir* were being performed about the same time in London. If Shakespeare saw both plays, this may have given him the germ of the idea for a play in which these two figures were drawn into parallel.

Further inspiration for using the Job story to add complexity to his *King Lear* must have come from a play that Shakespeare certainly knew, Christopher Marlowe's *Jew of Malta*. Written sometime between 1589 and 1592, *The Jew of Malta* was a major hit; it was performed seventeen times between 1592 and 1593 and was still popular in 1594, when it was entered

in the Stationers' Register.[18] The play's allusions to Job are overt: the rich
Jew, Barabas, having had his goods seized by the Christian rulers of Malta,
curses his enemies but is counseled to "be patient" by three friends, one
of whom is named Temainte, which has been read as a variant of the
name for the home of Job's friend Eliphaz the Temanite (1.2.169).[19] One
of them urges, "Yet brother Barabas remember Job" (1.2.180). Barabas
then launches into a comparison of himself to Job (concluding that he
himself has been far richer than Job and is therefore more afflicted).
Like Job, Barabas curses his "fatall birth-day" and dismisses his friends
(1.2.192). Marlowe's extraordinarily wicked Barabas is hardly a mirror of
the perfect and upright Job, and Marlowe's allusive parallel is "cited in
order to present Barabas as the opposite, as an Anti-Job, characterized by
his *impatience* (1.497), and choosing the road, not of Christian patience,
but of its opposite, revenge."[20] As will be discussed below, Job himself is
hardly patient, despite his reputation, but the idea of writing a play about
an "Anti-Job" seems to have attracted Shakespeare. Indeed Shakespeare's
allusive practice, like Marlowe's, often is contrastive, drawing attention to
how his characters fail to measure up to various biblical models.[21]

A Constellation of Allusions

The more one reads in Job, the likelier it seems that, as Muir suggested,
Shakespeare had this book in mind and ear as he wrote *King Lear*. One of
the play's more obvious allusions to the book of Job (noted by Shaheen,
Marx, Colie, and Holloway) is Gloucester's comment on the heath, when
he and the old man leading him first encounter "Blind Tom," that he saw
a person in the storm, "Which made me think a man a worm" (4.1.35).[22]
Although the Bible contains other comparisons of worms and men ("I
am a worm and no man," for instance, in Ps. 22:6), such self-loathing
worm references are particularly prominent in Job.[23] For instance, Job's
friend Bildad the Shuhite says that, if even the stars are unclean in God's
eyes, then "How muche more man, a worme, even the sonne of man,
which is but a worme?" (Job 25:6). Earlier in the book, Job himself
states, "I shal say to corruption, Thou art my father, and to the worme,
thou art my mother and my sister" (Job 17:14).

Colie cites several other allusions to Job, including Kent's remark in the stocks that "a good man's fortune may grow out at the heels" (2.2.157). (The expression "out at heels" means "worn out," so Kent is playing on both his "worn-out" fortune and his actual heels, which are sticking out of the stocks and therefore the mark of his condition.) Similarly, Job complains to God that, figuratively speaking, "Thou puttest my feet also in the stockes, and lokest narrowly unto all my paths, and makest the printe thereof in the heeles of my fete" (Job 13:27).[24] Furthermore, when Lear is out on the heath, he faces, according to the anonymous gentleman Kent encounters, a "night wherein the cub-drawn bear would couch, / The lion and the belly-pinched wolf / Keep their fur dry" (3.1.12–14).[25] Likewise, Elihu says in Job that when God raises a storm, "Then the beasts go into the denne, and remaine in their places" (Job 37:8). Lear is also "a comrade to the wolf and owl" (2.2.399), just as Job is the "brother to the dragons, and a companion to the ostriches" (Job 30:29).[26] Colie's study is not exhaustive, however. Job can also be heard behind Gloucester's fatalistic statement that "a man may rot even here" (5.2.8). Job says of people like himself who are persecuted by God: "Suche one consumeth like a roten thing" (Job 33:28). Tellingly, this verse from Job immediately follows Job's statement about the stocks. The second half of this verse—"and as a garment that is motheaten"—also parallels *King Lear*, with its complex thematic treatment of clothing and nakedness.[27]

The intertextual relationship between the book of Job and *King Lear* is a complicated one, mediated not just by overt allusions but also by additional biblical passages associated with the ones alluded to, and by non-biblical books that cite or comment on Job.[28] Shakespeare and other early moderns read the Bible as people today surf the Web; the Bible, especially the Geneva Bible, with its marginal notes and cross-references, was essentially an early hypertext. In "The H. Scriptures II," George Herbert describes this reading practice as one of associative or (in theological terms) typological reading in which no part of the Bible is read in isolation; rather, each is read in conjunction with related earlier or later passages, and these passages lead in turn to other passages in a kind of interpretive chain:

Oh that I knew how all thy lights combine,
    And the configurations of their glorie!

Seeing not onely how each verse doth shine,
But all the constellations of the storie.
This verse marks that, and both do make a motion
  Unto a third, that ten leaves off doth lie:
  Then as dispersed herbs do watch a potion,
These three make up some Christians destinie.[29]

In the case of Job, the most obvious such "motion" a reader would make
is to the Epistle of James, which cites Job in its discussion of patience,
the only other explicit biblical reference to Job being a passing mention
in Ezekiel. The Geneva preface to Job ends by noting, "Ezekiel commen-
deth Job as a just man, Ezek. 14,14, and James setteth out his pacience
for an example, Jam. 5,11." If the "motional" reading process Herbert
described is applied to *King Lear*, one can perceive an allusive "constellation" in Gloucester's and Job's aforementioned comments on rotting,
Job's moth-eaten garment, and James's condemnation of rich men: "Go
to now, ye riche men: wepe and howle for your miseries that shal come
upon you. Your riches are corrupt: and your garments are motheaten"
(James 5:1–2). Furthermore, as does James, Lear condemns the rich
using the metaphor of clothing: "Thorough tatter'd clothes small vices
do appear; / Robes and furr'd gowns hide all" (4.6.166–67). Moreover,
Lear's "howl, howl, howl" (and another "howl" in the Quarto [5.3.255])
echoes James's "wepe and howle for your miseries."[30]

   There are further lights in the intertextual "constellation" linking
King Lear and Job. Some editions of the Geneva Bible—1603, for instance, with Tomson's revised New Testament and the New Testament
notes of Franciscus Junius—included a brief essay entitled "How to take
profit by reading of the Holy Scriptures," by T. Grashop. Grashop urges
the reader to "marke and consider the agreement that one place of Scripture hath with an other," agreement of the sort indicated above between
Job and James. But Grashop also recommends that his reader "take op-
portunitie to read interpreters, if he be able."[31] Shakespeare seems to
have taken Grashop's advice, since *King Lear* echoes not only Job and
James but also *The Sermons on Job* by Jean Calvin. They were translated into
English by Arthur Golding, the translator of one of Shakespeare's most-
used sources, Ovid's *Metamorphoses* (1565/67). Golding's translation of

The Sermons on Job appeared in London in 1574 and sold well: there were five more editions in the next decade.

Calvin's *Sermons* provided Shakespeare with some specific language for *King Lear* and seems to have influenced his choice of certain prevalent themes and imagery. In chapter 32 of Job, for instance, the brash, young Elihu condemns Job's three old friends "because they colde not finde an answer, and yet condemned Job" (Job 32:3). In his commentary on this section, in which he develops the debate between youth and age, Calvin paraphrases Isaiah, who writes that if the elderly do not act in the fear of God, "the aged shall not see any whit, and . . . the wise shal become brutishe and utterly dull." Calvin returns to this topic in a later sermon on Job 32:4–10: "Now if God doe blinde the olde men, great men, and such as are in authoritie after that sorte, what shall become of them (I pray you) if God give them not his holy spirite?"[32] Shakespeare's answer is that they end up alone and suffering on the heath, like Gloucester and Lear. Blindness is a recurrent theme in the *Sermons on Job*, but Calvin also writes many times of God's stripping men naked: "I say, it becommeth us to suffer God too strippe us out of all, even to our bare and naked skinne, and to prepare our selves to returne to our grave in the same state" (30). Lear, stripped of much himself, sees the more totally "bare and naked" Edgar and comes to a conclusion similar to Calvin's: "Why, thou wert better in a grave than to answer with thy uncovered body this extremity of the skies. Is man no more than this?" (3.4.99–104). Of course, unlike Calvin, Lear doesn't attribute Edmund's stripping down to God, nor does he see it as a beneficial preparation for death. The lesson about the essential, existential nakedness of humanity is similar, however, as is the language of graves and naked bodies. In a further image of nakedness, Job responds to the news that his children are dead: "Naked came I out of my mothers wombe, and naked shal I returne thether" (Job 1:21). When the blinded Gloucester and the mad Lear meet again on the heath, Lear similarly reminds Gloucester of the experience of leaving the womb: "We came crying hither: / Thou knowst the first time that we smell the air / We wawl and cry" (4.6.174–76).

In his 101st sermon (on Job 27:19–28:9), Calvin writes more that is suggestive of Lear's recognition scene with Edgar as Poor Tom: "Truely there are many even of the smallest and lowest thinges, which wee cannot conceive, except GOD give us abilitie: according as wee see howe there are many simple idiots (as man termeth them) which know no more than brute beastes. Such manner of folk are set of God before our eyes as lookingglasses, to humble us withal. When wee see a starke idiot, that hath no wit nor reason, it behoveth us to looke wel upon him, for hee is a mirrour of our nature" (476). Lear's encounter with Edgar works in just this way, as does his sympathy with the suffering of his Fool (both Tom and the Fool are "starke idiots" in their different ways). Lear turns from these particular "mirrours" to consider humanity in general, thinking of all the "poor, naked wretches" out in the storm and recognizing that "I have ta'en too little care of this" (3.4.28, 32–33). In a later sermon, Calvin continues his meditation on how every man needs to consider the "starke idiot": "but yet notwithstanding though he be a King he must have brotherhood with the poorest sheepheards and neatherds in the world, except he can put off his owne nature. And out of doubt, as for the chiefe and excellentest thing a King hath in him, that is to say, manhood: hath not the shepeheard it aswel as he?" (511). Lear is of course a king, as Job is not, and it is precisely his kinship with the poor that he finally recognizes in his meeting with Poor Tom. Lear longs to "put off his owne nature," since "Man's nature cannot carry / Th'affliction, nor the fear" of the storm (the one in his mind as well as the one on the heath). All he can actually "put off" are his clothes: "Off, off, you lendings: come, unbutton here" (3.2.48–49; 3.4.106–7). He recognizes the link between himself and Edgar that Calvin notes—his "manhood"— realizing that "man is no more than this": "Thou ow'st the worm no silk, the beast no hide, the sheep no wool, the cat no perfume. Ha? Here's three on's us are sophisticated; thou art the thing itself. Unaccommodated man is no more but such a poor, bare, forked animal as thou art" (3.4.101–6). But such a recognition seems beyond Lear's power to retain, and he continues to struggle against the "mortality" of which his hand smells, as he tells the blind Gloucester (4.6.129).

In addition to Golding's Calvin, a possible source for this speech by Lear is a sixteenth-century commentary on rejecting worldly goods that makes liberal reference to Job. The critical consensus has been that Lear's catalog of animal products derives from Montaigne's essay "An Apologie of *Raymond Sebonde*": "Miserable man; whom if you consider well what is he? . . . when I consider man all naked . . . We may be excused for borrowing those [i.e., from those creatures] which nature had therein favored more than us . . . and under their spoiles of wool, of haire, of feathers, and of silks to shroud us."[33] John Florio's translation of Montaigne was published in 1603, so Shakespeare could have read it. But a similar passage appears in Edmund Bunny's Protestantized version of Robert Parsons's *A Book of Christian Exercise*, which had already been immensely popular for twenty years: "What vanitie is it then for us, to be so curious in apparel, and to take such pride therin, as we do? We rob and spoil al creatures almost in the world, to cover our baks, and to adorn our bodies withal. From one, we take his wool: from another, his skin: from another, his fur: and from some other, their very excrements; as the silk, which is nothing els, but the excrements of woorms."[34]

The list of materials for clothing is similar in both Montaigne and Parsons and perhaps simply makes sense in terms of contemporary garments, but while Montaigne's list includes silk and wool, as Lear's does, it also includes feathers, which Lear's doesn't, and Parsons's "skin" is closer to Lear's "hide" than Montaigne's "haire." Furthermore, the syntax in Parsons is closer to Shakespeare's, stringing together clauses rather than just the nouns, as in Montaigne. Finally, the context in Parsons is telling. Seven pages earlier (286), Parsons cites Job's "I said unto rottenness, thou art my father: and unto worms, you are my mother and sisters" (Job 17:14), so the reader would likely still have Job's worms in mind while reading about the excrement of silk.

Parsons's immediate use for this quotation, however, is to support an argument against the vanity of nobility, the very argument Lear has come to in meeting Poor Tom: "He that wil behold the gentrie of his ancestors: let him look into their graves, and see whether Job saith truly or no" (i.e., that rottenness is his father, worms his mother and sisters) (286). There follows, in the *Christian Exercise*, a discussion of fools, based on Paul's advice in 1 Corinthians that "the wisdom of this world is folly with God," and then a section on the vanity of beauty, concluding that "yet quickly commeth on old age, which riveleth the skin, draweth in the eies, setteth out the teeth, and so disfigureth the whole visage" (291). Then follows the aforementioned section on apparel, which begins by focusing on the lesson offered by a beggar, in appearance like Poor Tom: "If Adam had never fallen: we had never used apparel: for that apparel was devised to cover our shame of nakedness, and other infirmities contracted by that fal. Wherfore, we that take pride and glorie in apparel, do as much as if a begger should glorie and take pride of the old clouts that do cover his sores" (292). Later, on the page following the passage on excrements, Parsons cites James 5:1–3 ("Now go to, you rich men: weep, and howl your miseries," etc.), and, on the same page, Job 1:21 ("We came in naked unto this world, and naked we must foorth again") and Job 27:19–21 ("When the rich man dieth he shal take nothing with him, but shal close up his eies, and find nothing. Povertie shal lay hands upon him, and a tempest shal oppresse him in the night: a burning wind shal take him away, and a whirl wind shal snatch him from his place").

Several pages further on, Parsons turns his thoughts to "concupiscence of the flesh" and again cites several passages from Job, as well as Tobias: "And old Tobias insinuateth yet another cause, when he saith; *What joy can I have or receive, seeing I sit heer in darknes?* Speaking literally of his corporal blindnes, but yet leaving it also to be understood of spiritual and internal darknes" (299). Parsons's citation of Job and Tobias (or Tobit, as he is named in the Geneva Bible) together is no accident: the two figures were often linked as parallel exemplars of patient and righteous suffering, as in a poem by Robert Henryson:

> Job was moist riche, in writ we find,
> Thobe moist full of cheritie—
> Job wox peur and Thoby blynd,
> Baith temptit with adversitie:
> Sen blindes wes infirmitie,
> And povertie was naturall,
> Thairfoir in patience baith he and he
> Obeid and thankit God of all.[35]

Parsons's (or Henryson's) pairing of Job and Tobit, the beggar and the blind man, two biblical patterns of patience, is suggestive of Shakespeare's Lear and Gloucester (also of Gloucester and "Poor Tom"), though in this particular instance neither can necessarily be proven to be a direct source.[36]

There is another echo of Calvin's *Sermons on Job* in Shakespeare's Gloucester subplot, one specifically recalling Golding's dedicatory epistle. For example, Gloucester blames the pernicious astrological influence of the "late eclipses of the sun and moon" for bringing about the conflicts he has witnessed: "Love cools, friendship falls off, brothers divide: in cities, mutinies; in countries, discord; in palaces, treason; and the bond cracked 'twixt son and father. This villain of mine comes under the prediction—there's son against father. The King falls from bias of nature—there's father against child" (1.2.106–12). But the skeptical Edmund has a different perspective on nature and privately dismisses his father's astrology as an "admirable evasion of whoremaster man": "This is the excellent foppery of the world, that when we are sick in fortune, often the surfeits of our own behaviour, we make guilty of our disasters the sun, the moon and the stars, as if we were villains on necessity, fools by heavenly compulsion, knaves, thieves and treachers by spherical predominance; drunkards, liars and adulterers by an enforced obedience of planetary influence; and all that we are evil in by a divine thrusting on" (1.2.118–26). On the same subject, and in a passage that sounds similar to Edmund's critique, Golding criticizes those who, like Job, complain that their life is hard but who, unlike Job, search for some explanation besides God's will:

> Do we looke up to the hand that smiteth us? do wee consider the causes why they be layd upon us? . . . wee eyther . . . impute them to the influence of the skies, or father them upon fortune, or attribute them unto men, or write them uppon the unhappinesse of the tyme, or tie them to the place, or finally stand amazed at the afflictions themselves, surmizing any thing rather than the truthe, as who should say that God eyther could not or would not governe all things by his onely will and providence, which is as much as to denie that there is any God at all. (A2)

Golding here identifies the perspectives of both Gloucester and Edmund. In Golding's interpretation of Calvin, however, both characters should be condemned: Gloucester for his superstitious belief in the "influence of the skies," and Edmund for denying there is "anie God at all."[37] Shakespeare thus draws on a variety of sources—Job, James, Calvin, Golding, and Parsons—in fashioning his exploration of human suffering and providential justice. Some of these are alluded to and are thus important in understanding *King Lear*: the various verses from Job and James especially. Others were sources Shakespeare seems to have consulted, and borrowed from, in his preparation for and writing of the play. Astute and well-read members of the audience might have recognized echoes of Calvin, in Golding's translation, or of Parsons's, or Bunny's adaptation of Parsons's, but these echoes are most significant in revealing the remarkable extent of Shakespeare's reading as well as the way in which he assembled, appropriated, and adapted his materials in writing his plays.

The Pattern of Patience

Shakespeare's "constellation" of allusions to Job and its interpreters reflects his representation of Lear in terms of familiar and authoritative (since biblical) "patterns of patience"—patience in its root sense of "suffering" (from the Latin *patiens* and ultimately *patior*, "to suffer").[38] Perhaps the clearest reference to Job in *King Lear* is again "constellated" with Golding's Calvin and the Epistle of James. James urges his readers to be patient and cites the model of Job: "Behold we count them blessed which endure. Ye have heard of the pacience of Job, and have knowen what end the Lord made. For the Lord is verie pitiful and merciful" (James 5:11). Naseeb Shaheen hears James's statement behind Lear's cry that "I will be the pattern of all patience" (3.2.37).[39] But Shakespeare's specific wording is identical to Golding's dedication in Calvin's *Sermons*, in which Golding describes Job as "a perfect patern of patience" (A2ᵛ). (Calvin himself writes that "Job shoulde be set foorth unto us as a pattern" and that in him God has set us "a certaine portrayture of pacience" [27].)

Lear may wish to be the "pattern of all patience," but the pattern was already established for Shakespeare's audience by the proverbial "patience of Job," a familiar idiom in early modern English.[40] Bartholomew Chappell, for instance, in his *Garden of Prudence* (1595), used the example of Job (along with David) to urge the rejection of worldly vanities and the patient acceptance of suffering:

But if with want thou be opprest,
if pinched eke with povertie,
Let all by sufferance be redrest,
when it shal please our God on hie,
For *Job* by patience wan great praise,
cruel *Pharoah* could not *David* daunt,
By patient hope they both had ease,
and al their foes could not once vaunt,
Or say, loe here we have prevailed
loe here is he, whom we subdued.[41]

Falstaff makes humorous reference to Job's proverbial patience in Shakespeare's *2 Henry IV*, admitting to the Lord Chief Justice, "I am as poor as
Job, my lord, but not so patient" (1.2.101).[42] A more conventional reference occurs in *The Conflict of Conscience* (1581), a "most lamentable Hystorie, of the desperation of Frauncis Spera, who forsooke the trueth of
Gods Gospell, for feare of the losse of life and worldly goods" (long
title), by Nathaniel Woodes, a Norwich vicar. Woodes interpreted Job's
sufferings in the fashion made popular by Gregory the Great's *Moralia in
Job*: whether Job deserved suffering is irrelevant, since suffering is a gift
from God (and besides, he got everything back in the end):

For trouble bring[s] forth pacience, from pacience dooth insue
Experience, from experience Hope, of health the ankor true.
Againe, oftimes, God doth prouide, affliction for our gaine,
As *Job* who after losse of goodes, had twice so much therefore:
Sometime affliction is a meanes, to honor to attaine.[43]

Another straightforward reference to Job's patience occurs in Nicholas
Breton's *The Soules immortall crowne consisting of seaven glorious graces* (1601; the
fifth "grace" is entitled "The Praise of Patience"):

By patience *David* had a Princely fame,
And, *Job* his patience had a worthy praise:
But Christ his patience hath a Glorious name,
That ever lives to never ending daies.[44]

(Along with David, Job was traditionally interpreted as a type of Christ, which is significant for *King Lear*, as will be explained below.) Clearly, the virtue preeminently associated with Job in the sixteenth and seventeenth centuries was patience.

The virtue of patience is likewise prominent in *King Lear*. Lear's vow to be "the pattern of all patience" is one of six references to "patience," in addition to five references to other forms of the word, making it a key word in the play. For example, Regan tells Lear, after he has complained about the indignity of his servant Caius/Kent being in the stocks, "I pray you, sir, take patience" (2.4.327). Earlier, when Lear is railing against Goneril, Albany urges, "pray, sir, be patient" (1.4.254). For his own reasons, having more to do with staving off tears and madness than heeding his daughters, Lear himself desires to stay patient, saying (more to himself than anyone present), "I can be patient," and later calling, "you heavens, give me that patience, patience I need" (2.2.419, 460). Out on the heath, Kent (as Caius) urges Lear to remember his promise that he "will be the pattern of all patience," saying, "Sir, where is the patience now / That you so oft have boasted to retain?" (3.6.57–58). In addition, characters other than Lear either demonstrate patience or are urged to do so. Before his deluded suicide attempt, Gloucester tells the gods that he will "shake patiently my great affliction off" (4.6.36). Gloucester seems to use *patience* in a sense of stoic suffering dispassionately borne, though of course to commit suicide might well be considered an impatient act, as Edgar (disguised) reminds him, redefining the crucial term: "Bear free and patient thoughts" (4.6.80). Lear himself seconds Edgar's advice in the lines borrowed from Job cited above: "Thou must be patient. We came crying hither: / Thou knowst the first time that we smell the air / We wawl and cry" (4.6.174–76). By the final act, Albany's use of the word to Edmund is ironic: the long-scheming Edmund has been as patient (in waiting for the fruition of his plots and in "suffering" the consequences of bastardy) as anyone: "Sir, by your patience, / I hold you but a subject of this war, / Not as a brother" (5.3.60–62).

Thus Shakespeare connects Job and Lear through allusions to patience. While Job proverbially is patient, however, Lear's patience is obviously lacking. On the other hand, it is important to realize that, despite the English proverb and James's epistle, any attentive reader of Job must realize that Job is not actually patient at all, a realization that troubled many early commentators, including Calvin.[45] The biblical Job does not go so far as to follow the advice of his wife, who tells him to "Blaspheme God and die," but he nevertheless curses the day he was born with an invective vehemence that rivals any of Lear's curses:

> Let the daye perish, wherein I was borne, and the night when it was
>   said, There is a manchild conceived.
> Let that day be darkenes, and the shadowe of death staine it: let the
>   cloude remaine upon it, and let them make it fearful as bitter day.
> Let darkenes possesse that night, let it not be joined unto the dayes
>   of the yere, nor let it come into the count of the moneths.
> Yea, desolate be that night, and let no joye be in it.
>
> (Job 3:3–7)

In the Middle Ages, many retellings of the Job story, apparently disturbed by Job's intemperate passion, omitted his curses, as well as the colloquy with the three friends that follows.[46] The early modern Protestant attitude to passion was generally more accepting, because of various intellectual developments, and Job's outrage was not seen as necessarily blasphemous.[47] For instance, Samuel Rowlands used the example of Job both to counsel patience and to justify the open expression of grief by Mary at the foot of the cross:

> If holy Job himselfe so patient bore,
> To give meeke care to many a grievous crosse,
> Destruction of his cattell, flockes, and store,
> Untill he heard his deerest childrens losse,
> And then his greefes extreamest did abound,
> Renting his garments, falling on the ground.
>
> Needs must (in mournfull sorrow's dire complaints)
> The blessed Virgin farre excell all other,
> What soule (with dolours ever so acquaints)

As this most carefull comfort wanting Mother,
To see her God, life, father, love and sonne,
By bitt'rest torments unto death be donne.[48]

In other words, Job and Mary are linked by having one of the best-justified causes for grief, the death of a child, a cause that, at the end of Shakespeare's play, Lear also shares. Thus Job and Lear are more alike than might at first appear to be the case. What seems at first a contrastive allusion—Lear suffers as Job does, but not as patiently—turns out to be more complex: Job himself isn't so patient after all, even if Calvin might wish him to be ("But by the way let us holde this for a rule, that to be pacient, it behoveth us to moderate our sorrow" [28]).

Moreover, in writing *King Lear*, Shakespeare seems to have had in mind the etymological relationship between patience, passion, and (Christ's) passion, all of which derive from the same Latin root (*patior*, "to suffer").[49] That Shakespeare had the Latin in mind is supported by its actual inclusion in the play, in Lear's fear of *"Hysterica passio"* (2.2.246). There has been speculation about what medical condition Shakespeare had in mind and where he gained knowledge of it, but he may have particularly liked this disease because its name included the Latin root of the "patience" Lear desires, the "passion" that prevents him from attaining it, and the "passion" of Christ that provides the model for Christian suffering.[50]

The only character who is genuinely patient is Cordelia: she suffers without complaint her father's curse, the hatred of her sisters, rejection by a suitor, banishment, defeat, and an ignominious death. In a scene cut from the Folio text, a gentleman tells Kent how Cordelia took the news of her father's condition:

> It seemed she was a queen
> Over her passion, who, most rebel-like,
> Sought to be king o'er her. . . .
> . . . patience and sorrow strove
> Who should express her goodliest.
>
> (4.3.13–17)

Not only is Cordelia's patience appropriate to her character in general terms, but it also links her, through a number of prominent biblical allusions, to the passion of Christ. For instance, in both Quarto and Folio Cordelia states to her absent parent, from whom she has been separated, "O dear father, / It is thy business I go about" (4.4.23–24). Shakespeare's audience would likely have heard this as an allusion to Christ's remark to his parents in the temple, where they found him after becoming separated: "Knewe ye not that I must go about my father's business?" (Luke 2:49). Another example occurs when an anonymous gentleman states of the mad Lear (who has just fled the stage), "Thou hast one daughter / Who redeems nature from the general curse / Which twain have brought her to" (4.6.201–3). The twain in question are most obviously Goneril and Regan, who have "cursed" nature by their unnatural behavior, but in biblical terms the twain are Adam and Eve, whose sin brought a "general curse" (original sin) upon humanity, from which humanity is redeemed by the sacrifice of Christ.[51] Though as a redeemer Cordelia is likened to Christ, her redemption is a secular one: she redeems the anonymous gentleman's (and our) opinion of humanity, and she may redeem her father in some fashion, if we believe that Lear is a better man at the end of the play.[52] Lear further associates Cordelia with Christ in terms of their respective sacrifices, even if we aren't quite sure precisely what sacrifices Lear has in mind: "Upon such sacrifices, my Cordelia, / The gods themselves throw incense" (5.3.20–21).[53] Finally, the figure of the dead Cordelia in Lear's arms has been likened to a gender-inverted Pietà, a speculative suggestion that would nevertheless make visual sense on stage if Cordelia's qualities have already been established as Christlike.[54] This is not to say that Cordelia represents Christ allegorically, simply that she is similar to him in terms of her entirely innocent and patient suffering on another's account.

Ironically, a comparison between Lear himself and Christ is also implied by the allusive link between Lear and Job, since, as mentioned above, Job was a traditional type of Christ, the ultimate "pattern of patience" through his passion.[55] More explicitly, Lear and Christ are linked by Edgar's exclamation in response to the mad Lear, "O thou side-piercing sight!" (4.6.85), which recalls the piercing of Christ's side by the soldier

(John 19:34), though the allusion requires some puzzling out. Christ's side is pierced by the soldier, and the sight of this, in accordance with standard meditational practice (both Catholic and Protestant), "pierces" us, just as the sight of Lear does Edgar. This scene would also be visually allusive on stage if Lear wears a crown of wildflowers, as Cordelia suggests, and as many productions have staged it; such a crown of "burdock, hemlock, nettles" (4.4.3–6) suggests a crown of thorns rather more than flowers. Another association between Lear and Christ is encouraged as Lear refers to his "pelican daughters" when he meets Edgar as Poor Tom (3.4.74). The reference is to a popular myth dating back at least to Isidore of Seville: the pelican kills her young, grieves for them for three days, and then restores them to life by piercing her own breast and feeding them with her blood.[56] During the Middle Ages, this bit of imaginative nature lore acquired a Christian allegorical meaning, and the "pelican in her piety" became a familiar symbol of the sacrifice of Christ. Shakespeare would have seen this common image in any number of places. (One example is on a carved and painted boss in Southwark Cathedral, then St. Saviour's, where Shakespeare's brother is buried and where a number of his theatrical colleagues were vestrymen.)[57] However, in Lear's case, these allusions to Christ are mainly contrastive. Lear doesn't willingly feed his daughters with his own blood, as does the pelican; rather, they are devouring him. The play is Lear's "passion" in a more limited sense than it is Cordelia's; Lear suffers, but he doesn't suffer on anyone else's behalf, and he redeems no one. It is at the level of allusions that the patience, passion, and suffering (Passion) of Lear, Cordelia, Job, and Christ are both drawn to our attention and contrasted with each other.

A Hidden God

Shakespeare explored the existential problems of suffering, providence, and divine justice using historical and literary sources, as one might gather from Bullough's *Narrative and Dramatic Sources of Shakespeare*. But to this constellation of secular authors should be added at least Job, the Epistle of James, Golding's translation of Calvin's *Sermons on Job*, and Bunny's edition of Parsons's *Booke of Christian Exercise*.[58] Situating the play in the context of Job and its interpretations reveals how *King Lear*, whatever the theological beliefs of its author, is firmly rooted in the ground of religious and biblical ideas. An awareness of *King Lear*'s many sources also reveals some sense of Shakespeare's reading practice and the gestation process of his plays. Even if one remains skeptical about the influence of these sources on Shakespeare—though one shouldn't be, given the obvious range of Shakespeare's reading—knowing these works can help us understand the cultural, intellectual, and theological contexts from which the play emerged in its own time and may affect our response to some interpretive debates about *King Lear*.[59]

One long-standing interpretive debate, for instance, concerns whether the play is or is not "Christian," and whether it affirmed or challenged the prevailing Christian beliefs of its original audience. Elton's *"King Lear" and the Gods* has made naive "neo-Christian" readings (like Wilson Knight's) hard to take seriously, but more subtle Christian readings of the play persist. Seán Lawrence, for instance, assimilating Elton's analysis of *King Lear*'s characters as pagan or pre-Christian, has argued that the play's critique of religion is directed only at those specific religious views that in Christian terms are idolatrous.[60] René E. Fortin decides *King Lear* is fundamentally ambivalent, subject only to a kind of "hermeneutical circularity." Fortin nevertheless allows that "the Christian reader who is responsive to the Biblical echoes of the play may view the play as an attempt to demythologize Christianity, to reassert the hiddenness of God against the presumptuous pieties and shallow rationalism of the Edgars and Albanies of the world."[61] This seems undeniable (Lawrence is perhaps a case in point). But the notion of the "hiddenness of God"—a kind of theological escape hatch—raises as many troubling questions for *King Lear* as it seems to answer.[62]

Luther and Calvin both believed in a God (the Father, the God of Judgment) who was profoundly alien to and hidden from humanity, although they also believed in a God (Christ, the Word) who was loving and infinitely merciful. It was precisely the kind of problems expressed in Job that led Luther to develop a theology of the *deus absconditus* ("hidden God"), a God whose nature, judgments, and justice were essentially unknowable. In *De servo arbitrio* (1525), his famous response to Erasmus's *De libero arbitrio*, Luther wrote about the problem of trying to reconcile human and divine notions of justice. We must simply recognize, he argues, that divine justice is beyond us and trust in faith over our limited reason, otherwise we may be led to dangerous speculations:

> I will give an example to confirm this faith and console that evil eye which suspects God of injustice. As you can see, God so orders this corporal world in its external affairs that if you respect and follow the judgment of human reason, you are bound to say either that there is no God or that God is unjust. As the poet [Ovid, *Amores*] says, "Oft I am moved to think there are no gods!" For look at the prosperity the wicked enjoy and the adversity the good endure, and note how both proverbs and that parent of proverbs, experience, testify that the bigger the scoundrel the greater his luck.[63]

Luther then cites Job 12:6, "The tents of the ungodly are at peace," and goes on to say that we must remember that there is a life after this life in which all is set right. Despite the appearance of confidence here, however, it is clear elsewhere in Luther's writing that "there was terror in his encounter with the hidden, predestinating God and that the emotional, religious, or spiritual content of the experience burst the limits of the merely rational and conceptual."[64]

Calvin was similarly anxious, even terrified, by "the sovereignty of Job's God," which made it difficult not to see God as a tyrant.[65] Calvin tried to quiet his anxieties by several means. First, the premise of Job's perfection, with which the book of Job begins, was simply unacceptable in terms of Reformation theology. Both the narrator and God himself, in the opening wager with Satan, describe Job as a man preeminently virtuous. In the Bishops' Bible Job is "perfect and just" (Job 1:1). "Perfect" accurately reflects the Hebrew word *tam*, but the idea that any man besides Christ could be perfect was irreconcilable with Calvin's understanding of original sin and human corruption after the Fall. For Calvin, Job, like any human, could not aspire to perfection; he could at best be "upright." (The Geneva translators followed his lead, calling Job "upright and just.") As a result, if Job is admitted to partake of original sin, he cannot be perfectly innocent, and if he is not innocent, his suffering cannot be entirely unmerited.[66]

Calvin's most disturbing response to the problem of innocent suffering, as it appears in Job, was his theology of God's "double" or "secret" justice. Akin to Luther's concept of the *deus absconditus*, Calvin's idea was a means of reconciling divine providence with the obvious injustices of everyday life. Not only is God ultimately inscrutable and alien, but he operates by a principle of justice we cannot comprehend:

> There is also another kind of rightuousnesse which we are lesse acquainted with: which is when God handleth us, not according to his law, but according as he may do by right. And why? Forasmuch as our lord giveth us our lesson in his law, and commandeth us to do whatever is conteined there: although the same do farre passe al our power, and no man be able to performe the thing that hee hath commanded us: yet notwithstanding we owe him yet more, and are further bound unto him: and the law is not so perfect and peerlesse a thing, as is the said infinite rightfulnesse of god, according as we have seene heretofore that by that he could find unrightuousnesse in the Angels, and the very daysunne should not be cleere before him. Thus ye see how there is a perfecter rightuousnes than the rightuousnesse of the lawe. And so God listed to use that: although a man had performed al that is conteined in the law: yet should he not faile to be condemned. (413)[67]

In getting himself out of one theological bind, however, Calvin created further problems for himself. If God can operate according to a kind of justice that is above his own law and essentially equivalent to his will, how can he escape the label of tyrant? Accordingly, Calvin, like his medieval predecessors commenting on Job, is reluctant to describe Job's suffering as "punishment," preferring to think of it as a test or even as a means of grace (since suffering may lead to spiritual improvement). As Susan Schreiner points out, "Every time Calvin verges on saying that Job was judged for sins against God's secret justice, he switches vocabulary and says that God 'tested' Job according to 'another regard,' a 'higher cause,' or a 'secret intention,' namely as a model for future generations."[68] So in one sense, for Calvin, Job isn't really about justice at all. Golding takes this view further in his preface: "God never forsaketh us in our troubles, but upholdeth and maintaineth us even in our uttermost extremeties, by a secret and incomprehensible working, not always seen of the worlde, nor presently perceived of our selves: and that his afflicting of us is not for any hatred or ill will of purpose to destroy us, but of a fatherly loving kindnesse, too make us knowe better both ourselves and him."[69]

Job himself would have had little patience for the false comfort of Golding or Calvin. Nor was he the only figure in the Bible who felt that God's plan was often not only difficult to discern but sometimes difficult to credit. Jeremiah questions, "Wherefore doeth the waye of the wicked prosper?" and the Psalmist asks, "Then have I clensed my herte in vayne and washed my handes in innocency? All the daye long have I bene punished, and chastened every morning?" (Ps. 73:13–14). The complaint of Habakkuk is still more radical:

> O Lord, how long shal I crye, and thou wilt not heare! Even crye
>   out unto thee for violence, and thou wilt not helpe!
> Why doest thou shewe me iniquitie, and cause me to beholde
>   sorowe? for spoyling, and violence are before me: and there are
>   that raise up strife and contention.
> Therefore the Law is dissolved, and judgement doeth never go
>   forthe: for the wicked doeth compasse about the righteous:
>   therefore wrong judgement procedeth.
>
> (Hab. 1:2–4)

Of those who pose such questions about innocent suffering and the prosperity of the wicked, Job is the only one who gets a definitive response, at least in the sense that it comes directly from God, speaking from a whirlwind. The problem is that God's answer is no answer at all. Job asks, Why am I being punished since I have not sinned? God's "answer" is, "Where wast thou when I layed the fundacions of the earth? declare if thou hast understanding" (Job 38:4) and more of the same. In other words, Who are you to ask such a question of me? However problematic God's nonanswer, the response nevertheless comes directly from God himself, so Job is finally granted at least the audience he has demanded from the beginning. In legal terms, which Job often uses, he wants to bring his case before God and hear God's defense; Job is finally told that God is beyond any human jurisdiction. This seems to satisfy Job (perhaps especially since his comforters are chastised and his goods and health restored to him).

But *King Lear* is like Job without God's voice from the whirlwind. There are no answers, no voices from heaven, in *King Lear*. Instead, Gloucester says that the gods "kill us for their sport" (4.1.39). This is in fact what we see in Job, which begins with gaming—a heartless wager between God and Satan about the extent of Job's perfection. But there is no such explanatory "justification" in *King Lear*. Lear asks, "What is the cause of the thunder" (3.4.151). Yet while God tells Job that he "hathe devided the spowtes for the rain or the way for the lightening of the thunders" (Job 38:25), Lear's thunder does not speak. Calvin writes about thunder and God's voice in his commentary on Elihu's statement, "Heare the sounde of [God's] voice, and the noyse that goeth out of his mouth" (Job 37:2). In Calvin's interpretation, Elihu refers not to the voice Job has just heard but to thunder more generally: "This voice [of God] is none other thing, than the same noise that is made by the thunder: nevertheless it serveth too reprove men of their unthankfulnesse, in that they give not eare too Gods thundering: according also as it is a common proverbe when men play the madde men, too say that they are so lowde, that a man could not heare God thunder for them" (676). Although Lear says that it is "the great gods / That keep this dreadful pudder o'er our heads," this seems mere wishful thinking (3.2.49–50). It is not evident that Lear actually hears any deity in the thunder, nor is it clear that we should either.

Another difference between Job and Lear is that, even before God answers out of the whirlwind, Job never doubts that God does exist. Job also believes that God is just and all-powerful. (If Job didn't believe these things, his suffering would be less troubling.) But what does Lear believe in? Presumably not in a Christian God, since he lives before Christ's birth. Lear swears by Hecate, Jupiter, and Apollo, Roman deities who are certainly pre-Christian, yet Raphael Holinshed's *Chronicle*, another Shakespeare source, dates the beginning of Cordelia's reign from "the yeere of the world 3155, before the bylding of Rome 54." Leir's rule supposedly began in 3105, thus over a century before Rome was built, which makes it historically impossible that Leir could have heard of the Roman pantheon.[70] (All religious references in *King Lear*, whether Christian or

not, are thus anachronistic to the play's historical/geographical setting.)
When Lear curses Goneril, he invokes the goddess "Nature" (1.4.267).
Does Lear believe he is addressing an actual deity? In a later curse, Lear
addresses "You fen-sucked fogs" (2.2.356), but presumably he doesn't
actually credit fogs with agency, any more than he does the winds, cata-
racts, and hurricanes in his storm speech on the heath (3.2.1–2). So while
Job actually expects or at least hopes for an answer to his question about
divine justice, it isn't clear whether Lear does.

Yet, like Job, *King Lear*'s audience does desire an answer, whether
it comes from God or a character in the play. Which answer does the
play finally privilege? Gloucester's, that the gods are cruel and sadistic?
Edgar's, when he justifies to Edmund their father's blinding on the basis
of his adultery?

> The gods are just and of our pleasant vices
> Make instruments to plague us:
> The dark and vicious place where thee he got
> Cost him his eyes.
>
> (5.3.168–71)

(This affirmation of divine justice has a comforting Old Testament ring,
but after the onstage horror of Gloucester's blinding it has likely always
struck audiences as pat and cruel;[71] even in an age when seditious libelers
like Prynne were mutilated and branded, adulterers did not have their eyes
gouged out.) What of the apparent atheism of Edmund? It may be that,
as Lawrence suggests, *King Lear* represents merely a pagan world and has
no implications for true-believing Christians (though given its weight of
biblical and religious allusions this seems unlikely). Or perhaps the God
of *King Lear* is, as Fortin suggests, a Luther-inspired, inscrutable, hidden
God, a *deus absconditus*. (It would be theologically appropriate, then, that
there is no explanation for the suffering we see in the play.) Or perhaps,
like Calvin, we should not expect the suffering of Gloucester, Lear, and
Cordelia to seem just, since suffering is a blessing. Nor need it be justified
to us, since God has his own "secret justice," which we cannot comprehend. This is Elton's conclusion about how Shakespeare's audience likely
interpreted the play.

King Lear is as many-faceted a play as has ever been written, and Shakespeare's audience was likely not homogenous in its response to these interpretive options. But Elton admits, importantly, that "an unhistorical, Christian-conditioned Renaissance author and audience could only with difficulty have objectively and detachedly viewed a presentation of religious problems without converting them to some extent into Christian terms," and he goes on to suggest that Shakespeare's "audience would have the more sympathetically regarded the heathen's difficulties with his gods insofar as the Jacobean age was experiencing an analogous crisis in religion and the idea of providence."[72] Calvin's theology was one way out of the religious crisis, though as indicated above it was not without its anxieties, anxieties that troubled Calvin in his reading of Job to the extent that he felt compelled to write 159 sermons on it: How does one distinguish between a God whose justice is inscrutable and one who is unjust? How does one distinguish between an absent God and one who simply doesn't exist? The answer for Calvin is faith, the same faith that seems to lie behind Christian or specifically Calvinist interpretations of *King Lear*.

Faith, as the Epistle to the Hebrews puts it, "is the grounde of things which are hoped for, and the evidence of things which are not sene" (Heb. 11:1). In the theater, however, things seen tend to outweigh "things which are not sene," just as in the theater our emotional response to the drama tends to outweigh our theological positions. Calvin would see Lear's suffering as justified in light of the overwhelming sin shared by all humanity. Yet audiences have always seen *King Lear* as a tragedy, and many have felt, like Johnson, that the death of Cordelia is almost unbearable. The closing lines of the play (whether spoken by Albany or Edgar) urge us to "Speak what we feel, not what we ought to say" (5.3.323), and this point might be applied to the play's fundamental questions about God's justice and providence. What a good Protestant Christian "ought to say" in response to *King Lear* has been voiced by a number of critics, whether Christian, neo-Christian, or historicist. What we may "feel," though, is that all such readings are inadequate to the tragic power of Shakespeare's play. No theological argument proves convincing in the face of innocent suffering; neither Job's comforters, nor the voice from the whirlwind, nor commentators like Calvin provide a satisfying answer to Job's basic question, "Why me?" The questions posed by *King Lear* prove to be equally intractable. But this is likely because Shakespeare was a more skeptical reader of Job than was Calvin, and a skeptical reader of Calvin too, probing the anxieties about Job that the reformer was not quite able to argue away.

Notes

1. Prynne reinterpreted the initials as "Stigma of Laud."

2. [William Prynne], *A new discovery of the prelates tyranny* (London, 1641), n.p. The pamphlet was published anonymously and written in the third person, but Prynne was the author, and the account is his own. See William M. Lamont, *Marginal Prynne, 1600–1669* (London: Routledge and Kegan Paul, 1963), 38–40.

3. Prynne, *New discovery*, n.p.

4. Quoted in the New Variorum *King Lear*, ed. H. Howard Furness (Philadelphia: J. B. Lippincott, 1880), 419.

5. G. Wilson Knight, "The *Lear* Universe," in *The Wheel of Fire: Interpretations of Shakespearian Tragedy*, 4th ed. (London: Methuen, 1949), 191; John Holloway, *The Story of the Night: Studies in Shakespeare's Major Tragedies* (London: Routledge and Kegan Paul, 1961).

6. Holloway, *Story of the Night*, 85.

7. Arthur Kirsch, *The Passions of Shakespeare's Tragic Heroes* (Charlottesville: University Press of Virginia, 1990), 105.

8. Rosalie Colie, "The Energies of Endurance: Biblical Echo in *King Lear*," in *Some Facets of "King Lear": Essays in Prismatic Criticism*, ed. Rosalie Colie and F. T. Flahiff (Toronto: University of Toronto Press, 1974), 117–44; W. R. Elton, *"King Lear" and the Gods* (San Marino, CA: Huntington Library, 1966), esp. 30, 68, 263; Kenneth Muir, ed., *"King Lear": Critical Essays* (New York: Garland, 1984), 289. John D. Rosenberg, in "Lear and His Comforters," *Essays in Criticism* 16, no. 2 (1966): 135–46, casts *King Lear*'s neo-Christian critics themselves in the role of Job's wishful-thinking, naive friends.

9. Steven Marx, *Shakespeare and the Bible* (Oxford: Oxford University Press, 2000); Kenneth Gross, *Shakespeare's Noise* (Chicago: University of Chicago Press, 2001); Robert Pack, "Betrayal and Nothingness: The Book of Job and King Lear," in *The Long View: Essays on the Discipline of Hope and Poetic Craft* (Amherst: University of Massachusetts Press, 1991), 251–76; Naseeb Shaheen, *Biblical References in Shakespeare's Plays* (Newark: University of Delaware Press, 1999). Marx

cites further brief remarks by Jan Kott and Harold Bloom on the relationship between *Lear* and the book of Job. See Marx, *Shakespeare and the Bible*, 59.

10. Charles Lamb, quoted in Furness, New Variorum *King Lear*, 421. Stanley Cavell, *Disowning Knowledge in Seven Plays of Shakespeare* (Cambridge: Cambridge University Press, 1987), 68.

11. Marx, *Shakespeare*, 59.

12. Pack, "King Lear."

13. Richard Knowles, "How Shakespeare Knew *King Leir*," *Shakespeare Survey* 55 (2002): 12–35; W. W. Greg, review of *"The Chronicle History of King Leir": The Original of Shakespeare's "King Lear,"* by Sidney Lee, *Modern Language Review* 5, no. 4 (1910): 515–19.

14. Scott McMillin and Sally-Beth MacLean, *The Queen's Men and Their Plays* (Cambridge: Cambridge University Press, 1998), 160–66.

15. Leonard Siger, "The Image of Job in the Renaissance" (PhD diss., Johns Hopkins University, 1960), 230–53.

16. Annaliese Connolly, "Peele's *David and Bethsabe*: Reconsidering Biblical Drama of the Long 1590s," *Early Modern Literary Studies* [e-journal], Special Issue no. 16 (October 2007), article 9, http://extra.shu.ac.uk/emls/si-16/connpeel.htm.

17. Ibid., par. 8.

18. Roma Gill, introduction to *The Jew of Malta*, in vol. 4 of *The Complete Works of Christopher Marlowe*, ed. Roma Gill (Oxford: Clarendon Press, 1995), xvi–xvii.

19. All citations to this play are from the Gill edition.

20. G. K. Hunter, "The Theology of Marlowe's *The Jew of Malta*," *Journal of the Warburg and Courtauld Institutes* 27 (1964): 219.

21. For a study of this allusive practice in another play, see Hannibal Hamlin, "The Bible, *Coriolanus*, and Shakespeare's Modes of Allusion," in *Never Again Would Birds' Song Be the Same: Essays in Early Modern and Modern Poetry in Honor of John Hollander*, ed. Jennifer Lewin (New Haven: Beinecke Library, Yale University, 2002), 73–91.

22. William Shakespeare, *King Lear*, ed. R. A. Foakes, Arden 3rd series (Walton-on-Thames: Thomas Nelson and Sons, 1997); all citations to the play are from this edition. More has been written about the different textual states of *King Lear* than about those of any of Shakespeare's other plays; see, for instance, Gary Taylor and Michael Warren, eds., *The Division of the Kingdoms: Shakespeare's Two Versions of "King Lear"* (Oxford: Clarendon Press, 1983). The arguments for two entirely distinct and authorial versions of the play are not entirely convincing or, for the purposes of this chapter, especially relevant. Passages present in only one or the other version (Q and F) will be noted.

23. Unless otherwise noted, all biblical citations are from *The Geneva Bible: A Facsimile of the 1560 Edition*, ed. Lloyd E. Berry (Madison: University of Wisconsin Press, 1969).

24. The figure of Kent in stocks does have other possible sources, including Geoffrey Whitney's emblem on the "golden shackles" of courtly life, but these are not mutually incompatible. See Geoffrey Whitney, *"Aurea compedes,"* in *A Choice of Emblemes and Other Devises* (Leyden, 1586), 202. The figure of a courtier in stocks obviously resembles *King Lear* 2.2, though Kent doesn't actually look like a courtier in the scene, and the motto ("golden shackles") is not appropriate to the play. In his Arden edition (note to 2.2.153–71), Foakes cites Maynard Mack's comment that Kent in the stocks is emblematic of "Virtue Locked Out," but neither critic cites an actual emblem.

25. These lines are not in the Folio text.

26. Colie, "Energies of Endurance," 130, 131.

27. See Maurice Charney, "'We Put Fresh Garments on Him': Nakedness and Clothes in *King Lear,*" in Colie and Flahiff, *Some Facets of "King Lear,"* 77–88. Judy Kronenfeld also explores clothing and nakedness in *King Lear* in an extended attempt to link the play to Eucharistic controversies: *"King Lear" and the Naked Truth: Rethinking the Language of Religion and Resistance* (Durham: Duke University Press, 1998).

28. Intertextuality may include a wide range of potential relationships between texts, some seemingly intended for the reader to recognize, some perhaps not, but reflecting nevertheless the reading and thinking of the author. These latter fall into the broader category of sources.

29. *The Works of George Herbert*, ed. F. E. Hutchinson (Oxford: Clarendon Press, 1941), 58.

30. As Alan Ginsberg remembered (in his *Howl*), there is analogous howling in Isaiah, Jeremiah, and other prophets.

31. T. Grashop, "How to take profit by reading of the Holy Scripture," in the Geneva-Tomson-Junius Bible (London, 1603), STC (2nd ed.), 2190.

32. *Sermons of Maister Iohn Caluin, vpon the booke of Iob, translated out of French by Arthur Golding* (London, 1580), 538; all page citations are from this edition and are hereafter given parenthetically in the text. Susan Schreiner, in "Calvin as an Interpreter of Job," in *Calvin and the Bible*, ed. Donald K. McKim (Cambridge: Cambridge University Press, 2006), 68–72, points out that Calvin clearly identified with Elihu and argued that his words were not included in the criticism God directs at the friends in Job 42:7.

33. In *The Essayes of Michael Lord of Montaigne, Translated by John Florio*, 3 vols. (London: J. M. Dent, 1921), 2:169, 181. The editorial interpolation is from Foakes, ed., *King Lear*, note to 3.4.101–3. On the relationship between Shakespeare and

Montaigne, see Leo Salingar, "King Lear, Montaigne and Harsnett," in *Dramatic Form in Shakespeare and the Jacobeans* (Cambridge: Cambridge University Press, 1986), 107–39.

34. *A Booke of Christian Exercise . . . by R.P.* [Robert Parsons]. *Perused and accompanied now with a Treatise tending to Pacification: by Edm. Bunny* (London, 1584), 293; all citations are from this edition, though the passages cited are identical in Parsons's *The First Book of Christian Exercise* ([Rouen], 1582), and are hereafter given parenthetically in the text. The similarity between these passages is noted in passing in a little-known essay by Christopher Devlin, "Hamlet's Divinity," in *Hamlet's Divinity and Other Essays* (London: Rupert Hart-Davis, 1963), 41. On the curious history of Parsons's book, lightly Protestantized by Bunny (the book was not polemically "Catholic" to begin with), see Robert McNulty, "The Protestant Version of Robert Parsons' 'The First Booke of the Christian Exercise,'" *Huntington Library Quarterly* 22/4 (1959): 271–300. More recently, Brad Gregory argues that Bunny's adaptation of Parsons's was in fact more polemical than has been realized. See "The 'True and Zealouse Seruice of God': Robert Parsons, Edmund Bunny, and 'The First Booke of the Christian Exercise,'" *Journal of Ecclesiastical History* 45, no. 2 (1994): 231–69.

35. Robert Henryson, "The Abbey Walk," lines 17–24, in *The Poems of Robert Henryson*, ed. Denton Fox (Oxford: Clarendon Press, 1981), 157.

36. Beyond allusions and echoed sources lies the more nebulous intertextual field described by Julia Kristeva and Mikhail Bakhtin, in which an author may "borrow"—consciously or not—ideas, images, even language from the culture in which he exists. The resemblance between Lear and Gloucester and Job and Tobit may be a case in point. The more immediate source of King Lear's subplot is the story of the Paphlagonian king from Sidney's *Arcadia*, which has been recognized since at least Furness's 1880 Variorum edition. On the rich iconographic history (the intertextual field) that lies behind both Shakespeare's Gloucester and Sidney's Paphlagonian king, see Kahren Jones Hellerstedt, "The Blind Man and His Guide in Netherlandish Painting," *Simiolus* 13, nos. 3–4 (1983): 163–81.

37. Elton, *"King Lear" and the Gods*, chs. 6 and 7, describes and contextualizes both Gloucester's "pagan superstition" and Edmund's "pagan atheism."

38. For another exploration of these etymological and conceptual complexities, see Judith H. Anderson, "Patience and Passion in Shakespeare and Milton," in *Reading the Allegorical Intertext: Chaucer, Spenser, Shakespeare, Milton* (New York: Fordham University Press, 2008), 259–71. Anderson mentions Lear and Job in passing, but her interests lie elsewhere.

39. Shaheen, *Biblical References*, 611.

40. See M. P. Tilley, *A Dictionary of the Proverbs in England in the Sixteenth and Seventeenth Centuries* (Ann Arbor: University of Michigan Press, 1950), J59.

41. Bartholomew Chappell, *The Garden of Prudence* (London, 1595), B2.

42. Shakespeare, *The Second Part of King Henry IV*, ed. Giorgio Melchiori (Cambridge: Cambridge University Press, 1989). Once again, Shakespeare's biblical allusion is contrastive.

43. Nathaniel Woodes, *The Conflict of Conscience* (London, 1581), 1.2.221–5 (Bii). On the title page, Woodes's "lamentable Hystorie" is actually announced as "An excellent new Commedie." On Gregory's *Moralia in Job*, see Susan E. Schreiner, *Where Shall Wisdom Be Found? Calvin's Exegesis of Job from Medieval and Modern Perspectives* (Chicago: University of Chicago Press, 1994), ch. 1.

44. Nicholas Breton, *The Soules immortall crowne consisting of seaven glorious graces* (London, 1601), [G2v].

45. See H. L. Ginsberg, "Job the Patient and Job the Impatient," *Conservative Judaism* 21, no. 3 (1967): 12–28.

46. Siger, "Image of Job," 220ff.

47. On early modern attitudes to passion, in Erasmus and Luther as well as *King Lear*, see Richard Strier, "Against the Rule of Reason: Praise of Passion from Petrarch to Luther to Shakespeare to Herbert," in *Reading the Early Modern Passions: Essays in the Cultural History of Emotion*, ed. Gail Kern Paster et al. (Philadelphia: University of Pennsylvania Press, 2004), 23–42. Calvin, however, was as uncomfortable with passion as the Stoics, criticizing the excesses of both Job and David; see William Bouwsma, *John Calvin: A Sixteenth Century Portrait* (New York: Oxford University Press, 1988), 94–96.

48. Samuel Rowlands, "*Mulier ecce Filius tuus,*" in *The Betraying of Christ. Judas in Despaire. The Seven Words of Our Savior on the Crosse. With Other Poems on the Passion* (London, 1598), [E4v].

49. For a brilliant study of the history of these words and the ideas they represent, see Erich Auerbach, "*Passio* as Passion," trans. Martin Elsky, *Criticism* 43, no. 3 (2001): 295–308.

50. The disease is also called "the mother" (as by Lear himself, 2.2.245) and is one associated exclusively with women; in a play with no mothers, and in which gender and procreation are much at issue, "*Hysterica passio*" has obvious thematic relevance. From the medical perspective, see Kaara L. Peterson, "*Historica Passio*: Early Modern Medicine, King Lear, and Editorial Practice," *Shakespeare Quarterly* 57, no. 1 (2006): 1–22.

51. Roy W. Battenhouse recognized the allusion to Adam and Eve, citing the earlier argument of John Danby. Roy W. Battenhouse, *Shakespearean Tragedy: Its Art and Christian Premises* (Bloomington: Indiana University Press, 1969), 271.

52. But some, like Cavell, would argue that Lear does not learn enough from his experience, however changed he is in appearance and condition.

53. Cordelia sacrifices her happiness, her freedom, and (later) her life in her efforts to help her father, but it isn't clear that this is what Lear has in mind. On this suggestive but puzzling passage, see Philip Brockbank's British Academy Shakespeare Lecture, "'Upon Such Sacrifices,'" *Proceedings of the British Academy* 47, no. 4 (1976): 129–43.

54. For a recent argument, see Katherine Goodland, "Inverting the Pietà in Shakespeare's *King Lear*," in *Marian Moments in Early Modern British Drama*, ed. Regina Buccola and Lisa Hopkins (Aldershot: Ashgate, 2007), 47–74. The argument was made earlier by Helen Gardner (*King Lear* [London: Athlone Press, 1967]) and perhaps Maynard Mack (*"King Lear" in Our Time* [Berkeley: University of California Press, 1965]), as noted by Dennis Taylor, *Shakespeare and Religion Chronology*, "Post-Shakespeare 1900–2007" (www.bc.edu/publications/relarts/supplements/shakespeare/chronology.html).

55. On the iconographic relationship between Job and Christ, see G. Von der Osten, "Job and Christ: The Development of a Devotional Image," *Journal of the Warburg and Courtauld Institutes* 16, nos. 1–2 (1953): 153–58.

56. P. J. Heather, "Animal Beliefs (Continued)," *Folklore* 52, no. 3 (1941): 217.

57. For an online image, see Diocese of Southwark, "Southwark Cathedral," under "Tour," "Nave," "Roof Bosses," October 2004, www.southwark .anglican.org/cathedral/tour/bosses.htm. Among other uses of the image, there is an elaborate carved baptismal font with the pelican feeding her young in the church of St. Lawrence, Diddington, and a similar pelican on a font in St. Peter and St. Paul, Norfolk. The image remains in wide use in churches today. Queen Elizabeth I also wears a pelican jewel in her "Pelican" portrait, painted by Nicholas Hilliard. See Roy Strong, *Portraits of Queen Elizabeth I* (Oxford: Clarendon Press, 1963).

58. Additional biblical allusions lie outside the possible scope of this chapter. See, for instance, Susan Snyder, "*King Lear* and the Prodigal Son," *Shakespeare Quarterly* 17 (1966): 361–69, or Joseph Wittreich's *"Image of That Horror": History, Prophecy, and Apocalypse in King Lear* (San Marino, CA: Huntington Library, 1984), which focuses on the book of Revelation.

59. See, for instance, Robert S. Miola, *Shakespeare's Reading* (Oxford: Oxford University Press, 2000).

60. Seán Lawrence, "'Gods That We Adore': The Divine in *King Lear*," *Renascence* 56, no. 3 (2004): 143–59.

61. René E. Fortin, "Hermeneutical Circularity and Christian Interpretations of *King Lear*," *Shakespeare Studies* 12 (1979): 121.

62. Readers familiar with the long and substantial tradition of scholarship on apophatic or negative theology may find this characterization a little

dismissive, but it does seem justified in terms of the thought of Luther and Calvin, two particularly anxious theologians.

63. Martin Luther, "The Bondage of the Will," trans. Philip S. Watson in collaboration with Benjamin Drewery, in *Luther's Works* (American ed.), vol. 23 (Philadelphia: Fortress Press, 1972), 291.

64. B. A. Gerrish, "'To the Unknown God': Luther and Calvin on the Hiddenness of God," *Journal of Religion* 53 (July 1973): 274.

65. Susan Schreiner, "Exegesis and Double Justice in Calvin's Sermons on Job," *Church History* 58, no. 3 (1989): 326. See also Schreiner, *Where Shall Wisdom Be Found*, for a more extensive study. On Calvin's anxiety more generally, see Bouwsma, *John Calvin*, 32–48.

66. Calvin and other commentators based their argument for Job's imperfection on several passages where he seems to admit his sinfulness, e.g., "And why doest thou not pardone my trespass? and take away mine iniquitie?" (Job 7:21), and "If I wolde justifie my self, mine owne mouth shal condemne me: if I wolde be perfite, he shal judge me wicked" (Job 9:20).

67. Sermon 88 on Job 23:1–7, quoted (in a different translation) in Schreiner, "Exegesis and Double Justice," 332.

68. Ibid., 334.

69. Golding, "Epistle to Leicester," in Calvin, *Sermons on Job*, A2v.

70. Geoffrey Bullough, ed., *Narrative and Dramatic Sources of Shakespeare*, vol. 7 (London: Routledge and Kegan Paul, 1978), 319, 316.

71. See Rosenberg, "Lear and His Comforters," 138–39.

72. Elton, *"King Lear" and the Gods*, 338.

PART TWO

Chapter 6

The Wizards of Uz
Shakespeare and the Book of Job

JULIA REINHARD LUPTON

In his 1589 commentary on the book of Job, Theodore Beza associates the text with tragedy: "This whole discourse standeth of interchangeable speeches to and fro, the beginning and end of the booke only excepted: and if it were not that it is shut up with a joyfull and wished ende, it might rightly both for the matter, (then which nothing can be thought or imagined more grave and weightie) and also for the exceeding worthinesse of the persons, that here talk and reason together, be called a Tragedie."[1] In measuring the proximity between Job and tragedy, Beza notes the text's division between the prose frame, which is folkloric, exemplary, and ultimately comic in structure, and the central poetic sections, which consist of dialogue and are characterized by Job's vociferous complaints. Beza's generic analysis calls attention to the work's contradictions as well as its achievements: whereas the miraculous restorations of the prose frame imply a simple ethics of virtue exonerated and rewarded, the more difficult and substantial interior sections grapple with the fact that good people can suffer without cause—the position put forth by Job himself, in the form of argument, but also through the gestural genres of lament, complaint, oath, and curse, whose visceral pathos frays the extremities of discourse.

As Victoria Kahn has argued in a recent study of Job and *Paradise Regained*, both humanist authors like Sidney and exegetes like Beza frequently put forward the book of Job as an example of literary complexity native to scripture.[2] For Renaissance writers, Job thus becomes a key transitional text between scripture and secular literature; it is not only Job who is "tested" in this book, but also the normative theology and poetic conventions of biblical writing. The book of Job is generically affiliated with prose narrative, drama, and lyric; it relies extensively on irony and other rhetorical tropes for its emotional and argumentative effects; finally, set in the faraway land of Uz, the book is closer to imaginative fiction than to history. As Hannibal Hamlin notes in chapter 5 of this volume, Job dramas, common on the Continent, entered English theater as well; Robert Greene's *The History or Tragedy of Job* was recorded "in the Stationers' Register in 1594, the same year in which *King Leir* was played at the Rose." In his classic study of Shakespeare and the Bible, Richmond Noble argues that references to the book of Job, along with Ecclesiasticus, appear in Shakespeare's plays more often than any other biblical source after the Psalms.[3] Many of these references are passing and semantic, manifesting the kind of patterned thinking that travels easily from the Bible into everyday speech via the proverbial samplings of homily and liturgy. Yet Shakespeare also turns to Job's situation more systematically, in order to stage the psychic response of his characters to the terrible unraveling of the social institutions that had previously sustained them: the family in *Lear*, hospitality in *Timon of Athens*, the protections of civil society in *The Merchant of Venice*, and marriage in *Othello*. "Man is borne unto travail," Job laments in the Geneva translation: born out of his mother's labor and into his own trials (5:7), Job's travails signify both the subjective exertions of protest and complaint that he delivers from his dungheap and the traveling of his story among different epochs and communities whose borders are opened by his passage through them.[4] Shakespeare replays Job's predicament in distinct epochs and locales—the Venice of the Jew and the Moor, the pre-Christian Britain of Lear and his gods, and the classical Athens of Timon; taken together and separately, these experiments test the canonicity and elasticity, both emotional and geographical, of the Job story within the new domain of public theater. Pursuing the scars left by Job's travails in *Merchant, Othello,*

Timon, and *Lear,* I argue, can help us recover the religious intensities of Shakespeare's plays in both the singularity of their enunciation and the universality of their reach, in turn disclosing literature's own generative travails between the embodied, embedded singularity of specific expressions and experiences and the provisional universality produced by acts of iteration, adaptation, translation, and commentary, exercised in response to scripture as both model and antitype.

The Man from Uz

The book of Job takes place in the land of Uz, a fairytale location that most commentators locate somewhere outside the land of Israel. The 2009 Coen brothers film *A Serious Man,* which replays the book of Job in a Jewish suburb outside Minneapolis in 1969, goes so far as to equate Uz with Oz; the film culminates with the harried hero Larry Gopnik's long-awaited audience with the ancient and revered Rabbi Marshak, whose wisdom consists of intoning some lines from "Somebody to Love" by Jefferson Airplane. The Rabbi's postwar study is cluttered with mystical mementos reminiscent of the 1939 film, references that imply a kind of Frank Baum theology in which God is a good man but a very bad wizard whose gifts consist in making human beings discover their own resources. Although such a deeply humanist account of the book of Job (*Job: The Musical?*) would have been foreign to Renaissance readers, the Coen brothers' brilliant reading of Uz as Oz taps the secular potential of the enigmatic book that Kahn already sees operative in Milton, who, she argues, uses Job to keep the focus "on the horizontal dimension of secular time and on the questions about divine justice and ethical human action."[5] From Shakespeare and Milton to the Coen brothers, the secular edge of the book of Job has made it a rich resource for artists establishing their poetics in both creative and critical response to scripture.

For earlier Jewish commentators the story's indeterminate location meant that Job could emblematize human suffering as such while still offering a more particular embodiment of Jewish tribulations.[6] Calvin reads Job's redemption as proof that "there is no difference of the Iewe or Gentile, Greeke or Barbarous, learned or unlearned, high or lowe, or any other state or person before GOD"; for Calvin, Job's indeterminate location outside "the boundes of the visible Church" links him to Paul's universal mission.[7] Some commentators did cast Job as an Israelite, and we will see signs of a Jewish Job in Shakespeare's Shylock. For Muslims, Job (or "Ayyub") hailed from the pre-Mohammedan canon of holy prophets shared by Judaism, Christianity, and Islam. His name occurs four times in the Koran (4:163; 6:84; 21:84; 38:41–44), and a series of Islamic legends develop themes of testing, patience, illness, and divine healing that overlap with Job's cultic treatment in medieval Christendom and rabbinic Judaism.[8] All three religions link Job to the family of Abraham; indeed, the adjective *Abrahamic* rather than *Gentile* may best capture the form of regional universalism manifested by Job in his passage through neighboring traditions, including the three monotheisms and Near Eastern pagan wisdom cults. And it is not genealogy alone that renders Job "Abrahamic": as Ken Jackson argues in chapter 9 of this volume, the affinity between his story of unmerited justice and Abraham's encounter with a "call [that] shatters all reason" conjoins Job and Abraham in the ethical consciousness of monotheism.

The God that answers Job out of the whirlwind speaks of creation and its creatures, culminating in the visions of Behemoth and Leviathan; images of creation and createdness, both sublime and abject, abound in this teeming text, linking the book of Job to Wisdom literature, whose motifs Judaism shares with other Near Eastern discourses.[9] Job's God is nonetheless the Lord of the Covenant (Yahweh, the Tetragrammaton, the God of the J-Text), not the God of Creation (Elohim, the subject of the first sentence of Genesis, the God of the E-text).[10] Job insists not only that he, like Noah, has followed the "steppes" and "ways" of God but that he has never "departed from the commandement[s] [*mitzvot*] of [God's] lippes" (23:11–12). Job's claim implies his adherence to some form of revealed law organized by public cult, perhaps the seven Noachide laws instituted after the Flood, as was believed by John Selden, following both Jewish and Christian precedent.[11] The minimalism of the Noachide laws can be read in a universalizing direction, toward natural law, as Kahn emphasizes.[12] At the same time, God's initial covenant with Noah also anticipates the later covenant with Moses and hence implies the rudiments of a community-forming code that looks inward to its own regulation as well as outward to its affiliation with other forms of creaturely life. In the book of Job, covenant serves to signify the rule of law and the fact of relationship: between Job and God, between Job and his wife, and between Job and the community to which he belongs.[13] Covenant helps define Job's righteousness; it also gives Job something to fall back on when he makes his case. What covenant means for Job is the fact that an agreement exists: he has maintained his side of the bargain, and now he has a case in court. For Job, covenant defines righteousness, but it also invites protest.

What catapults Job from prose into poetry, and from patience into complaint, is not the death of his children but his affliction with skin disease (2:6–8). It is not that suffering bodily perforation is worse than the loss of children but rather that this final affliction re-signifies and brings into visibility the earlier sequence of losses, allowing these prior privations to speak through their inflamed openings: Job "open[s] his mouthe" when his own bodily integrity has been breached by disease. These sores bind together into a bodily image all the losses that Job has suffered, without in any way measuring them in an economic calculus. Job's sores, moreover, are not only a personal affliction; they also sign and seal his loss of status in the community in which he was once a master. In *Lear* and *Merchant*, Shakespeare is concerned with the loss of children, substance, and prestige; in *Othello*, he shifts attention to the spousal relation; in *Timon of Athens*, he focuses on bankruptcy alone. In each case, he takes his orientation from the passionately original voices of his creations, yet does so to gauge the fate of the social, the pressure that individual privation places on broader institutions and relationships. In both Shakespeare plays and the book of Job, privation is never purely private but always bears on the public world.

Inhabiting Job's sores and keeping them open is a host of worms, the most livid emblems of creaturely existence in a book rife with images of animal life. While the more exotic creatures demonstrate the wonder of God's creation, the worm, one of those "creeping things that creep on the earth" (Gen. 1:26; KJV) that the rabbis classed as *sheretz*, is a living ligature between disease, creatureliness, and complaint.[14] The worms, together with the sores that house them, define Job's "flesh" as the source and site of his complaint: "My flesh is clothed with worms and clods of dust; my skin is broken, and become loathsome" (7:5; KJV). We might take *flesh* here in the phenomenological sense that James Knapp develops in chapter 10 of this volume. Knapp cites Merleau-Ponty: "The flesh we are speaking of is not matter. It is the coiling over of the visible upon the seeing body, of the tangible upon the touching body, which is attested in particular when the body sees itself, touches itself seeing and touching the things, such that, simultaneously, *as* tangible it descends among them, *as* touching it dominates them all and draws this relationship and even this double relationship from itself, by dehiscence or fission of its own mass."[15] Phenomenology teases out the universal conditions of singular experiences, at once bodily, perceptual, and cognitive, trying to bring into view those aspects of living that by their very nature disappear from view or change in character as soon as we turn the instruments of reflective consciousness onto them. *Flesh* for Merleau-Ponty names the attempt to grasp the forms of appearance and disappearance that characterize the way we live with objects, environments, and our own bodies; phenomenological inquiry can occur in philosophy but also in visual art and in poetry when they try to capture or index the transient images left by human passion, pain, or thought.

The book of Job is phenomenological insofar as it records linguistic expression at the far edge of the endurable, a frontier defined by the somatic images left by the rim of the sore and the insistent protrusion of the worm. These orifices constitute the source of Job's complaints, the public loss of bodily integrity catapulting him into an idiom whose invective extremity remains close to the flesh that nourishes it. The Jobean topology of the worm in the wound that blossoms as the word of complaint provides a phenomenological image, a kind of bodily map, for the poetic experiments that flare up from sudden fissures in the bearable. This somatic topography belongs absolutely to Job, as its uniquely plaintive bearer and speaker; Theodore Beza recounts the legend attributing authorship to Job himself, a fiction that hits upon a certain truth about the text.[16] Yet this text also provides, quite literally, an opening for the voices of others, indexing Job's translatability across languages, traditions, and subject positions. Sores become mouths so that others can speak through their ache and arc: the dialogue as a form is a sequence of openings, a script that imagines its own iteration.[17] The commutativity of Job's plight and protest is signaled in the very status of the land of Uz as a locale without location, plagued by whirlwinds, bandits, and other refugees from a world in motion.

Job in Venice

Shakespeare, too, has journeyed to Job's country, setting up camp in the variegated yet oddly blank topography of Uz. In *Merchant*, Shakespeare focuses on Job as the subject of covenant (Shylock is Shakespeare's "Jewish Job"), but against the backdrop of a common creation defined by vulnerability to want and need and to the Jobean call to answer privation without rendering it meaningful. Shakespeare's two Venetian plays have long been linked as parallel explorations of the predicament of religious and racial outsiders in an urban zone committed to various forms of inclusion (economic, juridical, imperial), yet also fraught with autoimmune responses that expose the limits of Christian universalism. Precisely in marking those limits and bringing them into view, however, Shakespeare does not reject so much as renew the quest for universality as an ethical, political, and literary concern. As I argue at length elsewhere, it is no accident that both plays take up the book of Job as an instrument for exploring the phenomenology of complaint within a setting defined by both historical landmarks (Venice, Cyprus, Padua) and transhistorical claims to our attention, sympathy, and adjudication (injustice, privation, friendship, love).[18] Of all his Jobean experiments, Shylock is Shakespeare's most distinctively *Jewish* Job, signaling not only Job's origins in the Hebrew Bible but also the effective de-patriarching, the fall from a position of originary prestige and foundational hospitality, that Israel had suffered in the European diaspora.

As Hannibal Hamlin notes in chapter 5 of this volume, Marlowe incorporated many references to Job into his portrait of Barabas in *The Jew of Malta*, creating an "Anti-Job" by dislodging the plaintiveness of the patriarch from his righteousness. By apprehending Job as a narrative of Jewish travails in the tradition of Marlowe, Shakespeare delivers Shylock as a figure of historical as well as communal and subjective dislocation. Like Job, Shylock has lost both property and posterity, his daughter and his ducats. In the Jewish tradition, children who marry out are symbolically dead, and parents sit shiva for them to mark their permanent exclusion from the circle of the living. "I would my daughter were dead at my foot, and the jewels in her ear!" Shylock exclaims in a fantasy of restitution that serves to literalize rather than reverse the symbolic death of Jessica (3.1.80–81). In a beautiful reading of *Merchant*'s scriptural intertexts, Kenneth Gross associates Shylock's cry at the realization of his daughter's loss, "the curse never fell upon our nation till now, I never felt it till now . . . loss upon loss!" (3.1.78–84), with the cascade of privations suffered by Job.[19]

Shylock exhibits no plague sores. Yet his most famous complaint is emblematized by the image of flesh punctured and stigmatized: "If you prick us, do we not bleed?" (3.1.47). Like Job, he declares his right to protest, and he does so, moreover, via the image of pierced flesh, whose prick marks a perforation not only in the skin but also in the routines of living that such a provocation indexes. In drawing blood, the prick also provokes the flinch and the cringe, along with the forms of language appropriate to such gestures of reactive response. Shylock's query echoes an earlier claim by the Prince of Morocco, suitor to one Portia of Belmont: "Let us make incision for your love / To prove whose blood is reddest, his or mine" (2.1.6–7). In both passages, though to different purposes, the vulnerability of the flesh indicates the common creatureliness of those who declare themselves through it. Like Job's complaints, Shylock's protest is what issues when Merleau-Ponty's flesh recoils not in self-reflexivity but in shock, anger, or bewilderment, its "dehiscence" (both blossom and rupture) becoming an opening through which others can make themselves heard. The prick in question, moreover, involves interpersonal rather than physical stigmata: Shylock has been pricked into protest by his humiliation at the Rialto as well as the loss of his daughter to those who scorn him, echoing the social dimensions of Job's debasement and abandonment while discarding the physical losses.

If the pricked flesh indicates the creatureliness that Shylock shares with his tormenters, it also refers him back to covenant, via the suppressed allusion to circumcision as the physical sign and seal of membership in Israel. Shylock, like Job, is a *creature of covenant*, voicing from within the law the conditions of his own substantial belonging to both Judaism and the community of men. The pricking of the flesh, which spirals outward to include all of creaturely life while circling inward to circumscribe citizenship in Israel, instantiates the paradox that would come to be called "the Jewish question" during the period of Jewish emancipation. Can Shylock be both Jew and citizen? Shakespeare can find no good way out of this impasse. Marlowe simply kills off his Jewish Job, after making sure to poison his daughter Abigail in lieu of marrying her to her Christian suitors. Shakespeare chooses to convert both his Job and his Jessica to Christianity instead. Although many readers have found Shakespeare's solution less honest than Marlowe's, there is at least an attempt on Shakespeare's part, however clumsy, to recovenant with his own creation, to make his limited peace with Shylock by trying to imagine the conditions under which Shylock might enter into, and in the process rezone, a more inclusive community.[20]

Othello is also riven by crises of covenant in the republic of Venice. One of Job's symptoms was the blackening of his skin: "I am a brother to the dragons, and a companion to the ostriches. *My skinne is blacke upon me*, and my bones are burnt with heat" (30:30; emphasis added). The Geneva commentary compares Job's affliction to the plague of boils visited against the Egyptians. Indeed, we could say that Job's situation smacks of Egypt, since he suffers the death of his cattle and his children as well as an affliction of the skin, placing him once again at the suburbs of Sinai, both outside of and prior to its bonds. Othello, too, roams at the edges of covenant, insecurely included within Christianity from out of an ambiguous ancestry of Semitic cults that include not only Islam but also the Gnostic and pagan influences that fed into Hebrew Wisdom literature.[21] As Daniel Boyarin has recently reasserted, both Shylock and Othello belong to what Paul refers to in Philippians as "the circumcision."[22] Like Shylock and like Job, Othello is both allied with creaturely life as such and insistently marked as one who is fiercely faithful to both divine and domestic covenants. By characterizing Othello as a type of Job, Shakespeare simultaneously includes Othello within the scriptural universe and points to the precariousness of that inclusion, at once normalizing Othello through the force of a canonical reference and indicating the mixed nativity of that reference itself.

Othello breaks into Jobean complaint in act 4:[23]

Had it pleased heaven
To try me with affliction; had they rain'd
All kinds of sores and shames on my bare head,
Steep'd me in poverty to the very lips,
Given to captivity me and my utmost hopes,
I should have found in some place of my soul
A drop of patience: but, alas, to make me
A fixed figure for the time of scorn
To point his slow unmoving finger at!
Yet could I bear that too; well, very well:
But there, where I have garner'd up my heart,
Where either I must live, or bear no life;
The fountain from the which my current runs,
Or else dries up; to be discarded thence!
Or keep it as a cistern for foul toads
To knot and gender in! Turn thy complexion there,
Patience, thou young and rose-lipp'd cherubin,—
Ay, there, look grim as hell!

                              (4.2.49–66)

The word *patience* signals the Jobean prooftext, which Othello rightly takes as a cue not for quiescence but for complaint. The "sores and shames" name Job's double stigmatization: the enflaming of his body and the shaming of his person in the eyes of the community. Such horrors, Othello claims, he could have endured. The inner festering of jealous ecstasy, however—plague sores sunk inward—pushes him beyond the bounds set by the propriety of patience.[24] We expect worms to speak from those wounds, but we get toads instead, more references perhaps to the sorry plagues of Exodus. Job's sores act again as phenomenological images of the interface between bodily pain, the shaming gaze of witnesses, and the urge toward a language that is both expressive (issuing out of a welling pathos) and rhetorical (aimed at listeners, both in the present and for the future). Such sores become what Othello calls "fixed figures," a tracery that translates without sublating the stigmatization of the skin—whether by ritual pricking and cutting, by racial "complexion," or by viral plague sores—into an invitation to speech that can be taken up by others.

Othello, of course, suffers not from real sores but from imagined wounds, the blistering heat of jealousy. When Job declares, "I made a covenant [*brit*] with mine eyes; why then should I thinke on a maid?" (31:1), he is simultaneously asserting his marital fidelity to his wife and his cultic fidelity to the God of *chesed*, covenant love. He is also declaring marriage as an arena of social and psychic testing, a theme explored as well in *A Serious Man*, where the wife's affair with an unctuous older colleague represents both a personal loss and a public humiliation to the Job character. The book of Job provides Othello with a language of extremity, shame, and isolation as he falls out of relationship with Desdemona, Venice, and Christianity. At the same time, the scriptural provenance of the allusion secures Othello's place within the pale of a strained and struggling monotheism, a monotheism wrestling with its own universal claims. In this sense, the land of Uz becomes literally a common place, a *locus communis* where Othello can find a provisional place in the Abrahamic imagination. Yet this common place is riddled with fissures in tradition and transmission that ultimately expel Othello from the haven it appears to offer. In the terrible progression of the play, covenant as a form of love (*chesed*) becomes covenant as a form of jealousy, linking Othello's sacrificial rage to the God of the Old Testament "whose name is Jealous" (Ex. 13:14).

In both *Othello* and *The Merchant of Venice*, the forms of covenant signed by circumcision pose a limit to full inclusion in the universe promised by Christianity. If the Venetian polity grudgingly holds open a place for the Jewish Job, but only at the price of his Jewishness, no such place appears to exist for the black Ayyub. Nonetheless, Othello's resonant rain of sores serves to keep the land of Uz somewhere on Shakespeare's map of literary possibilities. By allowing Shylock and Othello to speak through Job's singular stigmata, Shakespeare assembles a far broader and more varied scene for monotheism than that acknowledged, say, by a Brabantio or a Gratiano. In both plays, Shakespeare keeps open a wound in Job's textual passage from the Hebrew to the Christian Bible and stages that passage on a varied terrain occupied by a wealth of other cults as well as competing destinies for monotheism. Through the rim of that wound, perhaps we can begin to glimpse a universe *other than* yet nonetheless *imagined by* the Venetian one, a cosmos that manages to bear the impress of a common creator while continuing to harbor a bewildering variety of places, persons, traditions, and genres within its aggravated yet elastic edge.

Shakespeare's Gentile Jobs

As Hannibal Hamlin argues at length in this volume, and as Steven Marx demonstrates, *King Lear* has long been associated with the book of Job.[25] We move here from modern Venice to pre-Christian Britain. Lear's passionate tirade against his daughter Goneril graphically compares his ungrateful daughter to a boil and a plague sore, an eruption in and of his very flesh:

> I prithee, daughter, do not make me mad:
> I will not trouble thee, my child; farewell:
> We'll no more meet, no more see one another:
> But yet thou art my flesh, my blood, my daughter;
> Or rather a disease that's in my flesh,
> Which I must needs call mine: thou art a boil,
> A plague-sore, an embossed carbuncle,
> In my corrupted blood. But I'll not chide thee;
> Let shame come when it will, I do not call it:
> I do not bid the thunder-bearer shoot,
> Nor tell tales of thee to high-judging Jove:
> Mend when thou canst; be better at thy leisure:
> I can be patient; I can stay with Regan,
> I and my hundred knights.
>   (2.4.199–213)

Lear's visceral language of erupted skin recalls the afflictions that seared Job's flesh into a living emblem of bodily and psychic suffering; when Lear lays claim to the virtue of patience, he brands his own travails with

Job's moral trademark.[26] Like Othello, Lear sees the sore as a source of shame, a scandal to place and standing that at once isolates the sufferer from social contact and exposes him to public scorn. Lear, like Job, is more sinned against than sinning; it is not, however, the death of his children but rather the indignities inflicted by them—paternity ingrown and metastasized—that inspire his Jobean outrage. Whereas Job loses his substance to accident and nomadic incursion, Lear has divested himself of his kingdom in order to take succor in his daughters' households. (Recall the rotating feasts that hold together the generations of Job.) Job finds himself de-patriarched by external events; Lear orchestrates his own bankruptcy, rendering himself open to neglect and abuse by his daughters. Such humiliation is public as much as personal, and Lear's emphasis in these early scenes necessarily falls on the blows delivered to dignity rather than on the wounds of physical suffering.

Inflaming the sores of his rage against Goneril is his own treatment of Cordelia, who, through her folkloric links to Griselda and Cinderella, is the play's female Job. The love she expresses in act 1, scene 1, is closer to Hebrew *chesed*, or covenant love, than to Greek *agape* or charity, and her mistake is to express *chesed* in the most minimalist form she can muster: "I love your Majesty / According to my bond; no more nor less" (1.1.91–92).[27] And Lear's mistake is to devalue and misrecognize *chesed* as no love at all. In psychological terms, he wants his daughter to love him as a mother would, without bounds or bonds. She instead asserts the love due to and from fathers, which is covenantal to the core, involving the legal character of paternity and the rights and duties it confers. Like Shylock, the initial trauma to Lear's paternity is symbolic rather than real, though he is the author of his own situation more than Shylock is. Lear has not only divided his kingdom but disowned Cordelia, forcing the elopement and outmarriage that Shylock passively suffers. In all three plays, the sores of Job are metaphors, representing the interiorization and subjectivization of Job's privations into psychic wounds. Shakespeare does to Job's sores what Paul does to Abraham's circumcision: he makes them affairs of the heart. Yet they are metaphors that bear on the real, insofar as in each case the image of the plague sore also asserts a frontier that interiorization cannot cross, insistently tracing an "embossed carbuncle" that raises and puckers the bodily envelope without disappearing into its interior. Like Gloucester's "bleeding rings" (5.3.188), the sore exists at the angry edge between *privation* and *privacy*, refusing to allow external loss to sink completely into psychological isolation. Lear wants to disengage from Goneril, but he cannot because the paternal bond, when rejected, returns as disease: "But yet thou art my flesh, my blood, my daughter; / Which I must needs call mine; thou art a boil, / A plague-sore, or embossed carbuncle." Lear suffers his own violent and foolish rejection of Cordelia's covenant love as it returns imploded and impostumed to his flesh.

Lear aspires to incarnate the saintly Job of the prose narrative, "the pattern of all patience," but he increasingly finds himself in a landscape of whirlwinds, nakedness, and exposure. As the play devolves, part of its work is to render ever more terrible and vivid the symbolic sores that Lear first identifies with his ungrateful daughters. Thus Edgar, seeking out "the basest and most poorest shape / That ever penury, in contempt of man, / Brought near to beast," studs his arms with "Pins, wooden pricks, nails, sprigs of rosemary," a "horrible object" borrowed from the practices of Bedlam beggars (2.3.7–9, 16, 17). And the symbolic affront to paternity returns in the real when Lear enters "with Cordelia dead in his arms." As he cradles her in a final paternal embrace, an Abraham with his Isaac in an *akedah* gone terribly wrong, the fantasy of restoration delivered by Job's prose frame mocks him with the promise of comic justice:

> And my poor fool is hang'd! No, no, no life!
> Why should a dog, a horse, a rat have life,
> And thou no breath at all? Thou'lt come no more,
> Never, never, never, never, never!
> Pray you, undo this button; thank you, Sir.
> Do you see this? Look on her, look, her lips,
> Look there, look there!
>
> (5.3.304–10)

Like Gloucester at the verge of Dover, Lear is killed by the fantasy, hit first by the power surge of the promised end and then by the horror of its final emptiness. Cordelia beckons here from the flooded ark of God's creation—dog, horse, rat—but the zoo is closed, and no breath remains. As such, *King Lear* remains truer to the essence of Jobean complaint, at once courting and resisting all consolation, than any other work by Shakespeare, as Hamlin and Marx have argued. In *Merchant*, we feel the cruelty of the difference between Job's restored household and Shylock's, and in *Lear* we savor for a moment the suppressed romantic impulse of the play toward restoration, only to see it evaporate in an instant, like breath on a mirror. Freud intuited a kinship between *King Lear* and *The Merchant of Venice*, a proximity that surfaces in both plays' terrible replays of Jobean comedy.

If *Lear* is the closest in spirit to Job, *Timon of Athens* is the closest in form.[28] Although precise verbal echoes are minimal, the two works manifest similar sets of generic admixture, tonal extremity, existential inquiry, and corporeal and creaturely imagery. Generically, the book of Job is theology bordering on drama, while *Timon of Athens* is drama bordering on philosophy. (The word *philosopher* appears four times in *Timon*, closely followed by three times in *Lear*, as if Shakespeare identified philosophy with the depths and verges rather than the heights of human experience.) In both plays, rich men with good hearts lose everything, and both engage in fruitless dialogue with a parade of inadequate friends. Falling out of the social networks that had sustained their great households, these cast-off lords suddenly find themselves reduced to a minimal existence whose exposure opens them to anguish and ardor. Timon's search for a pure instance of the gift is closely related to Job's complaint in despite of all consolation: both Timon and Job are good men who refuse to submit their virtues to economic itemization and calculation, a resistance that ends up driving them beyond the pale of civility and community.[29]

In chapter 19, Job catalogs the extent to which he has been stripped of every marker of recognition and eminence that had ensured his mastery in the summer of his content: "My neighbors have forsaken me, and my familiars have forgotten me. They that dwel in my house, and my maides toke me for a stranger. . . . I called my servant, but he wolde not answer" (19:14–16). He who had greeted the stranger—the patriarchal office of hospitality par excellence—has himself now become a pariah in his own household and in the loose alliance of households that make up the land of Uz. Like the book of Job, *Timon* tracks the effects of bankruptcy on a social world defined by the magnificence of a master, pursuing the reduction of the "good life" as exhibited by the liberality and munificence of a host to the "bare life" of an enraged hermit who turns against every social tie that previously defined his prestige. If the play indeed addresses itself to the paradigm of Job, it does so by subtracting Job's traumas of bereavement and illness in order to focus exclusively on problems of economy. Like the book of Job, *Timon of Athens* suffers a split. Whereas the book of Job is divided between prose and poetry, patience and complaint, *Timon* falls into two movements that reflect two faces or conditions of the play's hero. The first half of the play is overseen by *Timon philanthropos*, a wealthy man dispensing favors to his friends; its central setting, like that of Job's prose frame, is the banquet hall, a site of conviviality, communion, and gift exchange. The second half, which, like the central section of the book of Job, follows the host into his precipitous bankruptcy, is dominated by *Timon misanthropos*, a creature given over to hatred, subsistence, and the pursuit of a language capable of capturing their terrible rudiments. The critical histories of both works largely consist of efforts to calculate, mediate, and comprehend the vast stylistic, cognitive, and emotional spectra measured by each text as it follows its hero into the destruction of sociality.

Unlike Job, who is initially surrounded by wife and offspring, Timon has been alone from the start, and he never quite fits into the social world he has built, ever subject to exceptional extravagance rather than normal or normative giving. As such, his acts of themselves tear a hole in the fabric woven by the give and take, warp and woof, of reciprocity; he is his own Adversary, and he needs no bandits or tornados to destroy him. Both Job and Timon come to inhabit the pits and heaps of a wasted landscape, but Timon, as Coppélia Kahn puts it, "literally and figuratively digs his own grave."[30] Through the extravagant exorbitance of his philanthropy, he digs the cavern of his future misanthropy into the classical landscape of friendship, and in so doing creates subterranean synapses with the world of Job.

Timon makes universal claims for his misanthropy:

The gods confound—hear me, you good gods all—
Th'Athenians both within and out the wall;

And grant, as Timon grows, his hate may grow
To the whole race of mankind, high and low!
Amen.

(4.2.37–41)

Phrased as a prayer to the pagan gods, Timon's declaration ends with the Hebrew "Amen" familiar from Christian liturgy. Timon's assault begins with the Athenians, gyrating out beyond its walls to include all mankind; in a parody of Pauline inclusiveness, there is neither Greek nor Jew, neither slave nor free, in the great set drawn by Timon's sublimely mounting hatred. G. Wilson Knight seems to echo the Pauline scope of Timon's hatred when he notes, "The whole race of man is his theme. His love was ever universal, now his hate is universal, its theme embraces every grade, age, sex, and profession."[31] This is not a universalism to which any nation or culture could subscribe; instead, it takes shape as Timon's subjective response to his betrayal by his social circle, his way of assuming as his own the position of bare life to which he has been casually relegated by the reflexes of his neighbors. It is, in a phrase used twice by Knight, a "peculiar universality," a prospect of infinitude projected from within the deeply situated place of social exclusion. Such universality describes Shakespeare's land of Uz: a world produced when a specific space, time, and culture (Timon's Athens or Shylock's Venice) is turned inside out, not deprived of its specific texture but stretched, exposed, and inverted to the point of becoming something else.[32]

Is there a God in any of these texts? On one level, this is a silly question. After all, God actually *appears* at the end of the book of Job, giving what may be his most extended cameo in all of scripture if measured by sheer verbal output. And Shakespeare's plays were written in and for a Christian worldview, evident everywhere through the very scriptural netting that I have tried to disclose here. Yet it is perhaps worth noting that God's speech to Job likely constitutes its own late historical layer, philologically speaking. God *comes in*, out of his whirlwind, not quite *ex machina*, but certainly in a burst, a theophany, not fully contained by the script that houses it. This is not to doubt the unity of the text as we have it but to acknowledge the seams in its construction as signs of stress, places of problem as well as promise. And, as I have emphasized throughout this essay, none of Shakespeare's four Jobs is "Christian" in any straight-forward sense; Shakespeare's Uz is, quite strikingly and distinctively, a territory of mixed affiliations shared by diverse groups and possibilities.

Victoria Kahn argues that for Milton the book of Job became, per-haps paradoxically, a means of fashioning a secular place for literature, by which she means poetry that finally attains "an independent status as a purely human creation."[33] Although one could cast Shakespeare's Jobean experiments as a key moment in this secularizing process, one might also argue that Shakespeare uses Job, in all of its protosecular literary ambiva-lence, to create a religious zone in his texts that is not strictly theological, in which God enters as an afterthought, a late addition, and thus can be imagined as not entering at all. Milton can use Job to become secular because he is already writing from such a distinctly scriptural point of view. Shakespeare, on the other hand, is *already* writing secular literature; when he draws on Job, it is not to declare poetic independence but rather to acknowledge moments of radical interdependence: of each human on other humans, of the human on the creaturely, and of secular writing on sacred writing. Shakespeare's attraction to Job in these plays retains a "religious" dimension if we take that word not to identify a particular cult or confession, or to take direct aim at the divine, but rather to rec-ognize and address different forms of binding and rebinding (*re-ligare*), moments when we intuit individual life and poetic production in their bondage with and obligation to other instances that we do not fully au-thor ourselves. Such acknowledgment—exercised through allusion, for example—might then come to constitute a fuller and more valid form of authorship, poetically independent precisely in its subjectivization of multiple dependencies.

The word *religion* recurs three times in *Timon*, more than in any other play by Shakespeare.[34] One etymology derives religion from the language of binding; establishing obligations among members of a community or between the community and God, religion as religature always bears the signs of the constitutive incompleteness of collective life.[35] Timon seems to echo this meaning when he says of gold, "This yellow slave / Will knit and break religions" (4.3.34–35). Timon finds himself suddenly let loose, unbound, from the chain of beneficences that earlier sustained his fragile world. Yet the most absolute nonrelation can also be a means of relation. Thus in the wake of Timon's bankruptcy we see the Steward and the servants reforming a fellowship in honor of the terrible breach in the social order:

> Good fellows all,
> The latest of my wealth I'll share with amongst you.
> Wherever we shall meet, for Timon's sake,
> Let's yet be fellows.
>
> (4.2.22–25)

Released from the bonds of service by the failure of their master's finances, they reaffiliate as "fellows" by dividing the Steward's last paycheck. The dissolution of the very conditions of service becomes the means of a new form of relationship among them.

I would suggest that what Shakespeare learns from the book of Job is not a positive religious program. Rather, the book of Job represents for Shakespeare the scene of a singular tear in the social fabric—not the privations suffered by Job as such, understood as "private" losses, but rather the impossible strain they place on human conversation and relationship, fault lines that generate the rituals of mourning and consolation that too often remain inadequate to them. (Such rituals are not "for" the mourner but rather for the *socius* as such, which must find ways to tolerate, deny, and survive the pain of others.) In the book of Job, this tear in the social fabric becomes an aperture onto something larger, an existential encounter with the limits of friendship as a form of life, and hence a means for us to rethink, and relink, our social relations. It is in this aperture that God appears out of the whirlwind: in the breakdown of human communication and in the positive possibilities that such breakdown elicits. For Shakespeare's Jobs, friendship, kinship, citizenship, and marriage are resilient and necessary social systems that have nonetheless failed to provide from within their own reservoirs of custom and habit the measures that would mitigate the disasters visited upon them. Job's comforters are not the worst of men; they sit shiva with Job and then try to engage him in reconstructive conversation; others, apparently, have abandoned Job more completely to his sorrows. But the comforters' reliance on ordinary ethical frameworks, their parroting of a normative patois, is inadequate to Job's situation, and their embarrassed efforts serve to heighten rather than to ameliorate Job's isolation. God represents that force beyond human sociality that is drawn into the framework of civility not by trauma itself (the loss of wealth, health, and offspring) but by the failure of neighbor love to effect its own rebindings. If God is anywhere in *King Lear*, it is in Lear's storm, where even the power of linguistic association that we call rational discourse has broken down, along with, and because of, the crisis into which human association has been thrown.

What remains in *Lear* and in *Timon*, and perhaps in *Othello* and *Merchant* as well, is what God delivers in the book of Job: the sublime point of contact between creation and covenant, conceived at its most extreme verge, not as an answer to Job's complaints, but as a continued challenge for us to think the social precisely as an alternative to comprehending God fully. As Victoria Silver argues, covenant "returns us to relationship with divinity" but "does not in itself completely circumscribe or fully delineate our possible relations with God."[36] In Job, the sublime edge of covenant as it retracts from knowledge of God himself in order to return us to the call of the social bears the name "Leviathan":

> Canst thou draw out Liviathán with an hooke, and with a line which thou shalt cast downe unto his tongue? Canst thou cast an hooke into his nose? canst thou perce his iawes with an angle? Will he make manie prayers unto thee, or speake thee faire? Wil he make a covenant with thee? *and* wilt thou take him as a servant for ever? Wilt thou play with him as with a bird? Or wilt thou binde him for thy maides? Shal the companions banket with him? shal they devide him among the marchants? Canst thou fill the basket with his skinne? or the fishpanyer with his head? Laye thine hand upon him; remember the battel, and do nomore so. Beholde, his hope is in vaine: for shal not one perish even at the sight of him? (50:20–28)

Leviathan, a one-of-a-kind creature, represents the sublime limit of human understanding and the singularity of God's creation. The rhetorical questions that God poses to Job are meant to demonstrate the inadequacy of instrumental reason and of human accommodation: no man can catch Leviathan using the *techne* of the fisherman, nor can his flesh be sold in the marketplace or shared in the communal feast. The Leviathan is not subject to exchange, whether hospitable or monetary. Yet the feast that is refused in the here and now is promised elsewhere: in the messianic era, the rabbis tell us that we will eat the flesh of the Leviathan beneath a gorgeous sukkah or canopy crafted from its skin, recalling Abraham's open tent.[37] Some traditions associate Leviathan with the primordial forces of chaos that God overcomes in and as creation, making Leviathan both a consummate creature and that which creation itself abjures.

God's challenge to Job—"Wil he [Leviathan] make a covenant [*brit*] with thee?"—aims to measure, along with the other questions, the radical disparity between Job and God. Yet the question returns us to the possibility of covenant, and the whole negative cascade of queries reminds us of the forms of relationship that Job has indeed been capable of, as host and master, friend and father, hunter and husband, servant and psalmist. The Job of the prose tale could covenant with his household and his neighbors, and even perhaps with hostile tribes, and this same Job could covenant with God by obeying his commandments. The reference to Leviathan, then, becomes in part a sublime call to *re-ligare*: to rebind and rebuild the social in the face of personal and public trauma. In *Lear*, Cordelia has already named this possibility when she says that she loves according to her bond, no more and no less: an affirmation of bond as *chesed*, covenant love, whose painful minimalism nonetheless shelters the most absolute commitment behind it. Shylock, too, loves according to his bond, and at the end of the trial scene, Shakespeare awkwardly, even brutally, tries to find a way to *re-ligare* Shylock to a world that refuses to understand or honor the living legacy he represents. Othello represents the dangers of covenant love perplexed to the extreme, so that the very terms of intergroup relationship—is Othello an idolater at the well, or rather the most fierce of monotheists? Shabean at the gates or master of his house?—break down and return to destroy him. Finally, Timon is the philanthropist turned misanthrope, whose bare and brute insistence on nonrelation as such has the virtue of bringing into focus the tremulous necessity of the social bonds through which he has crashed with such pitch and moment, leaving us to imagine how we might want to pick up the pieces. Religious or secular? I am not sure the difference finally matters, insofar as the book of Job, and its Shakespearean renditions, challenge the norms of both in order to recall us, however, to the work of rebuilding such norms anew.

Notes

The readings of *The Merchant of Venice* and *Othello* put forward in this essay are developed in a different direction in my essay "Job in Venice: Shakespeare and the Travails of Universalism," in *Visions of Venice*, ed. Laura Tosi and Shaul Bassi (London: Ashgate, 2011). I would like to thank Ashgate for permitting me to revisit some of these readings here.

1. Beza goes on to give us the *dramatis personae*—"The Actors or speakers herein, are God himself, *Satan, Iob, Iobs* wife, and his fower friends"—and then divides its drama into scenes and acts, with the final prose conclusion as "the Epilogue or shutting up of the whole Tragedie." Theodore Beza, *Job Expounded* ([Cambridge]: John Leggatt, 1589), 3–4.

2. Victoria Kahn, "Job's Complaint in *Paradise Regained*," *English Literary History* 76 (Fall 2009): 625–60.

3. Richmond Noble, *Shakespeare's Biblical Knowledge and Use of the Book of Common Prayer* (1935; repr., New York: Octagon Books, 1970), 43.

4. Unless otherwise noted, all references from the Bible are from the Geneva Bible, 1560 edition, facsimile prepared by Lloyd E. Berry (Madison: University of Wisconsin Press, 1969).

5. V. Kahn, "Job's Complaint," 643.

6. Robert Eisen examines the universalist and particularist dimensions of Jewish medieval commentators in a separate subsection of each chapter of his excellent study *The Book of Job in Medieval Jewish Philosophy* (Oxford: Oxford University Press, 2004).

7. *Sermons of Maister John Calvin, Upon the Book of Iob*, trans. Arthur Golding (London: George Byshop and Thomas Woodcocke, 1580), A4.

8. The Geneva Bible notes the young friend Elihu's affiliation with Abraham, 33:2, note a. Both Jews and Muslims traced Job's lineage to the family of Abraham. Theologically, Abraham and Job were linked as objects of divine testing (Eisen, *Book of Job*, 23). In his study of Job in the Middle Ages, Lawrence Besserman refers to Aramaic, Coptic, Arabic, and Hebrew legends of Job; *The Legend of Job in the Middle Ages* (Cambridge, MA: Harvard University Press, 1979), 9. Modern biblical scholars emphasize the fertile contexts of other Near Eastern

religious traditions, including Egyptian and Akkadian; cf. Leon G. Perdue, *The Voice from the Whirlwind: Interpreting the Book of Job* (Nashville, TN: Abingdon Press, 1992).

9. On Job and Wisdom literature, see Leo G. Perdue, *Wisdom in Revolt: Metaphorical Theology in the Book of Job* (Sheffield: Almond Press, 1991).

10. See Robert S. Fyall, *Now Mine Eyes Have Seen You* (Downers Grove, IL: InterVarsity, 2002): "It is Yahweh, the Lord of the Covenant, who answers Job from the storm" (33).

11. Jason Rosenblatt, *Renaissance England's Chief Rabbi: John Selden* (Oxford: Oxford University Press, 2006), 154–57.

12. V. Kahn, "Job's Complaint," 638, writes, "In his *De jure naturali et gentium*, John Selden argued that Job kept all the Noachide laws—the seven natural laws incumbent on all mankind. (Selden's *De Jure*, as Jason Rosenblatt has argued, was 'the principal source of Milton's natural law thinking.')"

13. See Victoria Silver, *Imperfect Sense: The Predicament of Milton's Irony* (Princeton: Princeton University Press, 2001), 32: "His fierce self-righteousness does not pertain to the matter of his moral integrity, but instead to the very grounds of such justification: namely, the picture he sustains of God as the Lord of the ancient covenant, perpetually inclined toward human being in both wrath and loving-kindness but never oblivious to it." Victoria Kahn's secularizing reading of Job in Milton ("Job's Complaint") is in part a response to Silver's more theological reading.

14. On *sheretz*, see Aviva Zornberg, *Genesis: The Beginning of Desire* (Philadelphia: Jewish Publication Society, 1995), 7–10.

15. Maurice Merleau-Ponty, *The Visible and the Invisible*, ed. Claude Lefort, trans. Alphonso Lingis (Evanston: Northwestern University Press, 1968), 146.

16. Beza, *Job Expounded*, 3.

17. On the universality of protest in Job, see Antonio Negri, *Il lavoro di Giobbe: Il famoso testo biblico come parabola del lavoro umano* (Milan: Sugar, 1990).

18. Lupton, "Job in Venice."

19. See Kenneth Gross, *Shylock Is Shakespeare* (Chicago: University of Chicago Press, 2006), 24, on the relevance of Job to this passage: "A larger history of Jewish suffering becomes truly palpable to him only in its being translated both by the loss of his gold and his daughter and by the pain of trying to undo that loss; these contingent, private afflictions for Shylock point more truly to the sources of the curse. It is an apprehension by which he cuts himself off from Jewish history as much as he aligns himself with it. (In this he is a little like Job, refusing the comforts of a conventional, moralistic explanation of human suffering.)" He goes on to write, "Neither gold nor child is quite confused with the other; neither is tradable with the other; there is no easy logic of exchange here. The child is no longer a child; the jewels are more than jewels."

20. Gross poses the following challenge for contemporary readers of the play: "The crucial question remains what it means to keep faith with Shakespeare's fiction" (ibid., 124). On the question of Shylock's limited inclusion at the end of the play, see my book *Citizen-Saints: Shakespeare and Political Theology* (Chicago: University of Chicago Press, 2005).

21. On Job and the pagan sources of Wisdom literature, see Gerhard von Rad, *Wisdom in Israel*, trans. James D. Martin (London: SCM Press, 1972). In "Othello Circumcised: Shakespeare and the Pauline Discourse of Nations," I argued for the division of Othello between Islamic and pagan origins. Catherine Winiarski follows a similar line of thought in "Adulterers, Idolaters, and Emperors: The Politics of Iconoclasm in English Renaissance Drama" (PhD diss., University of California, Irvine, 2007). Daniel Boyarin, in "The Double Mark of the Male Muslim: Eraceing Othello," forthcoming in *The Political Theology of Race*, ed. Geoffrey Kaplan and Vincent Lloyd (Stanford: Stanford University Press, 2011), argues more forcefully that Othello is, unambiguously, a Muslim. What is interesting about Job is both the mixed sources of the text (combining pagan, monotheistic, and Wisdom elements) as well as Job's ambiguous status (as Jew, Gentile, saint, pre-Islamic holy man, etc.).

22. Boyarin, in "Double Mark," writes, "The original circumcised dogs, of course, are the Jews, called indeed 'the circumcision,' according to Paul: 'Beware of dogs; beware of evil-doers; beware of the circumcision' (Philippians 3:2). With this allusion, Shakespeare reveals the deep haunting of Europe by a dual figure, the Jew-Muslim, far far from the Jew-Christian vs. Muslim binary with which our theological politics works even today."

23. Noble, *Shakespeare's Biblical Knowledge*, 219, notes the allusion.

24. Peter Milward, *Biblical Influences in Shakespeare's Great Tragedies* (Bloomington: University of Indiana Press, 1987), 94, also notes the allusion to Job. On Job's sense of imprisonment, see the Geneva gloss to Job 10:7: "By affliction thou kepest me as in a prison, and restraynest me from doing evil, neither can any set me at libertie."

25. Steven Marx, *Shakespeare and the Bible* (Oxford: Oxford University Press, 2000), 59–78.

26. Jonathan Lamb, in his study of Job in eighteenth-century literature, *The Rhetoric of Suffering: Reading the Book of Job in the Eighteenth Century* (Oxford: Clarendon Press, 1995), 295, 298, notes the contiguities between Lear and Job in the writings of James Barry.

27. On *chesed* or covenant love, see, for example, Hans Urs von Balthasar, *The Glory of the Lord: A Theological Aesthetics*, vol. 6, *Theology: The Old Covenant* (Edinburgh: T. and T. Clark, 1991), 159–62, and Daniel Elazar, *Covenant and Polity in Biblical*

Israel: Biblical Foundations and Jewish Expressions (New Brunswick, NJ: Transaction, 1998).

28. I provide a longer reading of Timon and Job in my forthcoming book, *Thinking with Shakespeare: Essays on Politics and Life* (Chicago: University of Chicago Press, 2011).

29. On Timon and the gift, see Ken Jackson, "'One Wish' or the Possibility of the Impossible: Derrida, the Gift, and God in *Timon of Athens*," *Shakespeare Quarterly* 52 (Spring 2002): 34–66. My thoughts on Timon and Job are largely an extension of Jackson's coupling of Timon and Abraham.

30. Coppélia Kahn, "'Magic of Bounty': *Timon of Athens*, Jacobean Patronage, and Maternal Power," *Shakespeare Quarterly* 38 (Spring 1987): 34–57.

31. G. Wilson Knight, *The Wheel of Fire: Interpretations of Shakespearean Tragedy with Three New Essays* (London: Methuen, 1954), 221.

32. Ibid., 207–20.

33. V. Kahn, "Job's Complaint," 644.

34. See 3.2.78, 4.1.16, and 4.3.34.

35. See Graham Hammill and Julia Reinhard Lupton, "Sovereigns, Citizens, and Saints: Political Theology and Renaissance Literature," *Religion and Literature* 38 (Autumn 2006): 3.

36. Silver, *Imperfect Sense*, 35.

37. On the messianic banquet, see, for example, Howard Schwartz, *Tree of Souls: The Mythology of Judaism* (Oxford: Oxford University Press, 2004), 147–48, and Dennis Edwin Smith, *From Symposium to Eucharist: The Banquet in the Early Christian World* (Minneapolis: Augsburg Fortress Press, 2003), 261–67.

Chapter 7

Empson's Dog
Emptiness and Divinity in Timon of Athens

LISA MYŌBUN FREINKEL

A monk asked Zen Master Joshu, does a dog have buddha nature or not? Joshu replied, not.

This little story about Joshu and his dog is a koan—one of those legendary exchanges between Zen patriarchs and their students. In the Rinzai Zen tradition, such teaching words are used to break through habitual modes of thought and to facilitate the glimpse into nothingness and nonself that constitutes enlightenment. Here, Joshu's reply—"not" or "without" (in Sino-Japanese, the word is *mu*)—is impossible. Buddha nature is all-pervasive; how could any thing, even a dog, be without it? *Mu*, says the Zen master. *Mu. Not. Without. Nothing.* Within the Rinzai tradition, the koan of Joshu's dog is considered the *gateless gate*: it is the koan of all koans, initiating the practitioner into Buddhist study. At stake with Joshu's dog is a *not* that is not nothing—or at least not nothing as opposed to something. Joshu's *mu* is not relative to a *this* or a *that*; it does not find its determination as a thing of any sort, not even a non-thing. Instead, Joshu's *not* is not determined by the difference between "is" and "is not." *Mu* is indifferent to that difference. Does a dog have buddha nature or not? *Not.*

The monk who cares about puppy dogs wants, however, to catch a glimpse of their divinity. His question reveals that, for him, buddha nature is something hidden: an essence that lies beneath, or rests above, the surface truth of things. To pass the koan *mu*, however—to pass through the gateless gate itself—requires a glimpse into a divinity that is all-pervasive. Here buddha nature is at once so intimate and proximate—so immediately bound to things such as they are—that simply to stretch out our hands to touch it is already to have missed it. The indifference of *mu* is the unflinching stare of things as they are.

For the monk who likes dogs, this indifference looks suspiciously like cruelty. Indeed, in another koan of the same vintage, Joshu's dog finds its unhappy cousin in Nansen's cat: "Nansen saw the monks of the eastern and western halls fighting over a cat. Seizing the cat, he told the monks: 'If any of you can say a word of Zen, you will save the cat.' No one answered. Nansen cut the cat in two. That evening Joshu returned to the monastery and Nansen told him what had happened. Joshu removed his sandals, placed them on his head, and walked out. Nansen said: 'If you had been there, you would have saved the cat.'"[1] If buddha nature is all-pervasive, what is there to say? Any word of Zen, any expression of enlightenment, will fall infinitely short of this truth that is infinitely near. One single word transforms intimacy into dualism—and, in the words of the father of the Japanese Soto Zen tradition, the thirteenth-century monk Eihei Dogen, such a hair's breadth deviation from the all-pervasive Way is "like the gap between heaven and earth."[2] A miss is as good as a mile.

And so Nansen's students are stymied into silence. Quarreling over a cat, over the place of an animal in their settled monastic routine, they have more than enough to say. *Does a cat have buddha nature?* But when it comes to speaking Zen, no one says a word, and Nansen submits the cat to the fate that we all inevitably face: the fate of utter self-division. We cannot be both *this* and *that*, both here and there, both west hall monks and east hall monks, both human and divine.[3] Or more precisely, perhaps, we cannot *help* but be both here and there, both sacred and profane, both right and wrong—despite our wishes for purity and perfection. The very sentience with which we follow the Way inevitably splits us in two: body versus mind; flesh versus spirit; self versus other. If we insist on grasping enlightenment, the cat is already dead. If we insist on *not* grasping enlightenment, the cat is already dead. Only Joshu, the monk who guards the gateless gate, understands the master's lesson: we can't help but live in the world of dualism—in the world of *this* and *that*, of something and nothing. But it's only from *that* vantage point, that the cat is, indeed, worth saving.[4]

It is from just such a vantage point that I'd like to consider the dog in *Timon of Athens*. Is this dog a figure? a word? a theme? This question has puzzled at least one modern critic—one latter-day Joshu. Struggling with the puzzle of the dog in *Timon*, William Empson exposes the complicity of two problems in Shakespeare's work: the problem of words and the problem of God. For Empson, however, these problems remain separate and distinct. In contrast I would like to suggest that, taken together, the two problems disclose the very simplest and most intimate of unities: the kind of unity that only, perhaps, the sharpest edge of koan can reveal.[5]

Problem #1: The Structure of Complex Words

"A word may become a sort of solid entity," writes William Empson in 1951, "able to direct opinion, thought of as like a person; also it is often said (whether this is the same idea or not) that a word can become a 'compacted doctrine,' or even that all words are compacted doctrines inherently. To get some general theory about how this happens would clearly be important; if our language is continually thrusting doctrines on us, perhaps very ill-considered ones, the sooner we understand the process the better."[6] How do doctrines get into words—how are complex strands of thought carried forward in language? The question is one that has plagued my own research into the history of figural interpretation. In *Reading Shakespeare's Will*, my primary focus was not just the *idea* of figure but the *word* itself—*figura* (*figure*'s Latin etymon)—and the various strands of thought that word seemed to pull together.[7] The problem only seemed thornier because I found almost identical complexes of thought pulled together by other words—words with different derivations and yet startlingly similar etymological trajectories. Words like *model, type, copy, image*: a similar logic seemed to be carried by each of those terms—indeed, it was the similarity of this logic that rendered these words such neat synonyms one for the other—but then, what undergirded the synonymy? To ask the question again: How do words carry—or index—or otherwise sustain and reproduce complex cultural meanings?

It's no accident that this—the question of complex words—is one of the questions that Empson feels compelled to confront later in his career, for it is in many ways the question at the center of his career from the start, from his 1930 *Seven Types of Ambiguity* onward. What allows us to react differently, to glean different meanings from the same words? What allows those different meanings to cohere within a single word? How is ambiguity possible? How is complexity quite literally *articulated*?

Now, at issue here isn't merely the mechanics of definition, as Empson is quick to tell us. His example for this point will turn out to be significant: "One must read very deeply in Aquinas to know all of what he meant by [the word] God . . . and yet [Aquinas] would claim to mean all this complex idea even in a passing reference to God."[8] Over the course of his *Summa* Aquinas's terms become increasingly complex, but this complexity, Empson tells us, exists at the level of the idea, not at the level of the word. It is not so much the word *God* that is complex in Aquinas as it is the *concept* of God, the idea itself that unifies a bundle of properties within a single judgment—within an assertion. Over the course of the text, the word is defined. God is good, God is omnipotent, God is sovereign (etc.). The complexity of the word *God* in Aquinas ultimately coheres within a conceptual unity. Or, as Empson puts it, "The complexity of the word is simply that of the topic . . . [and] is therefore of no interest for my purpose here."[9]

To sort out the complexity of *words*, on the other hand, takes us away from concepts and definitions and instead toward linguistic usages. Instead of assertions, here we find what Empson calls *equations*: moments where two very different senses or contexts for a word exist side by side. In these moments what links the two meanings or uses is solely the *word itself*. No concept forms a unity here, no judgment underwrites the coincidence of meaning. Instead, by mere contiguity and accretion a word comes to mean several things at once. The word *dog* in *Timon of Athens* is a case in point. As Empson demonstrates, the play collates two different senses of the term: the pariah dog associated with the cynic—for example, the play's "churlish philosopher" Apemantus—and the fawning dog associated with the play's dim view of flattery.

At the beginning of the play, the two sides of the term—dog as flatterer and dog as cynic—are neatly summarized through the character of Apemantus. Apemantus's function in the play's opening is to "observe" (1.2.33), as he puts it: to witness in his currish and brutal way, to lay bare the sycophantic truth of Timon's court.[10] "Fie, thou'rt a churl," says Timon. "Ye've got a humour there / Does not become a man" (1.2.25–26). The anonymous painter, one of the parasites in Timon's circle, is even more direct with Apemantus, reminding the audience of the Greek etymology of the word *cynic*. "You're a dog," the painter tells Apemantus (1.1.203). For his part, however, Apemantus clarifies the doglike nature of flatterers like the painter. "Thy mother's of my generation," Apemantus retorts. "What's she, if I be a dog?" (1.1.204).

Even more pointedly, Apemantus reminds us that a flattering friend is but a sleeping dog: both are liable to wake and bite the hand that feeds them. "I pray for no man but myself," Apemantus declares in the mock grace he delivers at Timon's banquet.

> Grant I may never prove so fond
> To trust man on his oath or bond,
> Or a harlot for her weeping,
> Or a dog that seems a-sleeping,
> Or a keeper with my freedom,
> Or my friends if I should need 'em.
> Amen. So fall to't.
> Rich men sin, and I eat root.
>
> (1.2.62–69)

The sin of rich men, Apemantus makes us realize, is their participation in the generalized fawning flattery of the world. "He that loves to be flattered is worthy o'th' flatterer," Apemantus declares. "Heavens, that I were a lord!"

> *Timon:* What wouldst do then, Apemantus?
> *Apemantus:* E'en as Apemantus does now: hate a lord with my heart.
>
> (1.1.227–30)

The only escape from flattery is hatred, because only hatred bites sharply enough through the cords of human trust and interconnection. Yet by the end of the play, as Empson has pointed out, Apemantus's hatred gives way to flattery. "I love thee better now than e'er I did," Apemantus tells Timon in act 4. "I hate thee worse," says Timon. "Thou flatter'st misery" (4.3.233, 234). Indeed, by the play's end, Apemantus and Timon have traded places. Apemantus is now the fawning dog, and Timon has become the cynic.

From Empson's perspective, however, there's something quite unsatisfying about this exchange of meaning. For him it demonstrates the play's failure to unify its central term. Flatterer and cynic—that dog that fawns and the dog that snarls—the two determinations of "dog" have not found a higher ground upon which to reconcile their differences. Instead, the two meanings have remained separate, simply shifting their locations. "The striking thing," Empson writes, "is that the dog symbolism could be worked out so far and yet remain somehow useless."[11] Indeed, in Empson's view, *Timon*'s dog does not even manage, exactly, to become a true symbol but works instead as a mere "bridge" over which the different senses of the term "exchange puzzles."

And here at last we've articulated the problem of complex words. Empson's distinction between complex ideas (like Aquinas's notion of God) and complex words was initially crucial to him, for it allowed his verbal analysis free rein, enabling him to map out the sheer contiguity and accretion of verbal meaning without the constraint of staid conceptual categories like theme or character. Yet the notion of a "useless" symbolism should give us pause. Contrast *Timon*'s dog with *King Lear*'s fool, for instance, and you'll have a sense of the difficulties here. Upon close analysis, the ambiguity and polysemy of *fool* reveal a master trope, while the *dog* in *Timon* remains a mere "bridge" over which unresolved puzzles are exchanged. How can we explain this difference? At what point does sheer verbal complexity yield the clarity of "useful" symbol? What seismic or semantic pressure can transform the rough coal of ambiguity into the diamond brilliance of master trope? What Empson wants to uncover within the structure of complex words is precisely the stability of a concept. If verbal analysis is to serve a purpose, the sheer contiguity of meanings has got to deliver the unity of theme. In the end, then, Empson's distinction between concept and word cannot be maintained, and we are back where we started, asking how complex strands of thought are carried in language.

Problem #2: Milton's God

For Empson, the "Augean stable" of Christianity, the filth that he sees Milton as, unsuccessfully, seeking to purge, is its insistence on a God whose "justice" requires suffering and sacrifice.[12] "What is morally corrupting about Christianity," Empson writes in his 1961 text *Milton's God*, "is that the extreme difficulty of imagining the plan of its God, together with its ritual insistence upon torture, drive the worshipper at the back of his mind into treating God's motive as a sadistic one. . . . I see no hope before Christians," he writes, "until they renounce the Devil and all his works; that is, stop worshipping a God who is satisfied by torture, and confess in public that they have done so."[13]

But we miss, I think, the pith of Empson's argument—and as well the way in which a later text like *Milton's God* ties into his earliest work on ambiguity—if we focus solely on this moral condemnation. It's crucial instead to foreground the conclusion that Empson finally reaches in his reading of *Paradise Lost*: what makes the poem so great is that it makes the Christian God look so bad. How does it do so? According to Empson, Milton leaves out "only one major theological doctrine": the notion of God's supreme goodness. The western half of the Eurasian land mass," Empson writes,

> unlike the eastern, has long regarded its supreme God or ultimate reality as a person; but has also realized that this is a tricky belief which requires a subtle qualification. His Godhead must be mysteriously one with Goodness itself, so that he neither imposes moral law by [fiat] as a tyrant nor is himself bound by it as external to him. As regards his Godhead, he is the impersonal Absolute of Hinduism; he is built into the moral structure of the universe so as to be quite unlike other persons, and his other unique powers (omnipotence, omniscience and absolute foreknowledge) are merely a result.[14]

The double requirement within Christianity that God be *both* absolutely a person *and* impersonally absolute is what sets not just Christianity but the monotheism of all three Abrahamic religions apart from the religiosity of the eastern half of the Eurasian land mass. Personal *and* absolute, the Western God must be both the giver of the Law and the ultimate and only complete embodiment of the Law. He must manifest complete goodness at the same time that he is the very source of that goodness. This is the Creator God who is absolutely separate from his creation, yet is also the source of all that truly *is*. All of creation bespeaks his, the Creator's, utter glory, but only insofar as it also bespeaks its own distance, its *utter* distance, from that glory. Whence the injunction against graven images so central to all three of the Abrahamic faiths: if this God is supremely good, then our ability to recognize the goodness of his creation entails that we continually court the risk of idolatry.

This risk of idolatry is, however, sidestepped by the poet who "pursues / Things unattempted yet in prose or rhyme." Instead, as Empson argues, Milton does *not* take the supreme goodness of God for granted; he allows his God to look *bad*, and it is for this reason that his poem succeeds. In this way, for Empson, Milton's poem reveals nothing less than the deep trickiness of Christianity's most "tricky belief." Empson's beef against the Christian God thus runs deeper than the soteriology of torture. Instead I'd like to suggest that for Empson the problem is the utter independence or subjectivity of God.

The Abrahamic faiths give us a God who is defined by his absolute independence from creation. This is the God of Exodus 3:14 who says, "I am that I am"—who is entirely self-positing and self-predicating—at the same time that he creates all that *is* ex nihilo, from nothing.[15] This is a God whose very activity, whose spontaneity and self-determination as a subject, entails his crunching the nihility, the nothingness, of creation underfoot. In other words, the Creator God's activity in the world puts him over and against that world; insofar as his will is absolute, the world he has created can neither bespeak nor determine him. He is the giver of its moral laws but is not bound by those laws himself. Yet at the same time, if this absolutely sovereign God is to be morally good—and if there is to be a world as such—then he must also be embodied in this world he has created, built into (as Empson would say) its very moral structure. It is in this light that Christianity's "tricky belief" in a personal god reveals its thorniest difficulties.

Embodiment in creation poses no problem for a godhead understood in sheerly impersonal terms (like the absolute godhead of Hinduism, according to Empson). Such a deity simply *is* the moral law as such. But for the personal Creator God of Western monotheism, to be embodied in the moral structure of one's creation is to belie the principle of self-determination. It is here that the logic of sacrifice becomes so crucial: a supremely good sovereign must be a supremely passive one, one who suffers the moral law to the utmost in his own person. We've thus arrived at the trickiness that Milton's poem exposes and that Christianity articulates through the broken, bloody limbs of an absolutely passive— supremely patient—Christ.

What would it mean, however, to resolve these puzzles without the logic of sacrifice? A God that can be both active and passive, both subjective and impersonal: it seems all but certain that Empson articulated just this vision of godhead in a treatise called *Asymmetry in Buddha Faces*. The treatise was never published; up until very recently it was thought to have been lost.[16] Nonetheless, we have a fairly good idea of its contents. Writing from Japan in 1933, William Empson declared effigies of the Buddha to be 'the only accessible art I find myself able to care about." What impressed him about representations of the Buddha's face was the way that they combine "things that seem incompatible, especially a complete repose with an active power to help the worshipper."[17] In effigies of the Buddha, Empson found a congenial asymmetry capable of embracing the two sides of the Christian puzzle, the two sides of divinity: both absolute impassivity and the activity of grace.

Such faces precisely express the fundamental Buddhist standpoint of nonduality: a standpoint that is neither active nor passive, neither personal nor impersonal. A standpoint that, then, isn't properly so named, because it stands *nowhere*—it crunches *nothing* underfoot, not even the nothingness against which the absolutely sovereign subject posits itself. The Kyoto School philosopher Keiji Nishitani describes this nothingness that goes beyond the nihility of dualism in terms of the Buddhist concept of *sunyata*, or emptiness. *Sunyata* in Buddhism is "non-ego," Nishitani explains. "All attachment is negated: both the subject and the way in which 'things' appear as objects of attachment are emptied. Everything is now truly empty, and this means that all things make themselves present here and now, just as they are, in their original reality. They present themselves in their suchness, their *tathata*. This is non-attachment."[18] The emptiness that goes beyond the nihility of the subject and the attachment of the object is at one and the same time the suchness of all things.

Had he ever published his Buddha manuscript, William Empson might have given us a clear image of this self-emptying suchness. As it happened, however, what he left us with is not the congenial asymmetry of the Buddha but instead the "uninviting" (as he calls it) ambivalence of *Timon*'s dog. If *Timon*'s dog were more like *Lear*'s fool—if it were a master trope instead of a mere bridge between semantic contents—then we'd be able to reconcile the flatterer to the cynic. As it stands, however, the two senses of *dog* precisely articulate the discontinuity central to the play's vision of divinity. As it stands, there are two *gods* in *Timon*, just as there are two *dogs* in *Timon*.

The first god is Timon himself, in his guise at the play's beginning as pater or patron to all of Athens. As the play opens, Timon is envisioned by others the way he evidently envisions himself, as the very "magic of bounty"—as the source of all goodness, all *bonitas*, itself. "See," says the play's nameless poet in act 1, as virtually all of Athens assembles on Timon's doorstep looking for a handout: "Magic of bounty, all these spirits thy power / Hath conjured to attend" (1.1.6–7). Timon, we quickly learn, is "the very soul of bounty" (1.2.204), "the very heart of kindness" (1.1.274), not merely giving to all but veritably *pouring out* his goodness, as one lord puts it. Furthermore, in his universal patronage, Timon is "infinitely endeared" (1.2.223) to his followers—followers who marvel at the way in which Timon transforms all things to wealth. "Plutus the god of gold / Is but his steward," declares one lord.

> [N]o meed but he repays
> Sevenfold above itself; no gift to him
> But breeds the giver a return exceeding
> All use of quittance.
>
> (1.1.275–79)

Timon seems to define the very logic of wealth, the very meaning of worth.

Of course, at the root of Timon's bounty is no magic at all—no divinity more impressive than the power of credit, a power bound to the temporality of the promise. As his honest servant Flavius tells us, Timon's gifts derive from an "empty coffer,"

> Nor will [Timon] know his purse, or yield me this:
> To show him what a beggar his heart is,
> Being of no power to make his wishes good.
> His promises fly so beyond his state
> That what he speaks is all in debt, he owes
> For every word.
>
> (1.2.188–94)

Bound up in the temporal arc of the promise, the bubble of Timon's divinity will have to burst. This god will reveal his mortality after all, and all his bounty, all his goodness, and all his wealth, material and otherwise ("I am wealthy in my friends" [2.2.179], Timon declares)—all his bounty can't help but evaporate. Like the Creator God of Genesis, Timon as god engenders the entire world with his speech. But his words are mortal, and his world as transient as a broken promise. "The world is but a word," Flavius explains. "Were it all yours to give it in a breath, / How quickly were it gone" (2.2.146–48). In short, the god of the play's first half is the god of flattery: the god who buys his friends, who feeds on praise, and whose divinity is as mortal as breath. "When the means are gone that buy [your] praise," warns Flavius, "The breath is gone whereof this praise is made" (2.2.164–65). Timon can no longer flatter with his wealth, nor be flattered again by his purchased friends. The god of bounty is gone.

In the play's second half, however, a new divinity emerges. This one appears indestructible. I'm thinking, of course, of gold. Money. The bounty that Timon loses in the play's first half—an illusory bounty, one conjured up in the smoke of promising—reappears in the play's second half as the wealth that Timon neither wants nor can give away fast enough. Transformed now from flatterer to cynic, Timon digs in the earth for the bitter roots that Apemantus taught him how to eat. Famously, he finds instead of a bottomless vein of gold.

O thou sweet king-killer, and dear divorce
'Twixt natural son and sire! thou bright defiler
Of Hymen's purest bed! thou valiant Mars!
Thou ever young, fresh, loved and delicate wooer,
Whose blush doth thaw the consecrated snow
That lies on Dian's lap! thou visible god,
That solder'st close impossibilities,
And makest them kiss! that speak'st with every tongue,
To every purpose! O thou touch of hearts!
Think, thy slave man rebels, and by thy virtue
Set them into confounding odds, that beasts
May have the world in empire!

(4.3.374–85)

Karl Marx adored this passage, and was no doubt influenced by its logic when he declared in *Kapital* that the commodity is a "born leveler and cynic," since it is "always ready to exchange not only soul but body with each and every commodity." And as the commodity of commodities, money is the ultimate leveler—the ultimate cynic—making possible the exchange of anything for everything else, reducing all to an originary prostitution where all goodness is defiled by the universal traffic in goods. If gold is a visible god, then, it is so only insofar as it is the ultimate cynic.

"Nobody pretends that *Timon* is a very good play," Empson reminds us,[19] but the trajectory it traces is a deeply instructive one. From flatterer to cynic, from the word as mortal promise to gold as indestructible commodity, from the flattering emptiness of Timon's magical bounty, to the leveling cynicism of gold as "visible god": what we find in *Timon* is the problem of dualism laid bare. Over the course of the play what we realize is that *Timon*'s dog is not a symbol at all, but a cipher: a placeholder for a division—what Derrida might call a *différance*—that cannot, by definition, be embodied. Indeed, the complexity of *Timon*'s dog is neither concept nor trope. It is the complexity of the Zen koan. At issue is nothing less than the impossible division between subject and object: the breach between activity as the annihilating source of value (Timon's as the god of the play's first half), and passivity as that value mystically reflected in the world of things (gold as the ultimate cynic in the play's denouement). This is a breach that cannot in truth be symbolized because, in the end, there is no distance between subject and object—there is no span to bridge between flatterer and cynic. The two are as intimate as the two sides of Nansen's sword.

Or perhaps, if we're fond of *différance* in a gentler key, the distance between East and West, action and contemplation, like the two sides of a falling leaf. "As the maple leaf falls," writes the eighteenth-century Zen master Ryokan, "It shows its front side and its back side." The magic of bounty is just the front side of gold's visible divinity. As the leaf falls we realize that the flatterer is already the cynic.

Writing in 1242, in Koshohorinji, the first Soto Zen temple in Japan, Eihei Dogen offers a slightly different formulation of Ryokan's maple leaf insight. "All things," Dogen tells us, "appear as their own eternal life."[20] If everything rises and falls away, if all things are impermanent, are mere appearances that come and go, how then is it possible for them to embody the eternal? The question most profoundly misses the mark. The point for Dogen is instead that eternity *only* appears. There is no eternal life that isn't also the life that dies. There is no divinity—no buddha nature—apart from the frail appearance of all things. We've come back to Joshu's dog, which neither embodies divinity nor does not, since to speak of embodiment is already to create too much distance between the eternal and the transient.

Joshu's dog, *Timon's* dog: thus far the only link I've adduced between the two is William Empson, whose dozen years of teaching in East Asia left a firm Buddhist imprint on the bulk of his research. Lately my own research has been exploring an even earlier Buddhist imprint. I've been examining what we might call the Renaissance's other Other: amid the contacts with the New World, with Africa, with India, the West was also encountering the Buddhist East. These contacts did not begin (as most early modernists still seem to assume) in the eighteenth century. They began instead with Portuguese missions to Sri Lanka at the beginning of the sixteenth century and were furthered when the Jesuits sent missionaries to Japan midcentury. The first Englishman in Japan was William

Adams, who, inspired by Dutch trade with India, piloted a Dutch vessel to East Asia in 1598. After a disastrous voyage, in which he lost 80 percent of his crew, Adams landed in Japan. He spent the rest of his life there, becoming the first foreign-born samurai and opening Japan up for trade with the Dutch East India Company. He even helped establish an English trading factory.

Adams's story is stunning—novelistic enough to provide the basis for James Clavell's blockbuster *Shogun*. Less dramatic, but of greater significance, perhaps, for the dissemination of Buddhist thought in Shakespeare's England, is the writing of the Flemish Franciscan missionary William of Rubruck. William was exploring "Tartary"—that is, central Asia—around the same time that Dogen Zenji was describing the eternal life of all things in Japan. The first English translation of his account appeared in 1598 (the year that William Adams set out for Asia), published in volume 2 of Hakluyt's *Principal Navigations*.[21]

In chapter 27 of William's account we read about idolaters clad in "saffron coloured garments": "They haue with them also whithersoeuer they goe, a certaine string with an hundreth or two hundreth nutshels thereupon, much like to our bead-roule which we cary about with vs. And they doe always vtter these words: *Ou mam Hactani*, God thou knowest: as one of them expounded it vnto me." Written in 1245, translated into English in 1598, this text narrates what is apparently the first Western encounter with Tibetan Buddhism. Priests in saffron-colored robes, carrying malas or prayer beads, chanting the mantra of the Buddha of compassion: *Om mani padme hum*. William doesn't quite get the mantra right—it doesn't mean "God thou knowest"—but he comes close. The literal translation is "Hail jewel of the lotus"—although Tibetan Buddhists maintain that the six syllables are ultimately untranslatable.

William's text also represents the first serious effort of a Westerner to grapple with Buddhist philosophy. The passage is brief enough and remarkable enough to be quoted in full:

> Now, after I had sit a while by the foresaid priests, and entred into their temple and seene many of their images both great and small, I demanded of them what they beleeued concerning God? And they answered: We beleeue that there is onely one God. And I demaunded

farther: Whether do you beleue that he is a spirit, or some bodily substance? They saide: We beleeue that he is a spirite. Then said I: Doe you beleeue that God euer tooke mans nature vpon him? They answered: Noe. And againe I said: Sithence ye beleeue that he is a spirit, to what end doe you make so many bodily images to represent him? Sithence also you beleeue not that hee was made man: why doe you resemble him rather vnto the image of a man then of any other creature? Then they answered saying: we frame not these images whereby to represent God. But when any rich man amongst vs, or his sonne, or his wife, or any of his friends deceaseth, hee causeth the image of the dead party to be made, and to be placed here: and we in remembrance of him doe reuerence thereunto. Then I replyed: you doe these things onely for the friendship and flatterie of men. Noe (said they) but for their memory. Then they demanded of me, as it were in scoffing wise: Where is God? To whom I answered: where is your soule? They said, in our bodies. Then saide I, is it not in euery part of your bodie, ruling and guiding the whole bodie, and yet notwithstanding is not seene or perceiued? Euen so God is euery where and ruleth all things, and yet is he inuisible, being vnderstanding and wisedome it selfe. Then being desirous to haue had some more conference with them, by reason that mine interpreter was weary, and not able to expresse my meaning, I was constrained to keepe silence.

William's God is the tricky Creator God of the West. Universal Lawgiver, He nonetheless *is* the Law; he rules all things, yet is invisible because he is "Understanding and Wisdom Itself."

In contrast, the Tibetans are not yet schooled in dualism; as William understands the matter, they are monotheists but do not yet grasp what their faith itself entails. They do not understand what it means to say that the soul is "in" the body; nor do they understand that, similarly, God as spirit rules all things, is "in" all things, and yet is not a thing himself. From William's perspective, the Tibetans worship a god of flattery and idolatry. From *their* perspective—it is quite literally hard to say. What words can explain nondualism? How—on what grounds, in what language, governed by whose rules—can East and West meet? According to

William, this particular meeting is cut short—and although the Western explorer has the last word, he feels himself nonetheless unable to express his meaning. Despite himself, he is constrained to keep silence.

"If you had been there, you would have saved the cat."

Notes

1. "Joshu's Dog" and "Nansen's Cat" are "cases" (i.e., koans) 1 and 14 respectively in the collection of forty-eight koans known in Sino-Japanese as the *Mumonkan* or *Gateless Gate*. The *Mumonkan* was published in the thirteenth century by the Chinese Zen monk Wumen ("Mumon" in Sino-Japanese). For the text of the Mumonkan, see Kenkei Shibayama, *Zen Comments on the Mumonkan* (New York: New American Library, 1974). I've modified Shibayama's translations somewhat.

2. "Universally Recommended Instructions for Zazen," in *Shobogenzo*, trans. Kosen Nishiyama and John Stevens, 4 vols. (Sendai: Daihokkaikaku, 1975–).

3. Zoketsu Norman Fischer suggests that the division between the west and east halls signifies the distinction between the monks who spent their time in formal practice and those who took care of temple duties: i.e., the difference between contemplative and active pursuit of the Way. See his essay "Quick! Who Can Save This Cat?" in *Buddhadharma: The Practitioner's Quarterly*, Spring 2003, www.thebuddhadharma.com/issues/2003/spring/zoketsu_norman_fischer_save_cat.html.

4. Or worth mourning, for that matter: to place sandals on one's head was, I am told, a sign of bereavement in ancient China.

5. In Fischer's terms, ultimately the sword of Nansen cuts us *in one*.

6. William Empson, *The Structure of Complex Words* (1951; repr., Ann Arbor: University of Michigan Press, 1967), 39.

7. Lisa Myōbun Freinkel, *Reading Shakespeare's Will: The Theology of Figure from Augustine to the Sonnets* (New York: Columbia University Press, 2002).

8. Empson, *Structure of Complex Words*, 39.

9. Ibid., 40.

10. All citations from Shakespeare are from Stephen Greenblatt, ed., *The Norton Shakespeare* (New York: W. W. Norton, 1997).

11. Empson, *Structure of Complex Words*, 183.

12. William Empson, *Milton's God* (New York: New Directions, 1961), 227.

13. Ibid., 273, 266.

14. Ibid., 93–94.

15. See Kenji Nishitani, *Religion and Nothingness*, trans. Jason Van Bragt (Berkeley: University of California Press, 1983), 54.

16. According to Sharon Cameron, Empson's biographer, John Haffenden, has recently unearthed a copy of the "lost" Buddha manuscript and is currently preparing it for publication. Cameron herself offers a lovely virtual reading of the manuscript—such as its contents can be deduced from extant drafts and notes—in her recent *Impersonality: Seven Essays* (Chicago: University of Chicago Press, 2007).

17. William Empson to John Hayward, March 7, 1933, quoted in John Haffenden, *William Empson: Among the Mandarin* (Oxford: Oxford University Press, 2005), 318.

18. Nishitani, *Religion and Nothingness*, 33, 34.

19. Empson, *Structure of Complex Words*, 176.

20. *Shobogenzo*, "Immo," 62.

21. All citations of Richard Hakluyt's *Principal Navigations* are taken from the Gutenberg Project e-text, www.gutenberg.org/etext/25645.

Chapter 8

The Passing of Falstaff
Rethinking History, Refiguring the Sacred

JOAN PONG LINTON

By all accounts, Falstaff is one of the most popular characters Shake-speare created for the Elizabethan stage. The character has a stage life that traverses the historical world of the *Henry IV* plays and the comic world of *The Merry Wives of Windsor*. And in *Henry V*, an offstage Fal-staff in his dying and death remains a subject of conversation on stage. From the street scene in which the Hostess announces his dire sickness (2.1) to the tavern scene in which his companions mourn his death (2.3), to Fluellen's Alexander the Pig reference in the field (4.7), the absent Falstaff remains very much a part of the lived experience of his tavern circle and the imagination of soldiers in the field. Such attention given to a character's passing is unprecedented in Shakespearean and early mod-ern theater, and it remains for us to explore the dramatic implications of Falstaff's absent presence. Scholars have surmised that Shakespeare wrote the play fully expecting the role would be filled by Will Kempe (the actor who most likely had played Falstaff in the *Henry IV* plays) and that Kempe's departure from the Chamberlain's Men shortly before the play opened required last-minute adjustments "to manage the audience's pos-sible disappointment."[1] This theory, plausible if unverifiable, testifies to the difficulty, if not impossibility, of replacing the physical presence on stage of a character-actor who had a "history," so to speak, with Elizabethan audiences. Indeed, one may go further to say that the vicissitudes of theater business only made a necessity of intentions that were already set in motion in the play by that personal history.

In this essay, I argue that the passing of Falstaff, already promised in the epilogue to *2 Henry IV*, raises profound questions that bear on the dramatic representation of history, questions that *Henry V* explores through its self-conscious reflection on its theatrical medium. Specifically, in the scenes of tavern and field mentioned above, the play asks what happens to the unrecorded past, the lives of those whose names do not appear in written record. This attention to the unrecorded past in turn prompts the question of what constitutes truth in written histories, a skepticism in keeping with contemporary chronicles' acknowledged failure to reach closure on the truth about the events they report.[2] Steven Marx has shown that "the Henriad alternates between propounding the Tudor myth of divine ordination and royal infallibility and acknowledging 'that the crown is always illegitimate, that is, always an effect of social relations and not their cause, and therefore must (and can) endlessly be legitimated by improvisations of each wearer.'"[3] I would further suggest that in staging the unrecorded past *Henry V* claims the position of fiction from which Shakespearean theater may comment on the truth of written and official histories. The result is a rethinking of historical experience in which the workings of the miraculous figure centrally in the play's two disjunctive projects of redemption: Henry's providentialist politics of redeeming time, and Shakespearean theater's redeeming of the unrecorded past.

As Walter Benjamin observes, official history belongs to the victors, and what is excluded from official record becomes the "debris" of history.[4] This insight speaks to the Tudor myth of history, which ascribes to Henry V the role of redeeming the Lancastrian line from the stain of usurpation left by his father, in anticipation of its union with the house of York in constituting the Tudor dynasty. For Benjamin, however, the unrecorded past has a claim on the present, a claim that thereby endows the present with a "weak messianic power" to redeem the past from oblivion.[5] By extension, even as Falstaff becomes a fictional version of the "debris" of history, his stage passing constitutes the play's appeal to audiences to redeem what lingers of the character, if only as traces of a felt absence. This appeal is most strongly felt in the fictive scenes above mentioned, which punctuate the play's dramatization of Henry's political and military action with stages of Falstaff's passing. Comical yet resonant with absence, these scenes inhabit the *platea*, that fluid, often nonrepresentational space of traffic between actors and audience.[6] Through this traffic, Shakespearean theater renders the representation of dynastic history—the history Shakespeare adapts from sources such as the chronicles of Hall and Holinshed—into a history of the everyday.[7] In other words, the scenes engage the audience in a temporal reorientation from the re-presentation of past events, the significance of which has already been determined by the historians, to history as an open-ended experience of events in passing, an experience in the present even as it is receding into the past. In a play so acutely aware of its own representational medium, this everyday experience of history is captured in the very ephemeral quality of performance itself, in what passes on, and from, the stage.

The temporal reorientation enacted in the fictive history of the everyday raises a further question of dramatic history's relation to its written sources, official or otherwise. This question comes to implicate theater's medium, its mediation between oral and written practices, especially when the play's fiction of unrecorded history is juxtaposed with the deliveries of a Chorus representing the official view of Henry as "the mirror of all Christian kings" (Cho. 2.6). In this connection, I am especially interested in the story of Falstaff emerging from tavern and field, one that connects his passing with the fate of soldiers in battle and speaks to their shared creaturely existence as subjects sacrificed to Henry's redemptive mission. In doing so, the story of Falstaff enacts his redemption from oblivion as an alternative destiny beyond sacrifice, the kind of miracle Benjamin hopes for amid the debris of creaturely existence. The story of Falstaff thus points to an emergence of the sacred in a world where "miracles are ceased" (1.1.68) and troubles the uses of miracles by which Henry defines his sovereign power.[8]

Conceived in this way, the redemption of Falstaff jars expectations of redemption in any sense that would be sanctioned by orthodox religion.

This would not be surprising, however, to audiences who were familiar with Falstaff's perverse relation to religious matters and institutions in the *Henry IV* plays. As Kristen Poole has shown, Shakespeare's audience saw Falstaff as both a "parody of the sixteenth-century puritan," and a "caricature of [Sir John] Oldcastle," a Lollard knight turned into a martyr after he was executed by Henry V for treason and heresy.[9] Both the parody and the caricature serve to familiarize and demystify the past for Elizabethan audiences by locating it in contemporary religious polemics and politics. Sir John Oldcastle was "widely identified as an early puritan" in Shakespeare's day, and the stage Puritan was a "comically grotesque figure" especially resonant of the Martin Marprelate pamphlet war.[10] My analysis will not specifically address the considerable scholarship on these topics but will rather build on the familiarizing and demystifying functions of theater that Falstaff so fully embodies. If in life "plump Jack" is "the world," this world of the flesh, of sinful humanity, has always been part of the religious thinking of the time (*1 Henry IV*, 2.5.438). In his death and dying, then, it is this world of the flesh that connects the absent Falstaff with his audiences, returning both to the fictive history of the everyday, to those profane spaces of tavern and battlefield, spaces of creaturely indulgence and creaturely sacrifice, where history remains open-ended in its unfolding and miracles may yet occur.

Falstaff and the Creaturely

In "Creature Caliban," Julia Lupton explores the creaturely as a politico-theological dimension of existence. Beginning with the derivation of the word *creature* "from the future-active participle of the Latin verb *creare* ('to create')," Lupton designates the creature as "a thing always in the process of undergoing creation; the creature is actively passive or, better, passionate, perpetually becoming created, subject to transformations at the behest of the arbitrary commands of an Other." Lupton traces the history of the concept through Judaism and Christianity, in which "creature marks the radical separation of creation and Creator." This separation generates further divisions, including, "in more figurative uses," the division "between anyone or anything that is produced or controlled by an agent, author, master, or tyrant." Lupton also draws from German-Jewish philosophers, including Benjamin, for whom "the Creature represents the flip side of the political theology of absolute sovereignty developed in the late-sixteenth and early-seventeenth centuries."[11]

While Prospero and Caliban represent an exemplary case of the sovereign-creature relationship, a similar if less obvious sovereign-creature relationship exists in the "friendship" between Henry and Falstaff. This relationship is not immediately apparent because friendship has traditionally been idealized as both above politics and beyond personal gain. But even when Hal is a sovereign in training, his friendship with Falstaff involves a giving that has always been part of an unannounced exchange, one that comes due over a long arc of time and exacts a return that exceeds all calculation. Falstaff becomes the prince's creature when the latter pays his tavern bills without being asked (*1 Henry IV*, 1.2) and thereby subjects him to a future of dependency. Hal envisions this eventuality from the start, when he discloses in a soliloquy that he will "imitate the sun," cloaking himself in the "base contagious clouds" of tavern fellowship, only to emerge transformed when "this loose behavior I throw off, / And pay the debt I never promised" (1.2.175, 176, 186–87). In this disclosure Hal already anticipates the assertion of power that will define him as sovereign. In effecting his own "scripted transformation" through his public rejection of Falstaff, "the bloated image of his former vices," Henry literally pays the debt he never promised, his material gift exacting from Falstaff a spiritual return, a sacrifice beyond calculation.[12]

At some level, Falstaff is aware of his creaturely existence, especially when he tries to convince the prince not to banish him. Hal's promise of banishment—his "I do, I will" (2.5.439)—sets a *telos* that controls Falstaff, as it were, from the future. In part 1 of *Henry IV*, however, Falstaff's comic energy and subversive wit deflect attention from his creaturely existence, and in part 2 his physical distance from Hal likewise obscures his condition. Physical distance does not undo the gift/debt that is given/incurred in this one-sided friendship, just as it does not mitigate the intimate abjection Falstaff suffers when the newly crowned Henry demands of him "not to come near our person by ten mile" (*2 Henry IV*, 5.5.63). Writing on the unconscious dimension of creaturely life, Eric Santner theorizes that what makes the condition "traumatic is ultimately the overproximity to the mysterious desire of the other," an other or "master" who inhabits the locus of power and a desire that interpellates the subject but that the subject is unable to "metabolize."[13] In Falstaff's case, Henry's rejection is a negative form of the interpellation, one that banishes even as it hails Falstaff as creature. Falstaff is unable to metabolize this negative interpellation because he has persuaded himself that "the prince is sick with desire to see me" and because he is "sweating with desire to see [Henry]" at his coronation.[14] The negative interpellation may have its first rehearsal in the episode of the Gadshill robbery, when Henry (then Prince Hal), having robbed the robber Falstaff, savors the moment at the latter's expense: "Falstaff sweats to death, and lards the lean earth as he walks along, wert not for laughing I should pity him" (*1 Henry IV*, 2.3.16–18). While Hal may have one or more things in mind—the sweating sickness (or plague), venereal disease often treated by sweating, the fever Falstaff eventually dies of, or a sign of his cowardice—the deadly outcome proves the jest to be prophetic at some level.[15] Falstaff has reason to fear, in light of the "ex-citation" he receives from Hal/Henry, to which Falstaff can hardly fail to respond. The epilogue's promise in *2 Henry IV* that "Falstaff shall die of a sweat" echoes Falstaff's "sweating with desire" in the tone of dead certainty, driving home an abjection so visceral it turns desire into disease, so that by *Henry V* Falstaff's creaturely existence becomes fully evident in his active passivity of dying.

To measure the depth of Falstaff's abjection one need only recall the scene in *1 Henry IV* when he plays dead to escape being killed in battle. This faked death, his famous exposition on honor, equating it with "a word" and with "air" (5.1.133, 134), and his boastful rationalization for counterfeiting death reveal his utter refusal to sacrifice himself to the king's cause: "Counterfeit? I lie; I am no counterfeit. To die is to be a counterfeit, for he is but the counterfeit of a man who hath not the life of a man; but to counterfeit dying when a man thereby liveth, is to be no counterfeit, but the true and perfect image of life indeed" (5.4.113–17). In this quintessentially theatrical moment Falstaff advances a bid for life and a logic of survival by "signifying on"—repeating in order to create one's own meaning—the word *counterfeit*.[16] Repeated six times, the word recalls in stark contrast the soldiers planted in the battlefield as "counterfeits" of Henry IV. In the previous scene the rebel Douglas refers to killing them just before encountering the real king face to face. Juxtaposed with the soldiers' sacrifice, Falstaff's counterfeiting constitutes a refusal not simply of sacrifice but of the logic of sacrifice underwriting providentialist history. Unlike the quintessential actor Falstaff, who performs his death to the life, the soldiers perform their death in the theater of real life, for the cause of the king as God's substitute on earth. This sacrifice is a gift beyond any economy of calculation, for a promised reward in heaven. To be sure, it is only in the fictive space of theater that a soldier can escape sacrifice by playing dead and comment on it for laughs. Hugh Grady sees in Falstaff's "playfulness th[e] ability to subvert ideological interpellation through theatricality."[17] Theatricality can thus be said to metabolize ideological interpellation for the audience, but it cannot do away with the emplotted relationship—that negative interpellation—that binds Falstaff to the prince. In this fictive intervention into the historical past, Falstaff is the comic who appeals to the audience with a punch line that cuts to the heart of the subject's creaturely existence. It is not clear at what point Hal realizes that Falstaff is faking, but in his farewell to "Poor Jack," Hal promises to have his "fat . . . deer . . . disemboweled" (5.4.106–8), confirming Falstaff's creaturely status as "protected" game singled out for royal use.

In staging the passing of Falstaff, then, Shakespearean theater registers the sacrifice he ultimately delivers off the field. In *Henry V*, Falstaff the creature becomes the focus of concern for his tavern companions, his staged absence making for moments of rare pathos in a play centered on the deeds of a king. While the presence onstage of a body would draw attention to the body, the absence of one foregrounds the passing of a life, literally from the stage. For the staging of an absence is not the absence of staging. Rather, like the photographic negative that reverses the values of salient and recessive details, such staging calls for a different kind of visual and aural sensibility. The analogy is not the most fitting, since the fixity of the photographic image fails to capture the fluidity of stage action. But it suffices to say that the verbal staging of a visual absence effectively reconfigures both the stage image and the stage action—in this case, around Falstaff's absent presence—in the process de-forming and re-forming the audience's visual and aural expectations.

Around his absent presence, then, a community gathers to attend to the ordinary business of death and dying. If in life, as Grady points out, Falstaff is "the character closest to the heavily plebeian popular audience of [*1 Henry IV*]," in his death and dying his companions continue to make a place for him in their conversations, even as they continue to take their places in the traffic of the *platea*.[18] Situated on the fringes of Henry's historical world, Falstaff's companions appeal to the same popular audience when Hostess Quickly summons Falstaff's tavern mates to "come in quickly to Sir John" (2.1.106–7), or when Pistol says his "manly heart doth ern. / .... / ... For Falstaff he is dead, / And we must ern therefore" (2.3.3–6). Here, theater at its most elemental—its interplay of presences and absences—comes into alignment with history as event, the unfolding of the "it happens" even as it simultaneously recedes from experience.

What renders the event of Falstaff's passing poignant in its immediacy is the sense of a community coming together in mourning. This sense of community is all the more remarkable if we consider that Falstaff's tavern companions have been a fractured group throughout the *Henry IV* plays. The situation is no better if we follow Falstaff into the comic world of Windsor, where his tavern companions are at odds with him. For personal interest each betrays Falstaff's roguery to the merry wives and participates in his ritual baffling. In *Henry V*, Nym and Pistol are drawing their swords over the Hostess, who promised herself to the former but marries the latter—until news of Falstaff's illness puts a stop to the fight. Falstaff's passing thus both unifies the group and calls forth in each member the creaturely kindness that in life he seldom enjoyed or even deserved. It is in this sense that the dead can be said to have a claim on the living. From the perspective of the living, Santner explains what it means to be responsive to another human being as the figure of the Other: "What makes the Other other is not his or her spatial exteriority with respect to my being but the fact that he or she is strange, is a stranger, and not only to me but also to him- or herself, is the bearer of an internal alterity, an enigmatic density of desire calling for response beyond any rule-governed reciprocity; against this background, the very opposition between 'neighbor' and 'stranger' begins to lose its force. . . .

It is precisely this sort of answerability that is at the heart of our very aliveness to the world."[19] In death, Falstaff has become the figure of the Other par excellence. He is the neighbor whom death has made strange, even as his dying speaks to the mortality, that internal alterity, within each person, calling forth a response that suspends the tacit rules of tavern reciprocity. This answerability, which Santner defines as "the psychotheology of everyday life," marks theater's fictive production of the sacred.

To locate this theatrical moment within a poetics of emplotment, the suspension of rule-governed reciprocity of the tavern world parallels what Paul Ricoeur describes in *Figuring the Sacred* as a trait of the parable: the logic of "the extraordinary within the ordinary" by which "the parable redescribes life through the fiction of its story." By bringing about an "epoché," or purposeful suspension "of natural reality," the parable "opens up a new dimension of reality that is signified by the plot."[20] Implicit in this formulation is the rhetorical figure of the *parabola*, which George Puttenham makes explicit by naming it the "resemblance misticall" in his *Arte of English Poesie*.[21] Even as the parable figures the mystical as both within and exceeding the ordinary, so the staging of Falstaff's passing opens his companions—and potentially the audience—to a momentary experience of the sacred in the midst of life.

Of course, whether audiences will read the reconfigured stage action in this way cannot be predetermined. Should they do so, however, they will have effectively repositioned themselves as witnesses to what goes unpresented, and is unpresentable, a kind of theatrical sublime. Again, whether such a reading does not risk idealizing the early modern stage is worth considering. The risk is certainly present, in view of theater's roots in religious and ritual performances, enactments that are prone to mystification. Especially in a play that so pointedly reminds audiences of the cessation of miracles, all productions of the sacred must ultimately be reconciled with this post-Reformation skepticism, a skepticism evident in Henry's Machiavellian manipulations of religion and miracles. At the same time, however, this skepticism should not be taken as a rejection of the sacred or miraculous per se. Rather, the play's demystification of Henry's manipulations provides the impetus from which a different understanding of the sacred and the miraculous may arise.

Sovereign Power and the Miraculous

When the archbishop of Canterbury says that "miracles are ceased," he imports a post-Reformation sensibility into the play's pre-Reformation historical world, a familiar anachronism in the history plays that speaks to contemporary religious politics. At issue here is the Protestant criticism of Catholic beliefs and practices as corrupt and demonic in their veneration of the saints and the miracles associated with them. As Helen Parish tells us, "At the heart of this criticism of the miraculous powers of the saints was the assertion that the age of true miracles had passed. The miracles of the apostles had ensured that the roots of the church would be firmly planted, it was argued, but once the church had been established, such wonders were not necessary." Yet Protestant theology and polemic did not invalidate miracles altogether. "There was certainly no obvious date at which ecclesiastical miracles should have ceased: the promise made by Christ to the apostles (Mark 16; Jn 14.12) did not suggest that the capacity to work wonders would eventually be withdrawn."[22] In other words, miracles were still possible for the period, however attenuated and problematical they had become from the Protestant perspective.[23] This gap between theology and scripture contextualizes the political manipulation of the miraculous in *Henry V*, and the archbishop's anachronistic comment neatly frames the play's inquiry into the politics of miracles.

Henry's own political use of religion is nothing if not cynical, when he calls for the archbishop's interpretation of the Salic Law to justify his claim to the French throne: ". . . we will hear, note, and believe in heart / That what you speak is in your conscience washed / As pure as sin with baptism" (1.2.30–32). His decision to invade France is clearly motivated by his father's dying instruction: ". . . to busy giddy minds / With foreign quarrels, that action, hence borne out, / May waste the memory of the former days" (*2 Henry IV*, 4.5.341–43). Henry's mixing of politics and religion anticipates Carl Schmitt's formulations on political theology: that "all significant concepts of the modern theory of the state are secularized theological concepts" and that "the exception in jurisprudence is analogous to the miracle in theology."[24] The sovereign is the one who decides the "exception," which designates "that condition in which what is outside the law—the exception to the rule—comes to define the very essence of the law."[25] In Henry's case, the interpretation of the Salic Law amounts to a suspension of the law, so that in deciding the exception he is in fact asserting his power as sovereign. The discovery of the traitors Cambridge, Scrope, and Grey (though "by interception" of intelligence) further provides a touch of the miraculous to inaugurate "a fair and lucky war" (2.2.7, 180). In comparing the treason to "another fall of man" (2.2.139), Henry fully inhabits the providentialist horizon as divine substitute.

Turning from punishing traitors to commanding the obedience and sacrifice of soldiers, Henry resorts to a miracle from the saints' lives in rallying his troops at Agincourt. The fourth-century martyrs Crispin and Crispianus were princely brothers who undertook missionary work in France, becoming shoemakers in order to serve the poor. After the martyrs were persecuted and executed for their faith, their bodies were miraculously recovered intact. Derived from the Latin *legenda*, the legend is a narrative that defines "what is to be read and said."[26] As such, the Crispin legend not only provides a religious gloss to Henry's military campaign but also reinforces his call to brotherhood, his promise to ennoble those who will fight with him. Even as the martyrs' bodies were recovered intact, so Henry's soldiers would, on St. Crispin's Day in years to come, "remember, with advantage" by their healed battle scars the feats they performed at Agincourt (4.3.50). The miracle thus enables Henry both to make a promise that exacts a sacrifice in advance and, glossing over the prospect of death, to create a "memory" of military victory before the fact. For Elizabethan audiences there would be additional resonance from the popular literature that celebrated shoemakers' ability to create their own saint's day. As Alison Chapman observes, "Henry concedes a holiday in honor of Saint Crispin and the warrior shoemakers that fight on his behalf, and this shoemakers' holiday attests to the dependence of any military leader on his foot soldiers. Yet this is a dependence that must be forgotten in order to glorify the king."[27]

Closer examination also reveals Henry's inverted application of the miracle: whereas the martyrs are princes who gave their lives in service to commoners, Henry's common soldiers are the ones to give their lives for the prince's cause. Nor are the dead soldiers remembered among the noble dead after the victory at Agincourt.[28] Here we may detect a familiar, sacrificial logic of redemption, one we have encountered before in Henry's dealings with Falstaff. If Falstaff's sacrifice redeems Henry's reputation from his former profligacy, the soldiers' sacrifice would secure the victory with which Henry may redeem his line from the stain of usurpation. This sacrificial logic underwrites an exorbitant exchange with his "band of brothers" in which Henry once again suspends the tacit rules of shared sacrifice. The miracle's inverted application pinpoints the manipulation necessary at the heart of Henry's political theology. Such manipulation might easily be overlooked but for the scene that precedes, and frames, his Agincourt speech. In this ostensibly fictive scene, an incognito Henry quarrels with the soldier Williams over the king's responsibility to his soldiers, his disguise allowing each party to "speak [his] conscience of the king" (4.1.113). For Williams, it is the king's responsibility to prosecute war with good cause, for "if these men do not die well, it will be a black matter for the king that led them to it; who to disobey were against all proportion of subjection" (136–38). Henry's response is that the king is not responsible: "Every subject's duty is the king's, but every subject's soul is his own" (164–65). As a framing device, the quarrel undercuts Henry's political use of miracles. In stark contrast to the martyrs' intact bodies, the monstrous body Williams conjures—"all those legs and arms and heads chopped off in a battle, shall join together at the latter day and cry all . . ." (129–31)—powerfully figures history's other, what remains unpresented and unpresentable in official history. The result is not simply a critique of Henry's political theater but one that connects the soldiers with Falstaff in their shared creaturely condition, their total subjection to Henry and their equally total exclusion from history.

In its ostensibly fictive moments, then, the play brings to the fore an excluded past of the creaturely—appropriately so, since to be excluded from historical record is to be as good as fiction, that is, to have no validity as historical fact. As Santner puts it, from the standpoint of the present, "this is a past that has, so to speak, never achieved ontological consistency, that in some sense has not yet been but remains stuck in a spectral, protocosmic dimension." Elaborating on Benjamin's idea that such a past has a claim on the present, Santner proposes "a new conceptualization of the nature of that which registers itself in historical experience, a rethinking of that which in such experience, in its dense, 'creaturely' materiality, calls out toward the future, constitutes—'temporalizes'—the dimension of futurity as a mode of response to a peculiar sort of ex-citation transmitted by the past (one needs to hear/read excitation in its derivation from *ex-citare*, a calling out or summoning forth)."[29] Signifi-cantly, this ex-citation from the creaturely past structurally parallels and reverses the demand that the sovereign or master makes of his creature. Unlike the sovereign, the dead can neither control the living nor exact a sacrifice, and it remains for the living to respond to the call from the past and resurrect it from oblivion. This ability to redeem the past is the "weak messianic power" that the present can activate, wherein lies the possibility of a miracle of the everyday working through the dense, creaturely materiality of living and dying. As Santner further indicates, Benjamin's idea of miracle is formulated as a critique of Schmitt's politi-cal theology. For Benjamin, "A miracle signals not the state of exception, but rather its suspension, an intervention into this peculiar topological knot—the outlaw dimension internal to law—that serves to sustain the symbolic function of sovereignty."[30] Santner understands this suspen-sion to "involve . . . an intervention into the realm of 'creaturely life' and the processes of its production."[31]

With respect to *Henry V*, we have seen that the play's attention to the creaturely is integral to its critique of Henry's political theology and that its staging of history's unpresentable has everything to do with the play's rethinking of historical experience against the ideological horizon of Tudor political theology. When Williams imagines the arms and legs "crying all," and when Falstaff's tavern friends mourn his passing, they give voice to fellow creatures excluded from recorded history and appeal to the future for redemption. Such redemption, if it is to avoid being sub-sumed by official history, would necessarily have to imagine an alternative destiny for Henry's creatures, one that goes beyond the sacrificial logic of the Tudor myth. This ideological reorientation within the play, I would suggest, represents Shakespearean theater's fictive intervention into the realm of creaturely life, the stage's version of the miracle. The vehicle for this intervention is the emergence of Falstaff's story as "unrecorded history." Told in the tavern and in the field, the story serves as a powerful counter to the play's representation of Henry's heroic action, champi-oned by the Chorus as the self-appointed voice of official history.[32]

Rethinking History and the Miraculous

The Chorus in *Henry V* cuts a curiously provocative figure. In asking to be admitted "Chorus to *this* history" (Cho. 1.32; emphasis added), it continually disparages the physical limitations of the stage and players, yet its account of history is often shown in the ensuing scenes to be faulty if not intentionally deceptive. The result is the contest between the Chorus and the stage on which scholars have commented. Noting the Chorus's coercive posture toward the audience, Andrew Gurr points out that the Chorus's aim to praise Henry is at odds with the stage's far more ambiguous and ambivalent representation.[33] Graham Holderness further points to the inherent contradiction between the Chorus's function "to create an epic space for the drama and in the imagination of the audience" and its awareness of the "theatrical nature" of the enterprise.[34] To figure out just why such contest and contradiction should exist, we might turn to act 5, in which the Chorus addresses a select group among the audience: "Vouchsafe to those that have *read* the story / That I may prompt them" (Cho. 5.1–2, emphasis added). In targeting the literate among the audience, the Chorus not only equates historical truth with the fixity of writing and print but also claims this single historical truth ("the story") for its official version of history. As the play unfolds, it is the Chorus's monological position that the stage engages in dialogical interplay.

Indeed, a literate bias is present in the Chorus's delivery from the start, motivating its apology for the inadequacy of the stage and players to the epic dimensions of Henry's history:

> O, pardon! since a crooked figure may
> Attest in little place a million;
> And let us, ciphers to this great accompt,
> On your imaginary forces work.
> (Cho. 1.15–18)

This translation of players into "ciphers" is itself a literate reading premised on mathematical logic, specifically, the concept of zero as a number that signifies both nothing and, through the operation of multiplication, "a million."[35] The Chorus's numerical literacy thus underwrites a disembodied and idealizing imagination that would both transcend the real presence of the players and exclude from its account the materiality of history as lived experience. It is this double exclusion that the play action contests, especially in its attention to the fate of Henry's creatures. In this light, the contest between Chorus and play action can be seen to frame a more fundamental issue of medium and truth value in the representation of history. In turn, the exploration of this issue has implications for theater, which integrates oral and literate practices not only in its representation of history but also in its rendering of the miraculous on stage.

The better to understand the stakes of this contest, we might turn to Benjamin's differentiation between *novel* and *story* as narrative technologies of the self, that is, narrative techniques and practices that shape distinct dispositions to knowledge and sociability. In his formulation, the source of story is "experience, passing from mouth to mouth," and in communicating experience the storyteller is one who has "counsel" for his listeners.[36] For him, counsel is "less an answer to a question than a proposal concerning the continuation of a story which is in the process of unfolding," for "counsel woven into the fabric of real life . . . is wisdom."[37] Benjamin sees "the decline of the story [a]s the rise of the novel," which, in its "essential dependence on the book," is linked to the rise of capitalism and the ascendancy of the middle class. Arising from "the individual in his isolation," the novel instances the incommunicability of experience (detached from the fabric of real life) and the "profound perplexity" ("Ratlosigkeit," literally "counsellessness") of the modern world.[38] For this reason, the novel develops around the meaning of a life as the *telos* that informs the narrative throughout.[39] Thus while the "moral" of a story remains open to reinterpretation, the question it poses being how one might retell the story, the novel's "Finis" imposes closure on the meaning of a life. A person listening to, or reading, a story is "in the company of the storyteller," while the reader of a novel, being "isolated more so than any other reader, . . . in fact looks for other human beings from whom he derives the 'meaning of life.'"[40] Finally, both the novel and the story have their narrative impulses in epic memory, the difference being the form that memory takes in each. While memory in the story operates through "short-lived reminiscences," in the novel it takes the form of "perpetuating remembrance" akin to that in the "invocation to the muse."[41]

In *Henry V*, Benjamin's concept of the novel applies well to the Chorus's recourse to written history in fixing the meaning of Henry's life within the telos of the imagined community of England as a Christian nation. An almost abstract entity in the play, the Chorus remains isolated from other characters, detached from the fabric of creaturely experience, in its celebration of Henry as an exemplary Christian warrior-king. While this idealization of Henry dominates all of the choric speeches, the prologue to act 4 most fully captures the coercive mechanism by which the Chorus would perpetuate such a memory of Henry in the audience. The speech moves from the fluidity of the aural sense to the fixity of visual and finally visceral inscription. The narrative begins with the "creeping murmur" of night, presenting a world of outward action. The armies "hum" with "stilly sounds"; the sentinels pass "secret whispers"; "fire answers fire," and "steed threatens steed" with "boastful neighs." These sounds, "piercing the night's dull ear," waken both camps to the day ahead, to hammers and cock's crow, the toll of clocks and the rowdy "chid[ing]" of the French soldiers, confident in their superior numbers (Cho. 4.2, 5, 7, 8, 10, 11, 20).

Outward action turns inward to "rumination," as the sensory appeal shifts from the aural to the visual. The "watchful fires" are said to disclose the "gestures sad" of English soldiers, whose "lank-lean cheeks" and "war-worn coats" suggest their weariness. Amid the inertia, the "gazing moon" fixes on the figure of Henry moving among his troops. The audience is directed to "behold" his "cheerful looks and sweet majesty" and to note the effect he has on his soldiers (Cho. 4.24, 23, 25, 26, 27, 28, 40):

> That every wretch, pining and pale before,
> Beholding him, plucks comfort from his looks:
> A largess universal like the sun
> His liberal eye doth give to every one,
> Thawing cold fear, that mean and gentle all,
> Behold, as may unworthiness define,
> A little touch of Harry in the night.
>
> (Cho. 4.41–47)

In the Chorus's narration, Henry's disembodied gaze, like the sun's rays, felt in the body of the soldier, has the power to touch and penetrate, thawing cold fear in the heart. Henry thus becomes the ideal leader in the eyes of every soldier, who "plucks" from him the meaning of honor and bravery. His "liberal eye" not only defines value but bestows it as a "largess universal." In turn, the soldiers provide the focus of perception through which members of the audience are subjected to the gaze and inscribed with a visceral memory, "a little touch of Harry in the night."

If we detect in this hypnotic gaze the psychodynamics of identification described in Lacan's "mirror stage," it reveals an imagination already inscribed in a symbolic order embodied by Henry as the Ideal-I. Misrecognized as the sun's plenitude, Henry's gaze is the absence that organizes the field of relationships. It operates as the vanishing point in a visual imagination that freezes historical time into perspectival space, the imaginary rays of Henry's "largess universal" extending through the awestruck and fear-thawed soldiers to the audience.[42] Through this perspectival extension of the gaze, the Chorus conscripts the imagination of its auditors as "individuals in isolation" into a collective fantasy. Yet the Chorus's control of the audience may likewise be illusory, for it already anticipates contradiction by exhorting the audience to "yet sit and see, / Minding true things by what their mock'ries be" (Cho. 4.52–53). Not only is the Chorus's "truth" mocked in the ensuing quarrel between Henry and Williams, but in the course of the play Henry's own royal image is continually haunted by the emerging story of Falstaff.

This haunting of Henry's image warrants a return to the tavern and battlefield, where we may discern, in Benjamin's terms, a sociodynamics of the story in its unfolding. Beginning in the tavern, the story of Falstaff develops around a community of tellers who are also listeners. Thus Mistress Quickly relates the details of his final moments to her tavern companions, and her report is followed by a debate on whether he died like "any christom child" or like a reformed sinner exclaiming against sack and women (2.3.11). In recalling Henry's rejection of Falstaff, they sympathize with Falstaff—"the king hath killed his heart"; "the king hath run bad humors on the knight"; "his heart is fracted and corroborate"— although Nym also allows that "the king is a good king" (2.1.70, 110, 113, 114). Without fixing the meaning of Falstaff's life, the conversation represents an exchange of counsel that enables a community to deal with loss and survival. Such an exchange works against the monopoly of any one opinion because it involves affects whose meanings cannot be prescribed. In Nym's words, "things must be as they may" (18). At one level expressive of the resignation of the subjected, Nym's words also carry a supplementary meaning. The temporal structuring of experience implicit in the placement of "must" before "may" suggests an open-ended view of history as lived experience. Twice spoken—the second time in reference to the contradictory views of the king (114)—these words project no preconceived horizon, no larger end, to which the disparate memories and judgments of individuals may be reconciled. These details are precisely the creaturely materiality of everyday life that eludes written record, but more than that they elude the ideological horizon that informs official history and determines what is presentable. In the shared reminiscences of his companions Falstaff finds an afterlife of sorts, as the occasion for story. The story thus produced is a fragile thing, however, since it depends for its survival on the continuity of the community from which it arises, and this continuity is threatened when its male members are pressed into Henry's war.

Yet Falstaff's story does find a retelling beyond its original community—an unexpected one—in Fluellen's comparison of Henry to Alexander the Pig. Modeled on Plutarch's *Parallel Lives*, the comparison presents, in David Quint's judgment, an unwitting parody of humanist historiography,[43] but the effect, I would suggest, is the staging of a miracle. Although Fluellen means to compliment Henry "in his right wits and his good judgments" as far surpassing his historical model, Alexander's killing of "his best friend, Cleitus," in a drunken rage recalls Henry's rejection of Falstaff (4.7.37, 32–33).[44] The parodic parallel thus opens to examination Henry's friendship with Falstaff—this time extended to the context of soldiers in the field, for whom Henry's pledge of enobled brotherhood never materializes. Fluellen's retelling thus brings together friendship and brotherhood as two sacrificial logics that inform Henry's political theology of the creature. The retelling puts into play elements of dialectical vision that Benjamin finds essential to the redemption of the past: "The past can be seized only as an image that flashes up at the moment of its recognizability, and is never seen again. . . . For it is an irretrievable image of the past which threatens to disappear in any present that does not recognize itself as intended in that image" (4.390–91). Although Fluellen does not grasp the import of his historical parallel, his comic ineptness invites the audience to do so. In fact, Fluellen has forgotten the name of the "fat knight," and the prompting he receives from fellow soldier Gower offers yet another reminder to the audience of "Sir John Falstaff" (4.7.40, 43). Gower's "Sir" returns Falstaff in his knighted status to the field, suspending if only posthumously his creaturely abjection. At the same time, in his Pig reference, Fluellen's Welsh accent demystifies Henry's idealized image, revealing the sovereign in his corporeality to be also a creature.[45] Transpiring within a makeshift story community of two soldiers, this simultaneous resurrection of Falstaff as creature and demystification of Henry as sovereign bear the marks of a miracle in Santner's terms of an intervention into the realm of the creaturely.

Whether the Elizabethan (or our own) present recognizes itself in the image of the fictive past or, indeed, whether individual auditors care enough to respond to the story of Falstaff is beyond the control of the stage. But within the play's fiction, Fluellen's retelling of Falstaff's story comes at a moment when his own tavern circle has finally been decimated by war and disease. Even as the story changes with the context of each telling, the different reminiscences confirm the sacrificial logic of the sovereign politics and the miraculous power of creature sympathy to redeem the past. In staging the passing of Falstaff, Shakespearean theater discovers the extraordinary amid the ordinary, the sacred in the everyday, the miracle that never appears, yet to which one can bear witness, embedded as it is in the fabric of lived historical experience. In the open-endedness of story Falstaff finds a differently imagined redemptive future surpassing the horizon of the Tudor myth that will ultimately kill Henry into history.

Notes

1. Melissa D. Aarons, "The Globe and 'Henry V' as Business Document," *Studies in English Literature* 40 (2000): 285.

2. Annabel Patterson, *Shakespeare and the Popular Voice* (Oxford: Basil Blackwell, 1989), 79.

3. Steven Marx, "Holy War in *Henry V*," *Shakespeare Survey* 48 (1995): 89.

4. Walter Benjamin, "On the Concept of History," in *Selected Writings*, 5 vols., ed. Howard Eiland and Michael W. Jennings (Cambridge, MA: Belknap Press, 2002–3), 4:392.

5. Ibid., 4:390.

6. Robert Weimann traces the development of *locus* and *platea* from medieval mysteries, liturgical drama, and moralities to Tudor interludes and the Elizabethan stage. See *Shakespeare and the Popular Tradition in the Theater: Studies in the Social Dimension of Dramatic Form and Function*, ed. Robert Schwartz (Baltimore: Johns Hopkins University Press, 1978), 73–97.

7. Michael Tomlinson, "Shakespeare and the Chronicles Reassessed," *Literature and History* 10 (1984): 46–58, discusses Shakespeare's relative independence in drawing on such sources as Hall or Holinshed.

8. All quotations of Shakespeare's plays are taken from *The Norton Shakespeare*, based on the Oxford edition, ed. Stephen Greenblatt et al. (New York: W. W. Norton, 1997).

9. Kristen Poole, "Saints Alive! Falstaff, Martin Marprelate, and the Staging of Puritanism," *Shakespeare Quarterly* 46 (1995): 54, 49. The caricature provoked both a stage response in *The First Part of Sir John Oldcastle* (1599), and the forced renaming of Shakespeare's character from Sir John Oldcastle to Sir John Falstaff, as scholars surmise, under the threat of legal action from the martyr's descendant, the seventh Lord Cobham, who was then Lord Chamberlain. Richard Dutton, *Mastering the Revels: The Regulation and Censorship of English Renaissance Drama* (Ames: University of Iowa Press, 1991), 102–7.

10. Poole, "Saints Alive!" 63.

11. Julia Lupton, "Creature Caliban," *Shakespeare Quarterly* 51 (2000): 1, 4.

12. Maurice Hunt, *Shakespeare's Religious Allusiveness: Its Play and Tolerance* (Aldershot: Ashgate, 2003), 28, 25.

13. Eric Santner, *On Creaturely Life: Rilke, Benjamin, Sebald* (Chicago: University of Chicago Press, 2006), 31–34.

14. Ibid., 77–78, 25–26.

15. Giorgio Melchiori, "Dying of a Sweat: Falstaff and Oldcastle," *Notes and Queries* (June 1987): 210–11.

16. My understanding of "signifyin(g)" draws from Henry Louis Gates's discussion in *The Signifying Monkey: A Theory of African-American Literary Criticism* (Oxford: Oxford University Press, 1989), 44–54, 68–88. While Gates locates "signifyin(g)" (from its African roots) within African American folk and literary

traditions, the device and its force as social commentary can certainly be extended to other literary instances.

17. Hugh Grady, "Falstaff: Subjectivity between the Carnival and the Aesthetic," *Modern Language Review* 96 (2001): 613.

18. Ibid., 617.

19. Eric Santer, *On the Psychotheology of Everyday Life: Reflections on Freud and Rosenzweig* (Chicago: University of Chicago Press, 2001), 9.

20. Paul Ricoeur, *Figuring the Sacred: Religion, Narrative, and Imagination*, trans. David Pellauer (Minneapolis: Augsburg Fortress Press, 1995), 60. The phrase "Refiguring the Sacred" in my subtitle is inspired by Ricouer's title.

21. According to Puttenham, "The Greekes call it *Parabola*, which terme is also by custome accepted of vs: neuerthelesse we may call him in English the resemblance misticall. . . . Such parables were all the preachings of Christ in the Gospell, as those of the wise and foolish virgins, of the euil steward, of the labourers in the vineyard, and a number more." George Puttenham, *The Arte of English Poesie*, facsimile ed. (1589; repr., Kent, OH: Kent State University Press, 1988), 3.19.205–6.

22. Helen L. Parish, "'Lying Histories Fayning False Miracles': Magic, Miracles and Medieval History in Reformation Polemic," *Reformation and Renaissance Review* 4 (2002): 235.

23. In "Miracles Happen: Benjamin, Rosenzweig, Freud, and the Matter of the Neighbor," in *The Neighbor: Three Inquiries in Political Theology* (Chicago: University of Chicago Press, 2005), 77–133, Eric Santner theorizes an approach to reading the sacred in the experience of the everyday. He begins by recapitulating the historical trajectory constructed by Franz Rosenzweig in tracing "the gradual attenuation of the miracle" through a series of "enlightenment moments": "The first in this series is the triumph of philosophy over myth in antiquity. . . . The second 'enlightenment' refers to the Renaissance and the Reformation, in which the calcified legacies of Aristotle (above all in scholasticism) were supplanted by the privileging of direct experimental encounter with nature, on the one hand, and of spiritual experience authorized only by scripture and the strength of faith, on the other. For Rosenzweig, the eighteenth century moment we have come to refer to as the Enlightenment signals the moment when the trust in the reliability of experience and the historical/scriptural record of experience itself begins, in its turn, to appear as a form of naïve belief. In each case, what first occupies the place of knowledge over against belief comes to be retroactively posited as a groundless form of belief." Santner further points out that, for Rosenzweig, "miracles truly become a problem for both knowledge and faith" only during the third moment, "since miracles ultimately depend on

the testimony of witnesses—the ultimate witness being the martyr" (78). With respect to this historical trajectory, *Henry V* seems both to echo the second moment and to present a postmiraculous sensibility in its foregrounding of a political theology informed by the Reformation doctrine that "miracles are ceased." In other words, although miracles are ceased in being made manifest, they are still tenable if problematic—except, that is, when engineered for political theater, as in Henry's case.

24. Carl Schmitt, *Political Theology: Four Chapters on the Concept of Sovereignty*, trans. George Schwab (Chicago: University of Chicago Press, 1985), 36.

25. Lupton, "Creature Caliban," 6.

26. Michel de Certeau, *The Practice of Everyday Life*, trans. Steven Randall (Berkeley: University of California Press, 1984), 186.

27. Alison A. Chapman, "Whose Saint Crispin's Day Is It? Shoemaking, Holiday Making, and the Politics of Memory in Early Modern England," *Renaissance Quarterly* 54 (2001): 1485.

28. This is not to minimize the play's exemplary image of Henry, which owes something to the contemporary secularization of the Crispin legend. Of particular interest is Thomas Deloney's highly popular version in *The Gentle Craft* (1597), which the play echoes in places. Deloney's fiction anglicizes the brothers and romanticizes their exploits, erasing their martyrdom in the process. In Deloney's story, the heroes are not Roman missionaries but displaced princes of Logria (today's Kent) in the time when Britain was under the Roman Empire. Having adopted new lives as apprentices to a shoemaker, Crispine later marries the emperor's daughter in secret, while Crispianus undertakes battle to defend France (which was likewise part of Roman territory) against Persian invaders. In the end, the brothers regain their rightful places in society when Crispianus returns victorious to England and Crispine produces a male heir to the Roman throne. Juxtaposed with Shakespeare's play, it would seem that the brothers' separate careers are recapitulated in Henry's combined role of warrior and husband. The appeal to bourgeois Englishness in the romance theme of hidden nobility is exemplified in the body of the king.

29. Santer, "Miracles Happen," 86.

30. Ibid., 102–3.

31. Santner, *On Creaturely Life*, 15–16.

32. I should mention that the Chorus's speeches appear only in the 1623 Folio version of *Henry V*, which is generally accepted as the authoritative text. For Annabel Patterson, this means that "we simply do not know . . . what the performative version of *Henry V* was like; the Quarto may very well be closer than the Folio to what the London audiences actually saw on the stage at the absolute turn of the century" (*Shakespeare and the Popular Voice*, 73). According to

Gurr, however, "The Choruses were in the manuscript prepared early in 1599, the text later printed in the First Folio." Introduction to *King Henry V*, ed. Andrew Gurr (Cambridge: Cambridge University Press, 1992), 7.

33. Gurr, introduction to *King Henry V*, 6–15.

34. Graham Holderness, *Shakespeare Recycled: The Making of Historical Drama* (New York: Harvester Wheatsheaf, 1992), 108.

35. In this dual capacity, the number zero functions as what Brian Rotman, *Signifying Nothing: The Semiotics of Zero* (New York: St. Martin's Press, 1987), 19, calls a metasign, a sign that, in signifying nothing, points beyond itself to the epistemic system in which it operates.

36. Benjamin, "The Storyteller," in *Selected Writings*, 3:144, 145.

37. Ibid., 3:145–46.

38. Ibid., 3:146.

39. Ibid., 3:155.

40. Ibid., 3:156.

41. Ibid., 3:155, 154.

42. Rotman, in *Signifying Nothing*, points to the adoption of the number zero, the invention of perspective, and the generalized use of money as the bases for the emergence of the metasubject in Renaissance thought. By *metasubject*, he means a subject beyond, or abstracted from, individual selves that can conceivably inhabit any number of subjective positions. As metasubjects, the soldiers and the auditors can thus be seen to substitute for one another.

43. David Quint, "Alexander the Pig: Shakespeare on History and Poetry," in *William Shakespeare's Henry V*, ed. Harold Bloom (New York: Chelsea House, 1988), 62.

44. Judith Mossman, "*Henry V* and Plutarch's *Alexander*," *Shakespeare Quarterly* 45 (1994): 69–73, rightly points out that the play consistently compares Henry V favorably to Alexander. Her claim does not take into account, however, the conflicting views of Henry in the play.

45. Lupton, "Creature Caliban," 6.

Chapter 9

Richard II, Abraham, and the Abrahamic

KEN JACKSON

Because Shakespeare's *Richard II* depicts the deposition of a king on the throne by "divine right," many have assumed that the play can tell us much about what is increasingly referred to as Shakespeare's "political theology," the extent to which theological concepts and beliefs underwrite or determine his political understanding.[1] This essay operates under that common and fundamental critical assumption.

It does not assume, however, the scholarly boundaries that have been set to explore this political theology. Generally speaking, *Richard II* scholarship limits the possible range of Shakespeare's political theology by setting a boundary at the medieval religious notion that the king somehow embodied the divine in his very being ("the king's two bodies") and another boundary at what seems to be a protosecular early modern understanding that "the Law" rather than the divine was the ultimate sovereign, responsible for the making and unmaking of kings.[2] According to most critical opinion Shakespeare either leans toward one boundary or another, backward or forward in history, or, alternately, is considered to be resolutely but brilliantly ambiguous on the whole matter, looking both forward and backward at once in accordance with his legendary "double-eyedness."[3]

The critical wager of this essay is that if one even briefly assumes a broader range of possible religious and historical understandings it will quickly become clear that Shakespeare's political theology in *Richard II* is organized around Genesis 22 and the story of Abraham's sacrifice of Isaac. That is, the critical terms, concepts, and images that shape Shakespeare's "political theology" do not derive primarily from the medieval notion of the "king's two bodies," or from the early modern English constitutional understanding of the "king-in-parliament," or from a prescient sense of a realpolitik to come, but from the long and still relevant interpretive tradition surrounding Genesis 22.

In Genesis 22, after many trials, God calls the aged Abraham to kill his son and heir, a demand that very often has been interpreted as a "test" of the patriarch's faith. But interpreters have long been troubled by their own interpretive efforts when it comes to this strange and incredibly influential text.[4] To interpret the call to kill Isaac simply as a test is insufficient. The call shatters all reason: it makes no sense, especially in that God already has promised Abraham that Isaac will inherit everything. In this strangeness, the text of Genesis 22 is akin to the prose and poetry surrounding Job. The call to kill Isaac, in short, requires Abraham to respond to God as a figure of the "Law" beyond the law, a Law that defies or precedes rationality or even a basic sense of fairness or reciprocity. This figure of the Law beyond the law that Abraham must obey certainly defies any postclassical Hobbesian sense of the law as a manmade system developed to forestall violence. This Law beyond the law defies economic thought itself and marks a distinctly religious and non-Greek world of Jerusalem, a thought outside thought, something completely alien and other, something that calls but cannot be fully answered or understood.[5] Abraham is not Agamemnon called to sacrifice Iphigenia for the common good. He is called to do this alone with no one around and with no guarantee of reward for his faith or his devotion. This is a sacrifice *without* sacrifice in the sense that Abraham can exchange nothing with God. He cannot even imagine in his heart of hearts that he is doing this for something, for God, lest he refigure this call from the Law beyond the law as a rational exchange. He must respond immediately. The Hebrew term *hineni*—"Here I am"—marks this responsiveness in the text.[6] The "reason" for this call must remain a "secret" even to Abraham. Part of the horror of the episode is that he cannot speak in Genesis 22 and explain or justify his actions to Isaac or to Sara. When readers of Genesis hear about Sara again, after Mt. Moriah, they hear only of her death.

These paradoxes, as suggested, have long troubled interpreters. Philo, Tertullian, Origen, and St. John of Chrysostom all acknowledged that they were, in fact, interpreting a secret that, by definition, could not be known. Martin Luther seems to be working within this interpretive tradition when he repeatedly turns to the difficulty or impossibility of thinking about Abraham's torment, saying, "We cannot comprehend this trial."[7] Of course, most Christian thinkers ultimately resolve this paradox by reading Genesis 22 and its interpretive problems as typological prefigurations of the mystery of the Crucifixion. That is how most English cycle drama treats the strange demand. There is, however, even within this early English dramatic tradition a precedent for returning to the paradox of Genesis 22 without the consolations of Christian typology. The Towneley or Wakefield *Abraham and Isaac*, for example, can be excruciating.[8] The figure of Abraham in that play never explains himself to Isaac. He looks crazed, half-mad. And no Christian explanation covers over the horror of the episode.

The best-known and perhaps most powerful interpretation in this long history is Søren Kierkegaard's reading in *Fear and Trembling*.[9] According to Kierkegaard, this absence of any sense of exchange between Abraham and God is the critical aspect of the narrative. For Abraham truly to respond to God's demand to sacrifice Isaac, Abraham must kill Isaac without believing he will get anything in return—salvation, for example. Abraham must move toward the absolutely other, God, without any (even secret) sense of a deal having been struck. He must be a religious actor and a crazed murderer in the same instant. If he economizes in any way and allows himself to hope for a reprieve or reward because of his gesture, he is lost, since this economizing negates the otherness of the divine other and implies a level of equality between man and God. Abraham is then (almost) impossible to think in that the call from God imposes on him a seemingly impossible demand of self-emptying.

The phrase "fear and trembling," of course, comes from Paul in Philippians 2:12. Paul's readings of Abraham's life illuminate the absolute separation, the relation without relation, the nonrelation, between God and man embedded in Genesis 22. This understanding of Abraham's blindness even to himself in Genesis 22—the utter distance between God and man—partly informs a whole series of Pauline motifs perhaps more familiar to readers of Shakespeare: faith versus works, wisdom in foolishness, knowing in full versus knowing in part, seeing face to face rather through a glass darkly, living "as if" the divine presence were here, and so on.[10] In many respects, Kierkegaard's reading of Genesis 22 derives from Luther's reading, which, in turn, derived from Paul.

It is precisely this kind of Kierkegaardian figure, I want to insist, that *Richard II* seems to conjure. The play conjures this figure first as a counterpoint to the aged Gaunt and then, later, as a more favorable, if potentially comic, contrast to Gaunt's brother York. In so doing, Shakespeare is sketching an Abrahamic figure to address the paradox of sovereign violence. That is, sovereignty always implies an initial act of violence that will allow the law and some form of "justice" to emerge. But the trace of this initial sovereign violence never disappears and, in moments of exception, will manifest itself quite dramatically.[11] Nonetheless, we still dream of a sovereign figure without violence, one that will impose law and justice without force. Shakespeare, I will try to show, imagines that nonviolent sovereign figure in terms of Genesis 22 and the Kierkegaardian Abraham.

Shakespeare's attention to Genesis 22 is almost everywhere present in *Richard II*. The play opens, for example, with a king on the throne by divine right calling on a father, Old John of Gaunt, to "sacrifice" his son Henry Bolingbroke.

> Old John of Gaunt, time-honored Lancaster,
> Hast thou according to thy oath and bond
> Brought hither Henry Hereford, thy bold son,
> Here to make good the boisterous late appeal,
> Which then our leisure would not let us hear,
> Against the Duke of Norfolk, Thomas Mowbray?
> (1.1.1–6)[12]

John of Gaunt, of course, is not asked to kill his son on the spot. He is called to follow "his oath and bond" to bring "his bold son" to "make good" Bolingbroke's charge that Mowbray acted in treason. Nonetheless, like Abraham, Gaunt is called to sacrifice his son, and it is a call he answers in the affirmative. Henry IV famously gestures toward the "Holy Land" in the play's concluding lines, but this is a play that *begins* there as well, specifically on Mt. Moriah.

Let us retrace the early course of events to better see how this ancient *religious* command is embedded in the play's opening, lines that ultimately help us see the play as a whole. Gaunt presents Bolingbroke to Richard as commanded. After Richard listens to Bolingbroke and Mowbray, he tries to force some kind of reconciliation between the two, but this is a reconciliation he seems to know will fail. As he remarks when it does fail, he cannot "command" (1.1.197) any to "make . . . friends" (1.1.198). This predetermined failure at reconciliation actually just sets the stage for another predetermined show: the famous ritual (non)combat between Mowbray and Bolingbroke. Richard directs the two to fight to settle the matter, only to quickly interrupt the battle to banish Mowbray for life and Bolingbroke for ten years—long enough to guarantee that the son will never see his "old" father Gaunt again. The decision to banish initially may appear to an audience to be spontaneous on Richard's part, but Shakespeare quickly makes it clear that a decision to settle the conflict in this way was made prior to this moment.

In turn, this decision to banish initially appears well conceived and well crafted *politically* speaking. Richard can dispose of Bolingbroke, who really wants to charge Richard with the death of his uncle Gloucester (Woodstock). And Richard also can get rid of Mowbray, the man who seems directly responsible for Gloucester's death. But the politico-theological complexity of Bolingbroke's banishment manifests itself strikingly when at the moment of actual banishment Shakespeare also makes it clear that the decision to issue the banishments was made under the advice of the council, including John of Gaunt. An audience is told rather suddenly that the father participated in the decision to banish his own son.

An audience does not know exactly how or when the shared decision to banish Bolingbroke was reached. What we do know or, more importantly, what we are led to consider about Gaunt's role in the banishment of Bolingbroke is provided in an earlier scene involving Gaunt and his sister-in-law, the Duchess of Gloucester. In act 1, scene 2, immediately *before* an audience watches the interrupted combat and the crucial moment when Bolingbroke is banished, we watch as the duchess pleads with Gaunt to revenge her husband and his brother, the Duke of Gloucester (Woodstock). Gaunt refuses because

> *God's is the quarrel*; for God's substitute,
> His deputy anointed in His sight,
> Hath caused his death; the which if wrongfully
> Let heaven revenge, for I may never lift
> An angry arm against his minister.
>
> (1.2.37–41)

Gaunt's absolute deference to God, a radical obedience that is inextricably intertwined with his political understanding of kingship, prompts him to forego any revenge for his brother. In short, the dramatist makes sure that an audience sees Gaunt choosing this deference to God over family just before it views the banishment of Bolingbroke.

In inserting this short scene here, Shakespeare encourages us to assume that the legal/theological sensibility underpinning Gaunt's choice also was employed in any conversation he had with the king and the council about Bolingbroke. Bolingbroke's situation does not differ greatly from Woodstock's in that both are potentially acting "illegally" against the king and Gaunt must choose either to respect the inscrutable, unknowable divine "other" that guarantees the crown—or to respond to his family. The parallel is marked. The seemingly absolute devotion to God that prohibits Gaunt from taking the part of his own brother against the king provides the context to understand Gaunt's subsequent participation in the banishment (sacrifice) of his own son. Even more, one could say that his absolute respect for this absolute other in some sense *requires* the sacrifice of a son. It is in this sense that we can begin to see how John of Gaunt, like Abraham, is called.

At the heart of Gaunt's political theology, I am suggesting, is a commitment to an unknowable, inscrutable God, a God who guarantees the crown. And Gaunt's commitment to this "other" is measured and understood, in at least two early and distinct instances in the play, against his devotion to family. Intriguingly, Richard also initially hints at a comparable political theology involving a commitment to an absolute justice that is measured and understood against the life of a son—a son, of course, that this "sun king" does not have. When Mowbray questions the king's impartiality because of his blood relationship to Bolingbroke, Richard responds:

> Mowbray, impartial are our eyes and ears.
> Were he my brother, nay, my kingdom's heir,
> As he is but my father's brother's son,
> Now, by my scepter's awe I make a vow,
> Such neighbor nearness to our sacred blood
> Should nothing privilege him nor partialize
> The unstooping firmness of my upright soul.
>   (1.1.115–21)

Richard says that his commitment to the notion of perfect justice embodied in his kingship would outweigh his devotion to a son and heir. If called to choose between this perfect justice and his son, he would sacrifice his son.

One could argue that these stated claims made by Gaunt and Richard are purely political performances on their part designed to cover and further their own ends. But even to the extent that we are allowed to imagine Gaunt's and Richard's motivations at the beginning of the play as being purely "Machiavellian" in this way, the fact of the matter is that Shakespeare eventually shows their claims of devotion to involve profound and horrific sacrifices for both figures. Gaunt loses a son and Richard loses the crown; both losses are set in the context of their stated commitment to an absolutely other sense of justice. That is, even if we interpret both these characters as not actually believing in the political theology they espouse, their supposed willingness to honor an absolutely other sense of justice over their own family, Shakespeare makes clear through his depiction of events that their very *claims* have consequences. The issue is not the psychology of individual characters but the political theology their words sketch out for us.

Frankly, though, Shakespeare does not seem interested in depicting Machiavels whose political scheming goes awry for them. This is

Richard II, not *Richard III*. If anything, Shakespeare seems interested in exploring a much more common, everyday psyche. He seems interested in both Gaunt's and Richard's simple inability to fully embrace the politico-theological claims they make. With Richard and Gaunt Shakespeare presents us with men surprised and confused when they are actually forced to live the demands of their stated political theologies. The actual moment of Bolingbroke's banishment is telling. Gaunt breaks down completely. He simply cannot say at that moment with either political or religious equanimity—as he did about his brother Woodstock—"God's is the quarrel." Shakespeare devotes the rest of the scene to this emotional breakdown of what heretofore has been an experienced and skilled courtier.

While on some minimal reflection it seems perfectly normal and expected that Gaunt might do something more than flinch at the actual banishment, we must acknowledge that Shakespeare instead makes it clear that this breakdown should be understood as a surprise, both to Gaunt himself and to Richard. Shakespeare gives the first, critical lines to the king: "Uncle, even in the glasses of thine eyes / I see thy grieved heart" (1.3.208–9). In what could or could not be a gesture of familial mercy, Richard then immediately cuts the length of Bolingbroke's banishment from ten years to six (1.3.211–12). Gaunt initially attempts to recover the polished, reserved tone of professional diplomacy in making a dark but simple point:

> I thank my liege that in regard of me
> He shortens four years of my son's exile.
> But little vantage shall I reap thereby;
> For, ere the six years that he hath to spend
> Can change their moons and bring their times about;
> My oil-dried lamp and time-bewasted light
> Shall be extinct with age and endless night;
> My inch of taper will be burnt and done,
> And blindfold Death not let me see my son.
>
> (1.3.216–24)

But Gaunt is only partially successful at masking his feelings. He explicitly rejects both the familial form and content of Richard's gesture, a matter Richard cannot ignore. Richard replies, again, as a blood relative, seeking to reaffirm ties in this troubling and, again, to him, surprising, moment: "Why, uncle, thou has many years to live" (1.3.225). Gaunt's tone and comments sharpen noticeably, and he seems to give up any attempt at courtiership:

> But not a minute, King, that thou canst give.
> Shorten my days thou canst with sullen sorrow,
> And pluck nights from me, but not lend a morrow;
> Thou canst help Time to furrow me with age,
> But not stop no wrinkle in his pilgrimage;
> Thy word is current with him for my death,
> But dead, thy kingdom cannot buy my breath.
>
> (1.3.226–32)

Gaunt not only suggests the limitation of Richard's powers, the fact that the king may be mistaking his divinely sanctioned position with divine power itself (a matter about to become increasingly important in the play), but also suggests that Richard's banishment of Bolingbroke is somehow bringing about Gaunt's own death.

Gaunt's sharp and apparently unexpected shift in tone and topic then prompts Richard, who heretofore has been every bit as diplomatic as Gaunt, to reveal that the father actually had a hand in the decision to banish the son. Richard makes the additional point along the way that as king he is acting well within and not, as Gaunt hinted, outside the law: "Thy son is banished upon good advice, / *Whereto thy tongue a party verdict gave.* / Why at *our justice* seem'st thou then to lour?" (1.3.233–35). Richard suggests here that he and Gaunt share a comparable sense of the law and justice and perhaps a political theology. The fact that Gaunt suddenly no longer seems to share this common sense of justice is what surprises Richard. And, again, Gaunt himself seems caught off guard by his own inability to honor the "justice" crafted in council.

Gaunt does not try to conceal his part in the decision to banish Bolingbroke, nor does he try to conceal his apparent sudden and profound change of heart about that decision. On the contrary, he reveals his innermost thoughts. Indeed, at this very uncourtier-like moment, he seems incapable of doing anything but speaking his innermost thoughts, even though those truths do not paint a particularly flattering self-portrait:

> Things sweet to taste prove in digestion sour.
> You urged me as a judge, but I had rather
> You would have bid me argue like a father.
> O, had it been a stranger, not my child,
> To smooth his fault I should have been more mild.
> A partial slander sought I to avoid
> And in the sentence my own life destroyed.
> Alas, I looked when some of you should say
> I was too strict, to make mine own away;
> But you gave leave to my unwilling tongue
> Against my will to do myself this wrong.
>
> (1.3.236–46)

Shakespeare is conveying a most important piece of information here, both about Gaunt as an individual character and about the larger complexity and demands of his political theology. It seems that Gaunt, in refusing to challenge Richard's justice on the basis of an unknowable, inscrutable, impossible, perfect sense of justice ("God's is the quarrel"), *also* clearly retained a very distinct sense that the unknowable, inscrutable, impossible justice would, in fact, go his way.

That is, Gaunt's stated commitment to the absolutely other justice of God was not a Machiavellian cover but simply an all-too-human compromise. One might note that we first caught some glimpse of Gaunt's willingness to translate the otherness of God's justice in a manner that suited his own interests when he expressed his hope for "hot vengeance" for Woodstock. Here, again, we glimpse this compromised nature of Gaunt's commitment in his explanation of how he came to agree to Bolingbroke's banishment. He says that he agreed to the judgment of banishment in part to avoid the appearance of bias ("a partial slander") but that secretly he hoped his friends would save him from himself. His stated commitment to the inscrutability of God's justice ("God's is the quarrel") is, it turns out, something less than absolute:

Alas, I looked when some of you should say
I was too strict, to make mine own away;
But you gave leave to my unwilling tongue
Against my will to do myself this wrong.

                              (1.3.243–46)

I am certainly not pointing out the compromised, economizing nature of Gaunt's commitment to the distinctness of God's justice to fault
him, nor am I suggesting that Shakespeare faults him. On the contrary, it
is almost impossible to imagine someone who would not (at least secretly)
hope that his or her own self-interests would coincide with an "objective" rendering of "justice." Or, to put this another way, it is almost impossible to imagine someone who would not hope or even expect that his
or her "sacrifice" actually would be rewarded. In fact, Shakespeare wants
to draw our attention not to a flaw or weakness on Gaunt's part but to
the very normality of Gaunt's response, for no father could avoid struggling
in some way with the contradictory demands of his political/theological
commitments and his own family feeling. The point the play seems to be
dramatically realizing here is that only a truly extraordinary person could
be expected to sacrifice his son *without any sense* that his gesture would
be compensated in some form. Only someone truly extraordinary could
have the absolute and total commitment to the inscrutable laws of God
alluded to by Gaunt earlier. In short, we are led to ask two very simple
questions: What could Richard have been expecting of Gaunt at the moment of Bolingbroke's banishment that made possible such surprise?
And what was Gaunt expecting of himself at this critical moment?

On the basis of their shared and expressed commitment to an inaccessible and absolute justice, I would suggest that Richard and Gaunt are
portrayed as expecting some manifestation of that absolute faith, perhaps with Gaunt having a complete, near-divine equanimity regarding
the loss of his son. Shakespeare imagines a more dignified version of
the unhesitating zeal with which Gaunt's brother York later offers his
son Aumerle in his devotion to King Henry IV. Richard and Gaunt appear to imagine what can best be termed an "Abrahamic" ideal, a father
willing to sacrifice a son for the call of an absolute and unknowable
God. But, importantly, both of them, the play begins to suggest at this

remarkably telling moment, misrecognize the *absoluteness* of this demand to the otherness of the Law beyond the law. Gaunt mistakenly conceives of that "otherness" as ultimately coinciding with his own self-interests, his own love for Bolingbroke. He does not fully understand that such a commitment actually can take a son and what that would feel like.

Similarly, we begin to see here that the sonless "sun king" does not fully understand that a true commitment to the absolute justice that guarantees the crown might entail the loss of the throne itself. It is, in fact, what I would call Gaunt's transformative Abrahamic experience that provides the audience with a new vantage point from which to see and engage the king and the king's claimed devotion to this "other" justice that is distinct from his own familial feeling, his own self. Gaunt becomes a "prophet new inspired" (2.1.31). As a new prophet, infused with a certain after-the-fact fear and trembling, a certain after-the-fact awe and respect for the absolute otherness of the God that guarantees the crown, Gaunt can see that Richard II, too, lacks sufficient respect for this alterity. Like Gaunt *before* the banishment of Bolingbroke, Richard still believes that that otherness coincides with his self-interests; indeed, Richard famously believes that that otherness coincides with his very being. In some sense, Richard believes he embodies this divine alterity. It is at this point that Gaunt begins charging Richard with conquering England "itself" (2.1.65), suggesting that Richard has become the "Landlord of England . . . now, not king / Thy state of law is bondslave to the Law" (2.1.113–14).[13] This last remark infuriates Richard II (2.1.115) and begins to shatter his diplomatic facade.

As a prophet Gaunt sees clearly what Richard does not: that a monarch is not equivalent to the "Law beyond the law" and that clinging to such a notion will bring disaster. But just because Shakespeare's "prophet" sees this impending disaster we should not assume, as so many have, that the playwright is then advocating or embracing a secular realpolitik on the historical horizon. Despite his recognition of the flaws in Richard's understanding of divine right theory, Shakespeare does not seem ready to separate the religious from the political altogether. The clear suggestion of the play's opening acts is *not* that the crown is utterly divorced from the divine but that Richard II has misconstrued the relationship of the crown to the divine. Hence, I think, the oft-noted sympathy Shakespeare generates for Richard, particularly in the deposition scene and then in the concluding scenes. The dramatic suggestion is not that there is no divine relation to the crown but that Richard wildly has overestimated the access he has to the divine. Gaunt's experience reveals that neither Gaunt nor Richard has sufficient respect for the absolute otherness of the "Law beyond the law" that legitimates monarchical power.

Correspondingly, Shakespeare begins to suggest through Gaunt's "prophecy" that a monarch should rule with a certain religious fear and trembling, a certain awe and unease with relation to the inscrutable, unknowable "other" that provides the throne.[14] A monarch is guaranteed nothing, has no deal with God, no particular access to God or God's quarrels. A true and absolute commitment to the "Law beyond the law" requires, *pace* Kierkegaard, an Abrahamic willingness to respond to that Law without expecting anything in return, a willingness to give oneself up and over to that Law without the slightest attention to self-interests, a willingness to give oneself up and over even if that costs one everything.

But how does one figure a sovereign so utterly willing to give himself up and over in fear and trembling, a sovereign who is in one sense so utterly submissive yet still, in some sense, sovereign? In short, a dramatic and political challenge emerges once Shakespeare stages Gaunt's Abrahamic transformation, a transformation that involves a self-critique and a ringing critique of Richard II: If the problem for both Gaunt and Richard is that they both misrecognize the absoluteness of the demand to respect the otherness of the "Law beyond the law," then how does one stage an appropriately contrasting figure? How does one begin to sketch a monarchical presence that has the requisite fear—and who also trembles?

Before Richard is deposed and cedes the crown to Bolingbroke, he gives authority to Gaunt's brother York. While recent criticism tends not to address the issue as terribly significant, it is in part Richard's willingness to use York as a proxy during his military excursion in Ireland that brings about his deposition. York facilitates the passing of the crown to Bolingbroke, and this is critical for tracing the Abrahamic influences on Shakespeare's political theology (2.1.220). Criticism has concentrated mainly on York's age, his weaknesses, and, ultimately, his role as some sort of comic relief rather than his role as pivotal political figure.[15] And

York certainly is old, weak, doddering, palsied, and, generically speaking, an altogether complicated figure. But to understand fully York's age, feebleness, and generic complexity we need to resituate him in the Abrahamic context that seems to govern the play's thought. In Abrahamic terms, York becomes a much more serious figure, a lens through which we can see Shakespeare's political theology.

When Gaunt dies York assumes the role of Richard's chief critic. York's initial criticism is prompted by Richard's plans to seize Gaunt's lands to help fund the war in Ireland. York reiterates much of his brother's critique, explaining simply that Richard II cannot break the Law that guarantees his own crown without risking the crown itself:

> Take Hereford's rights away, and take from Time
> His charters and his customary rights;
> Let not tomorrow then ensue today;
> Be not thyself; for how art thou a king
> But by fair sequence and succession?
>
> (2.1.195–99)

Failure to attend to that Law beyond the law, York prophesies, will "pluck a thousand dangers" on the king's head. And, on a more personal note, such inattention will "prick [York's] tender patience to those thoughts / Which honour and allegiance cannot think" (2.1.207–8).

But York is not the savvy and articulate courtier that Gaunt was, and his criticisms, not surprisingly, lack the sharpness of Gaunt's final speeches. Simply put, York is a less threatening political player for Richard. And it is this supposed weakness, many assume, that leads Richard to name York as governor in his absence immediately after York has warned that Richard's actions will lead him to think thoughts "which honour and allegiance cannot think" (2.1.208). The tendency is to read this as a suggestion that Richard simply does not take York's concerns or doubts seriously. Ultimately, this inattention or undervaluation may have been a political mistake on Richard's part, so, to the extent his decision has anything to do with his loss of the crown, it is considered, yet again, the king's poor decision making that matters here and not York's character.

If, however, we begin to consider the possibility that Shakespeare is mapping out an Abrahamic kingship in response to Richard's divine right theory, then York's appointment deserves more attention. In selecting York as governor, Richard II is not just making a calculated political decision. Richard is, in fact, giving the crown to the "just" person in terms of the utter selflessness already sketched out as a prerequisite for managing the royal prerogative: "Our uncle York Lord Governor of England, / For he is just and always loved us well" (2.1.220–21). York may not be a shrewd statesman or a commanding presence, but he embodies the devotion to the divine "Law beyond the law" that both Richard and Gaunt incorrectly assumed they possessed. If I am correct that Gaunt became aware that his commitment to the "Law beyond the law" was less than absolute only at the banishment of Bolingbroke, and that Richard still mistakenly assumes that his own being corresponds to this unknowable "Law beyond the law," then York stands out as a stark contrast to both in that his respect for the otherness of the Law beyond the law is unquestionably absolute. Consequently, we can speculate that Shakespeare imagines more at work than one would initially assume in this temporary transfer of power. In short, York figures the weak sovereign that helps Shakespeare resolve the dramatic and political paradox that Gaunt's Abrahamic critique of Richard produced. In York, Shakespeare comes to dramatic terms with the impossible demands of the royal prerogative, the demand that a monarch simultaneously use exceptional sovereign power and utterly abandon his self-interests.

Shakespeare clearly marks York as an "Abraham." Despite his frustration with Richard II, York notably accepts Richard's command to become governor without question. Speaking to the queen as he accepts his new role, York says:

Your husband, he is gone to save far off,
Whilst others come to make him lose at home.
Here am I left to underprop his land,
Who, weak with age, cannot support myself.
Now comes the sick hour that his surfeit made;
Now shall he try his friends that flattered him.
(2.2.80–85; italics added)

"Here I am" (*hineni*), the famous response of Abraham to God in Genesis 22, here marks York—as does his unquestioning obedience to authority. York, it starts to become clear, possesses Gaunt's only recently acquired Abrahamic understanding. Even more, one could say York embodies the significance of Abraham in Shakespeare's imagination.

Like Abraham, York is neither heroic nor tragic, but "neuter." In 2.3, when Bolingbroke arrives back in England, York sternly rebukes Bolingbroke for his "rebellion," just as Gaunt ruled against Bolingbroke's challenge to the king via Mowbray. But Bolingbroke does not give up on gaining some kind of support from York. Bolingbroke's manner of doing so is very intriguing. He calls York his father and asks him if he, like his true father, would sacrifice his own son in this situation.

> You are my father, for methinks in you
> I see old Gaunt alive. O, then, my father,
> Will you permit that I shall stand condemned
> A wandering vagabond, my rights and royalties
> Plucked from my arms perforce and given away
> To upstart unthrifts? Wherefore was I born?
> (2.3.117–22)

We need to keep in mind here that in Genesis 22 Isaac was also the heir to everything Abraham had earned, so his loss was not just emotional and familial but tied to property.

Bolingbroke then makes this even more personal, asking York about his own son Aumerle:

> You have a son, Aumerle, my noble cousin;
> Had you first died, and he been thus trod down,
> He should have found his uncle Gaunt a father
> To rouse his wrongs and chase him to the bay.
> (2.3.125–28)

In effect, Bolingbroke asks what York would want to have happen to his son in this situation, a question York will answer rather emphatically in act 5.[16]

York is the mysterious means by which the crown will pass from Richard to Henry IV in a legitimate fashion. York prevents this transfer of power from reducing kingship to a mere power struggle. Like his brother Gaunt earlier, York remains steadfast in his commitment to Law:

> My lords of England, let me tell you this:
> I have had feeling of my cousin's wrongs
> And labored all I could to do him right:
> But in this kind to come, in braving arms,
> Be his own carver, and cut out his way
> To find out right with wrong—it may not be;
> And you that do abet him in this kind
> Cherish rebellion and are rebels all.
>
> (2.3.140–47)

But York is in a weak position and he could not resist Bolingbroke and his supporters even if he zealously wished to do so. Thus he finds himself in the role in which Bolingbroke sought to put him at the beginning of their conversation: *a gracious uncle.* York is torn between his commitment to Law (grace, his title and responsibilities) and his family bond. Like Abraham, York is hopelessly caught in a contradiction, able only to respond, "Here am I." He "welcomes" them neither as friends nor foes (2.3.170).

York does help Bolingbroke capture Bushy, Bagot, and Green—"the caterpillars of the commonwealth"—but his support for Bolingbroke remains carefully measured throughout. Even when we hear that York has "joined with Bolingbroke" (3.2.200), Shakespeare depicts the tension, not the harmony, in this critical union. York reminds Northumberland to respect the crown and refer to Richard as King Richard: "It would beseem the Lord Northumberland / To say 'King Richard.' Alack the heavy day / When such a sacred king should hide his head!" (3.3.7–9). Bolingbroke, in fact, has to remind York not to express too much sympathy for Richard: "Mistake not, uncle, further than you should" (3.3.15). York, in turn, cautions Bolingbroke, reiterating Gaunt's initial concern that anyone claim or even assume access to the divine that would guarantee the throne: "Take not, good cousin, further than you should, / Lest you mistake the heavens are over our heads" (3.3.16–17). What York is pressing for is an Abrahamic model of kingship that is almost impossible to realize. He wants a sovereign who moves toward the crown with a certain respect, a fear and trembling for what the "heavens" think about all this. Importantly, Henry IV accepts this model: "I know it, uncle, and oppose not myself / Against their will" (3.3.18–19). It is a mistake, I think, to contemplate Bolingbroke's movement toward the crown without taking this partnership with the distinctly Abrahamic York into account.

While no one, to my knowledge, has discussed these biblical allusions before, I cannot say that is because Shakespeare is particularly subtle about the matter. In act 4 Bolingbroke announces the death of Norfolk, saying, "Sweet peace conduct his sweet soul to the bosom / Of good old Abraham!" (4.1.104–5). Upon conjuring the image of "good old Abraham"—a still familiar dramatic presence to an Elizabethan audience—stage directions call for the entrance of York, who, importantly, announces that Bolingbroke is now the king. In this play, Abraham and the Abrahamic willingness to give absolutely are intimately linked to divine and righteous kingship.

These pronouncements precede the famous mirror-breaking scene and Richard's relinquishing the crown. Richard's loss of the crown prompts York's son, Aumerle, to plot against the new king. After Richard II has been parted from his wife and sent to the tower, Aumerle appears in the home of his mother and father, the Duke and Duchess of York, where his father discovers his son's treason and rushes to Henry IV to have his son condemned as a traitor. Aumerle's mother, the Duchess of York, struggles to stop her husband, but York is more impaired by his inability to get his boots on. This scene leads to an even stranger and potentially comic scene wherein the king forgives Aumerle, only to endure one parent pleading for his son's death and another pleading for his life.

The scene is utterly Shakespeare's creation, and, in the context of this play, many have found it utterly bizarre, comic, or farcical, out of place with the rest of what is a solemn play, and very often it has been cut; it has been called, among other things, "geriatric slapstick."[17] Phyllis Rackin's response is rather common in criticism disconnected from religious sensibilities: "What we have here is not simply a comic interlude in a serious play but a degradation of serious characters and serious action to comic status, and that degradation marks a crucial stage in the affective process the play orchestrates for his audience."[18] What the playwright is doing with this scene, Rackin suggests, is turning audience sympathy from York:

> His zealous efforts to have his own son condemned to death are grotesque rather than comfortably funny. As long as Richard held the throne and York remained torn by loyalties divided between the old king and the usurper, his character remained sympathetic even when his behavior was comic; we could laugh lovingly at a gently comic representation of our own emotional predicament in the face of the dilemma the play represents. However, once Bolingbroke becomes king, York becomes a caricature, a moral automaton who carries his new allegiance to such absurd lengths that we can no longer sympathize with him or it. We repudiate York, and in so doing we also repudiate whatever allegiance we have paid to Bolingbroke; for the single-minded and irrational lengths to which York carries his loyalty to the new king discredit his cause by unwitting parody.[19]

But when one attends to the context of Genesis 22 it becomes clear that the strange scene reveals Shakespeare's engagement with the story of Abraham and Isaac that has organized the whole play and his political theology.[20] This is no degradation, in short, but an effort to point an audience toward the most affectively moving dramatic scene in the cycle tradition so that an audience can track the difficult, torn emotions the deposition of Richard elicits to a familiar biblical source.

In act 5, scene 2, the duke is describing to the duchess Bolingbroke's arrival in London as the newly crowned Henry IV and Richard's departure. York makes clear, again, that he is given over to the "Law beyond the law" that makes the king:

> Heaven hath a hand in these events,
> To whose high will we bound our calm contents.
> To Bolingbroke are we sworn subjects now,
> Whose state and honor I for aye allow.
> (5.2.37–40)

The duchess announces Aumerle's entrance: "Here comes my son Aumerle." York responds:

> Aumerle that was.
> But that is lost for being Richard's friend.
> And, madame, you must call him Rutland now.
> I am in parliament pledge for his truth
> And lasting fealty to the new-made king.
>
> (5.2.41–45)

The mother responds to a familial role, the father to a public.

In dealing with the paradox of the Law beyond the law, Shakespeare engages the religious in the dramatic form he knew best: the religious cycle plays. The crucial role of the Duchess of York in this scene might obscure somewhat the possibility that this is in many respects, perhaps, a borrowing straight from the cycle play tradition. Very few of the extant medieval cycle play versions of *Abraham and Isaac* portray Sara or even refer to her. But there is one that, tellingly, does depict Sara: the Northampton cycle (formerly known as the Dublin). In it Sara appears only briefly, but that brief appearance is important for act 5, scene 2, in *Richard II* in that her role clearly links the play in the figure of the Duchess of York to the long interpretive history of Genesis 22.[21] In the Norththampton play, Abraham returns from his encounter with, not God, but an angel, calling for Isaac's sacrifice. Sara greets him fondly with Isaac ("her dear son") at her side. Abraham immediately tells Sara that he has to go to sacrifice. Then he turns to his servants to prepare his transportation:

> And, therefore, sirs, maketh mine ass ready,
> And Isaac, son, thou never yet me saw
> Do no such observance,
> Therefore array thee and go with me,
> And learn how God should pleased be:
> For, son, and ever thou think to thee,
> Put ever God to honourance.[22]

Isaac immediately agrees, but Sara, not surprisingly, objects, quite vehemently:

Yea! But I pray you, gentle fere,
As ever you have love me deare,
Let Isaac abide at home here,
For I kept not he went in the wind.

"Peace, dame, let be!" Abraham yells. "Do way!" he says to this interference. He tells her that the child needs to know "how God should be pleased." Realizing she can't stop Abraham, Sara turns her attention to the servants, insisting that his horse be well trained and that Isaac suffer no unnecessary indignities on the journey. The Northhampton Abraham has to recapture the attention of the servants in this moment: "Get hither our horses and let us go hen. . . . Leapeth up! Have do, anon!" We are not sure how this is staged, whether the servants are diligently going about their business and only moderately distracted by Sara or whether her elaborate attentions to Isaac's comforts are holding up the trip. Either way, though, the scene corresponds rather strikingly to York's clumsy efforts to get his boots on and to the way his servant must fend off the duchess to get his job done.

What is especially telling about this (potential) dramatic borrowing, I think, is that Shakespeare chose to stage this particular "play within the play" in front of his version of the newly crowned monarch: Henry IV. In so doing, Shakespeare hints that *Abraham and Isaac* is the play every monarch should watch or consider. Paradoxically, however, the strange and seemingly comic manner in which he inserts this episode into his otherwise solemn drama also reminds us, per the interpretive history of Genesis 22, that this is the play no monarch should understand or interpret.[23] Shakespeare's Henry IV recognizes that a different play is being staged in front of him when York and the duchess approach, but, as various source studies have often noted, he gives this minidrama a title that does not really fit: "Our scene is alt'red from a serious thing, / and now chang'd to the 'Beggar and the King'" (5.3.79–80).[24]

Given all the prefatory Abrahamic allusions, one must assume that an early modern audience would have had a better sense of what the king was watching than he did. I am suggesting that a knowing audience watches as the king utterly misrecognizes the play he is in. This is to Shakespeare's purpose. To presume to interpret *Abraham and Isaac* is to presume the same access to the absolutely other presumed by Gaunt and Richard. Genesis 22, as Luther and so many others understood, must be observed but cannot be comprehended. To respond wisely and properly to *Abraham and Isaac*, Henry IV can only embrace this unreadable scene as he does here: that is, he can only respond to it as a piece of foolishness. And an audience would recognize his ultimately patient response to the duchess and her repeated demands to say "pardon" as an appropriate response to a certain Pauline foolishness (1 Cor. 1:25). The duchess insists that the king pardon her son Aumerle, but this is impossible: he has already pardoned Aumerle in exchange for Aumerle's future loyalty. He does not have the capacity the duchess imagines he does to forgive absolutely or, strictly speaking, to forgive in any sense; he already has done so. Still, at her insistence, Henry IV acts *as if* he does pardon Aumerle, he says his lines, he plays his part without any presumption that he has any relationship to the part she ultimately seeks to give him: that of a "god on earth" (5.3.136). In this "farcical" short play, then, we see a model of Abrahamic kingship. This king has a relation to the divine that is, in fact, a nonrelation. Henry IV acts as a divine sovereign in granting this pardon without any hint of having the actual proximity to the divine that tormented and confused Richard.

Work out your salvation in fear and trembling, Paul writes, without knowing or presuming that your work will be sufficient for God. Many, like Kierkegaard, have taken this admonition so far as to mean that one cannot even presume God. How is this possible? How are we to imagine a figure willing to respond to God *without* responding, without believing even in secret that he will receive anything in return, without believing in secret that he has some special relation to the divine? Harder still, how are we to imagine a divinely sanctioned monarch who will adhere to this admonition to move toward God in fear and trembling without any sense that he is supposed to be a "god on earth"? Richard could not accept that when he looked rather darkly into a glass he could not find a trace of the divine—only his own image (1 Cor. 13). In contrast, Henry seems to tolerate a mirror image, the distance between himself and the divine.

In the famous mirror-breaking scene it is Henry that—in an unusual moment of philosophizing or theological reflection—reminds Richard of the limits of the mirror.

> *Richard:* Mark, silent King, the moral of this sport:
> How soon my sorrow hath destroyed my face.
> *Bolingbroke:* The shadow of your sorrow hath destroyed
> The shadow of your face.
>
> (4.1.291–94)

Even Richard is forced to acknowledge the truth of this observation, that one does not yet see "face to face," and he is somewhat surprised at Henry's theological astuteness: "Say that again. / The shadow of my sorrow? Ha! Let's see. / 'Tis very true" (4.1.294–96). In brief, in the scene with the Duke and Duchess of York, Henry IV plays his role as "god on earth," the God in the *Abraham and Isaac* play who will ultimately pardon Isaac, but he has no sense that his actions in this play are divinely inspired. In fact, Shakespeare's rendering makes it impossible for him in the context of the scene to even think of his actions as such.

The pronouncement of the Duchess of York, then, that Henry is "god on earth," means nothing; it is, as so many have noted, a farce. Yet it *also* means everything, as it directs us toward the ideal sovereign figure who acts without acting, without knowing or believing—even in secret— that he is somehow tethered to the divine. The narrative that helps us understand this divine nonrelation is not the "king's two bodies" but Genesis 22. In insisting on reading the scene only as farce, disconnected from serious religious content, Rackin fails to see that the pronouncement by the duchess corresponds to the more general argument made in *Stages of History* that in the history plays women must authorize male rule: "Before the masculine voice of history can be accepted as valid, it must come to terms with women and the subversive forces they represent."[25]

I want to conclude, however, not with a theoretical flourish, but with an attempt to show the correspondence between this kind of theorizing and a more distinctly "historical" scholarship. The historian Paul E. J. Hammer, reexamining the famous production of the play by the Lord Chamberlain's Men's on February 7, 1601, the afternoon before the

so-called Essex Rising against Queen Elizabeth I, suggests that Shakespearean criticism has been correct in not choosing too hastily between a
secular, republican, pro-Bolingbroke *Richard II* and a medieval, religious,
monarchical pro-Richard *Richard II.*[26] Hammer does not point to Genesis
22, but he does suggest an immediate historical context in which my reading of Abraham's sacrifice beyond sacrifice makes sense. That is, what he
has to say about very specific events in 1601 suggests that an Elizabethan
audience would have understood *Richard II* in just such sacrificial terms.

The fact that many of Essex's supporters commissioned this particular play on that particular afternoon has suggested to many that the
play inspires rebellion and antimonarchical sentiments. But according to
Hammer, Essex and his men were distinctly not trying to launch a coup
d'état on February 8; on the contrary, they were trying to stage an "aristocratic intervention" to petition the queen to arrest Essex's "enemies
on charges of treason and corruption."[27] The form of this intervention
comes straight out of *The State of Christendom* (1594), a political manuscript that describes the means to "humbly" petition a monarch while
showing "proper reverence for the sovereign."[28]

The play functioned, then, Hammer concludes, as something of a
negative example for Essex's supporters in that the play shows how difficult, if not impossible, it can be to approach the monarch with such a petition *without* ultimately enacting some kind of violence toward the notion
of sovereignty connected to the crown: "If Essex was indeed to become a
Bolingbroke in the strictly limited sense of moving against men whom he
and his friends judged to be latter-day 'caterpillars of the commonwealth,'
one message intended by this performance was surely that Essex—unlike
his ancestor Bolingbroke—in 1399 would do it *properly.*"[29] If this is true,
we can say that the play manifested for an (at least aristocratic) early modern audience both a profound respect for the absolute and divine nature
of sovereignty as invested in the crown and a highly sophisticated awareness of the dangers of presuming some access to the source of that sovereignty. Implied in this historical contextualizing is the notion that true (or
proper) respect for sovereignty actually must involve the risk of violence
to be true and legitimate: other, easier displays of loyalty might involve the
sort of political calculation being contested ("caterpillars"). Henry IV, of
course, despite all his efforts to not do violence to Richard, ends the play

wanting to wash blood from his "guilty hand," thinking himself in some sense both a righteous king (and father) and a murderer.

Moreover, demonstrating this true or proper respect for divine sovereignty also requires that the petitioner expose him- or herself to potentially extraordinary sacrifices. Hammer suggests that Essex, an unusually good and experienced military commander, came to London in a "pitifully ineffective" military posture in part because he was displaying a willingness to make just such a sacrifice, not mount a violent attack. One term for this sort of gesture, I am suggesting, one that has been understood and embraced for thousand of years—although ignored almost entirely in our determination to render a secular Shakespeare—is the Abrahamic.

Notes

1. The term *political theology* derives mainly from the writings of Carl Schmitt, *Political Theology: Four Chapters on the Concept of Sovereignty*, trans. George Schwab (Cambridge, MA: MIT Press, 1985). For the most sophisticated account of political theology in early modern literary studies, see Julia Reinhard Lupton, *Citizen-Saints: Shakespeare and Political Theology* (Chicago: University of Chicago Press, 2005).

2. The *locus classicus* for the "king's two bodies" is Ernst H. Kantorowicz's *The King's Two Bodies in Mediaeval Political Theology* (Princeton: Princeton University Press, 1957). On the concept of "king-in-parliament" and its relationship to Shakespeare in particular, see Edna Zwick Boris, *Shakespeare's English Kings, the People, and the Law* (London: Associate University Presses, 1978).

3. For a good, concise review of issues in *Richard II* criticism, see R. Morgan Griffin, "The Critical History of *Richard II*," in *Critical Essays on Shakespeare's "Richard II,"* ed. Kirby Farrell (New York: G. K. Hall, 1999).

4. For a lucid review of the interpretive history of Genesis 22, see Carol Delaney, *Abraham on Trial: The Social Legacy of Biblical Myth* (Princeton: Princeton University Press, 1998).

5. The interpretive history of Genesis 22 is critical for Jacques Derrida and his attention to "otherness" that has informed so much of literary critical theory in the last fifty years. A trajectory of concern can be traced from his initial 1963 response to Emmanuel Levinas, most commonly read in "Violence and Metaphysics: An Essay on the Thought of Emmanuel Levinas," in *Writing and*

Difference, trans. Alan Bass (Chicago: University of Chicago Press, 1978), 79–153, to *The Gift of Death*, trans. David Wills (Chicago: University of Chicago Press, 1995), where Derrida discusses Genesis 22 in great detail.

6. For a discussion of "hineni" and how it relates to Continental philosophy, see Hilary Putnam, "Levinas and Judaism," in *The Cambridge Companion to Levinas*, ed. Simon Critchley and Robert Bernasconi (Cambridge: Cambridge University Press, 2002), 33–62.

7. Martin Luther, *Lectures on Genesis Chapters 21–25*, vol. 4 of *Luther's Works*, ed. Jaroslav Pelikan (St. Louis, MO: Concordia, 1961), 428.

8. *The Wakefield Mystery Plays*, ed. Martial Rose (New York: Norton, 1961). See, too, Edgar Schell, "The Distinctions of the Towneley Abraham," *Modern Language Quarterly* 41, no. 4 (1980): 315–27.

9. Søren Kierkegaard, *Fear and Trembling/Repetition*, vol. 6 of *Kierkegaard's Writings*, ed. and trans. Howard V. Hong and Edna H. Hong (Princeton: Princeton University Press, 1983).

10. Studies of Paul are many and varied. See, in particular, Gunther Bornkamm, *Paul*, trans. M. G. Stalker (Minneapolis: Fortress Press, 1995). See also Gregory Kneidel, *Rethinking the Turn to Religion in Early Modern English Literature: The Poetics of All Believers* (New York: Palgrave, 2008). Kneidel usefully reinvigorates the work of John S. Coolidge, *The Pauline Renaissance in England: Puritanism and the Bible* (Oxford: Oxford University Press, 1970).

11. Walter Benjamin, "The Critique of Violence," trans. Edmund Jephcott, in *Reflections: Essays, Aphorisms, Autobiographical Writings*, ed. Peter Demetz (New York: Schocken Books, 1986), 275–305. See also Jacques Derrida, "Force of Law: The Mystical Foundation of Authority" in *Acts of Religion*, ed. Gil Anidjar (New York: Routledge, 2001), 228–98. On the way constituting violence appears in "exceptional" situations, see Giorgio Agamben, *State of Exception*, trans. Kevin Attell (Chicago: University of Chicago Press, 2005).

12. All quotations from *Richard II* are from *The Complete Works of Shakespeare*, 4th ed., ed. David Bevington (New York: Longmann, 1997).

13. On these critical lines, see Donna Hamilton, "The State of Law in *Richard II*," *Shakespeare Quarterly* 34, no. 1 (1983): 5–17.

14. On the play's prophecies, see Henry E. Jacobs, "Prophecy and Ideology in Shakespeare's *Richard II*," *South Atlantic Review* 51, no. 1 (1986): 3–17.

15. For serious and substantial considerations of York, see Sharon Cadman Seelig, "Loyal Fathers and Treacherous Sons: Familial Politics in *Richard II*," and Sheldon P. Zitner, "Aumerle's Conspiracy," both in Farrell, *Critical Essays*, 154–71 and 171–89 respectively.

16. I would compare and contrast this moment with the opening act of *Titus Andronicus*, when Titus "answers" Tamara's plea for empathy ("O, if to

fight for king and commonweal / Were piety in thine [his sons], it is in these [her sons]" [1.1.114–15]) by unhesitatingly slaying Mutius when the boy comes between Titus and his commitment, not to God, but to the Roman state. See my "'Here Aaron Is': Abraham and the Abrahamic in *Titus Andronicus*," in *Cultural Encounters between East and West, 1453–1699*, ed. Matthew Birchwood and Matthew Dimmock (London: Cambridge Scholars Press, 2005), 145–67.

17. Zitner, "Aumerle's Conspiracy," 172–77.

18. Phyllis Rackin, "The Role of Audience in Shakespeare's *Richard II*," *Shakespeare Quarterly* 36, no. 3 (1985): 262–81, 275.

19. Ibid., 279.

20. Astute critics, such as Harry Berger, have noted the connection to earlier, more serious moments in the play: "The York/Aumerle episode, which ends in doggerelized comedy, is a compressed caricature, a skewed icon, of the Gaunt/Bolingbroke interaction. York screams for his son's death, while Gaunt reluctantly consents to his son's banishment." Harry Berger, "*Ars Moriendi* in Progress, or John of Gaunt and the Practice of Strategic Dying," in Farrell, *Critical Essays*, 238.

21. Six of the eight extant versions of *Abraham and Isaac*, including the Northampton/Dublin, are usefully printed together for comparison in R. T. Davies, *The Corpus Christi Play of the English Middle Ages* (Totowa, NJ: Rowman and Littlefield, 1972): 375–441.

22. Ibid., 410.

23. See Erich Auerbach, *Mimesis: The Representation of Reality in Western Literature*, trans. Willard R. Trask (Princeton: Princeton University Press, 1953). Auerbach uses Genesis 22 as one exemplar of the "two kinds of style" in Western literature, the other being the scene involving Odysseus's scar. "On the one hand fully externalized description, uniform illumination, uninterrupted connection, free expression, all events in the foreground, displaying unmistakable meanings, few elements of historical development and psychological perspective; on the other hand, certain parts brought into high relief, others left obscure, abruptness, suggestive influence of the unexpressed, 'background' quality, multiplicity of meanings and the need for interpretation, universal-historical claims, development of the concept of historically becoming, and preoccupation with the problematic" (23).

24. The reference is probably to "King Cophetua and the Beggar Maid," a ballad that does depict a beggar mother pleading with a king for charity for children. But the real focus of the ballad is the king's love for the maid. Shakespeare alluded to this ballad in *Romeo and Juliet* and *Love's Labour's Lost* as well.

25. Phyllis Rackin, *Stages of History: Shakespeare's English Chronicles* (Ithaca: Cornell University Press, 1991), 148.

26. Paul E. J. Hammer, "Shakespeare's *Richard II*, the Play of 7 February 1601, and the Essex Rising," *Shakespeare Quarterly* 59, no. 1 (2008): 1–35.

27. Ibid., 16, 11.

28. Ibid., 12.

29. Ibid., 34.

Chapter 10

Penitential Ethics in *Measure for Measure*

JAMES A. KNAPP

All difficulties are but easy when they are known.
—*Measure for Measure*, 4.2.204–5

Even before the play had begun, the very title of Shakespeare's *Measure for Measure* would have given its first audiences a reference point for the subsequent action: Jesus's words of caution in the Sermon on the Mount, "Judge not that ye be not judged, for with what judgment ye judge, ye shall be judged, and with what measure ye mete, it shall be measured to you again" (Matt. 7:1–2).[1] As the scriptural reference suggests, the play's ostensible theme is "proper judgment," and its extension, *justice*, especially insofar as the notion of justice pertains to the relation of the individual to the state. Moreover, this theme is placed squarely in the context of religious debate—specifically politico-theological debate—highlighted by the reference to the Sermon. The play's commentary on the state/subject dyad has been given serious consideration in important recent work on Shakespeare and political theology, notably that of Debora Shuger and Julia Reinhard Lupton.[2] Such work extends a long line of commentary about the play's position on religion's role in the sovereign's delivery of good rule and the application of law.[3] Specifically, recent work addresses how *Measure for Measure* might help clarify what early moderns saw as the proper balance between the application of earthly justice (the law of the world) and the distribution of mercy with its deferral of judgment to eternal justice (the eternal judgment of souls that is always to come).

For the present discussion, I seek to build on such critical discussions of political theology centered on historical debates by turning explicitly to the philosophical and spiritual (religious) questions that underlie early modern debates over political theology—questions that emerge from Shakespeare's engagement with ethics in *Measure for Measure* from the point of view of a dramaturge rather than a churchman or moral philosopher. My aim here is not to adjudicate the debate over Shakespeare's confession—judging the relative compatibility of his dramatic representation with Calvinist, Lutheran, or Roman Catholic theology—but rather to examine his treatment of ethics in the context of the swirl of theological and philosophical debate resulting from a century of Renaissance and Reformation. To isolate the theologico-philosophical questions raised by Shakespeare's play, I will focus rather narrowly on the temporal dimension of ethics as just action: the fact that action always precedes judgment, or to put it in slightly different terms, that judgment is always retrospective, while action is always future directed, always involved in the process of becoming. This temporal problem at the heart of ethics is also at the center of the scriptural source from which Shakespeare takes his title: for Jesus's cautionary advice to "judge not *that ye be not* judged" places judgment (of another's past action) in the context of one's own future judgment at the hands of another (ultimately the absolutely Other, God).

In what follows, I specifically focus on the ways in which *Measure for Measure* addresses the issue of ethical temporality by contrasting the visible and the invisible, through the play's emphasis on form and figurality. As Lisa Freinkel notes, "Judgment is only possible on the basis of comparison—what is alien is not familiar, what is new is not old."[4] In the context of the debate over the place of ethics in earthly and eternal justice, the basis of comparison is complicated by the paradox of Christian mystery: if we know the new by comparing it to what it is not (the old), then how can we accept Christ's claim in the Sermon on the Mount: "Think not that I am come to destroy the law, or the prophets: I am not come to destroy them, but to fulfill them" (Matt. 5:17). The answer, variously expressed by Christian authorities from St. Paul to Luther, is that what is being compared is comparable not in fact but only in figure. Take, for example, Paul's famous comparison in 1 Corinthians: "When I was a child, I spake as a child, I understood as a child, I thought as a child: but when I became a man, I put away childish things. For now we see through a glass darkly; but then *shall we see* face to face: now I know in part; but then shall I know even as I am known" (13:11–12). The comparison of "seeing then" to "seeing now" is incomprehensible without temporality. The difference between the two forms of vision is generated by their separation in time; unlike comparing two paintings side by side, the comparison of then and now is not simply a matter of the differences and similarities between two visual fields, it is also contingent upon the intervention of time in the process of perception. Moreover, while the comparison of childhood and adulthood offers an accessible illustration of the relational difference between developing and mature human understanding, the point of the passage is to inspire belief in that which cannot be known: what it will be like to be face to face with God.

In fact the concept of "being face to face with God" is a wholly material and intensely visual conceptualization of salvation, a future state that is unavailable to visual experience.[5] The incongruous comparison here is none other than allegory: human coming of age as an allegory of spiritual salvation. And in this way the problem of bridging the gap between Old Testament Law and New Testament Love melts away into the contours of figurality. But it does so in a formally specific manner that is important to the current consideration of ethics in *Measure for Measure*. As Freinkel points out, Paul's allegorical treatment of the relation of the old and new relies on a figure of chiasmus, which is further developed by Augustine in his articulation of Paul's revelation: "In the Old Testament there is a concealment of the New, in the New Testament there is a revelation of the Old."[6] Augustine's employment of chiasmus, what would become one of Shakespeare's favorite figures, appears to be no solution at all, as it "turns temporal difference back upon itself. Repetition becomes inversion and inversion takes us back to where we started."[7] But as Freinkel observes, "This suspension is, ultimately, an illusion—if only because of language's temporal dimension: AB comes before BA. Indeed, chiasmus relies upon the fact of this temporality, for it is only insofar as chiasmus enforces a revision . . . that the trope avoids tautology, yielding instead a sense of development: we feel we have *gotten somewhere*. In this way chiasmus, we might argue, is the trope built out of that recursive movement essential to construing linear syntax: its repetitions enforce rereadings—we double back and thus move forward."[8]

The thrust of my argument here is that Shakespeare dramatizes how a penitential comportment toward the ethical overcomes moral dogmatism at the same time that it complicates the demand that ethical experience poses to the subject. Shakespeare's dramatization of Angelo's and Isabella's movement toward penitential ethics relies on precisely the kind of opportunity that Freinkel identifies with "language's temporal dimension": the invitation to "double back and thus move forward" in the course of one's experience of the play. Specifically in *Measure for Measure* the penitent ethical subject that emerges toward the end of the play is concerned not with his or her responsibility to the law or a concept of justice but with responding to the singularity of the situation at hand while acknowledging that judgment of any course of action must be deferred to an inaccessible future. To adapt Freinkel's account of linguistic chiasmus to the kind of chiastic exchange in embodied experience that Shakespeare dramatizes in *Measure for Measure*, I will follow the lead of phenomenologist Maurice Merleau-Ponty in extending the figure of chiasmus to the phenomenological experience of the world. For Merleau-Ponty such experience is always embodied, and his account is particularly helpful in illuminating Shakespeare's exploration of the dynamic relation between embodiment and cognition on the early modern stage.

Excursus: Phenomenology, Religion, Ethics

For Merleau-Ponty embodied experience is also always a matter of doubling back and moving forward, in a process that he describes with the term *chiasm*, or *intertwining*. The chiasm draws on the rhetorical trope of chiasmus (and its attendant reversibility) while referencing the physiological point at which the world of vision becomes intertwined with conscious apprehension—the so-called optic chiasma in the eye. Merleau-Ponty

attempts to move beyond the conventional mind-body problem by pro-
posing an alternate mode for embodied experience, one inspired by the
"uncontested evidence that one must see or feel in order to think, that
every thought known to us occurs to a flesh."[9] What separates Merleau-
Ponty from straightforward materialist or behaviorist thinkers is his notion of "flesh." While a complete account of Merleau-Ponty's "flesh" is
beyond the limits of this essay, as a point of reference, consider this relevant passage: "The flesh we are speaking of is not matter. It is the coiling
over of the visible upon the seeing body, of the tangible upon the touching body, which is attested in particular when the body sees itself, touches
itself seeing and touching the things, such that, simultaneously, *as* tangible
it descends among them, *as* touching it dominates them all and draws this
relationship and even this double relationship from itself, by dehiscence
or fission of its own mass."[10] In this passage Merleau-Ponty articulates a
central insight of phenomenological thought: that an understanding of
embodied experience is contingent upon the double reflection that occurs when one is aware of the interaction between the conscious and the
sensual aspects of a particular phenomenal moment, when it makes sense
to describe the experience as one of "seeing oneself seeing." Despite the
level of abstraction required to delineate the conceptual relationships
Merleau-Ponty seeks to explain here, his analysis remains grounded in the
particularity of human experience.[11] His attention never strays from the
singularity of an individual's embodied interaction with the world in time.
Nevertheless, his account has overt religious—specifically Christian—
rhetorical echoes. The experience in which the "tangible descends among
them" recalls Christ's descent to earth in human form, and the resulting
"dehiscence or fission" of the mass (seemingly whole) prior to the exchange is not unlike the process of kenosis that resolves the paradox of
Christ's relationship to both God and man.[12]

It is not surprising, then, that the most important heir to Merleau-
Ponty's phenomenological enterprise, Jean-Luc Marion, has taken the
method in an explicitly Christian direction. Where Merleau-Ponty places
emphasis on the excess of perceptual experience—that which allows for
conceptual revision—Marion identifies the trace of the divine. Merleau-
Ponty notes that perception "asserts more things than it grasps," by
which he means that no perceptual experience captures the full range

of possible interrelations between phenomenon and apprehension.[13] The implication is that one must return to the experience on reflection and that a subsequent similar experience could result in radically different conceptual understanding. The stakes are overtly ethical, for, as Jorella Andrews argues, "Perception as he defines it . . . is . . . ethically productive. . . . The ethics in question challenges traditional positions in that it is not the discovery and application of 'universally valid' rules, principles, or rights that are presented as foundational, but involvement in perceptual acts experienced as ongoing and unstable."[14] For Merleau-Ponty such an ethics of perceptual instability is a condition of human embodied experience and its temporal embeddedness. Only when one seeks to extract systematic principles or laws from experience does one escape temporality, and then the price is far too high, for to escape temporality is to "withdraw into the core of our thinking," or, as Andrews puts it, to "relinquish our primordial embeddedness in perception."[15] From a Christian perspective, of course, the emancipation from temporality is the desired end, albeit always deferred. Thus for Marion the method of phenomenological reduction that serves Merleau-Ponty's goal of eschewing dogmatic philosophical proscription becomes the method by which to avoid the pitfalls of traditional onto-theology. Specifically, Marion seeks to recuperate the icon and the idol as visual categories by taking them out of the metaphysical and mimetic tradition. As long as the icon is predicated on a known prototype, its perceptual excess is denied (all effort to apprehend the image is constrained by the prototype and an attempt to judge how nearly the icon approximates the original). This, like all onto-theology according to Marion, approaches the divine from the wrong direction. Alternately, Marion suggests, "The icon is given not to be seen but to be venerated. . . . The 'respectful veneration' is not to be confused with adoration: the one, in effect, is concerned with a (real) nature, the other a (irreal [*sic*] intentional) gaze; before the icon, one should not adore, since the visible and real support (the image in its materiality) does not merit what a divine nature alone demands."[16] The process by which "respectful veneration" occurs is what Marion calls the "kenosis of the image." Emptied of its purported representational characteristics, the icon is able to suggest the trace of the invisible:

A dulled, dressed-down image . . . the icon allows another gaze, which it gives to be seen, to suddenly appear through it. . . . The self renunciation of the image itself—a condition of its transformation into an icon—is thus accomplished in the obedience of the one who shed his face, renouncing his visibility in order to do the will of God. By this paradoxical glory, Christ displays the logic of the iconic image. . . . In fact it is precisely at the moment that he loses his human appearance [*figure*] that Christ becomes the figure of the divine will: in him, it is no longer his human appearance [*figure*] that is imagined [*se figure*]; and shedding appearance, he gives shape [*donne* [*figure*] to a holiness that would have remained invisible without the shrine [*écrin*] (not screen [*écran*]) of his body.[17]

What becomes visible for Marion is the invisible truth of the Christian God, made visible precisely at the moment that the visible is effaced. For Merleau-Ponty, the invisible remains temporally bound in the figure of the unknowability of the future. For the purposes of the present discussion, I submit that Merleau-Ponty's phenomenology is more germane to Shakespearean theater, while simultaneously acknowledging its compatibility with the theological concerns so central to Marion. In each case a negotiation between the material body and the immaterial word (or truth, or spirit, or life) is central to the phenomenological method.

Dramatic Embodiment

Measure for Measure raises the issue of embodied experience in the opening scenes. The topic of judgment as temporal comparison (old and new) is expressed explicitly in terms of figural embodiment: Duke Vincentio requests that Escalus render a judgment of his future substitute, Angelo, with the question: "What figure of us think you he will bear?" (1.1.16). Interestingly, the Duke has already made up his mind to deputize Angelo, having

> . . . with special soul
> Elected him our absence to supply,

Lent him our terror, dressed him with our love,
And given his deputation all the organs
Of our power.

(1.1.17–21)[18]

The Duke's awareness of a dissonance between the outward features of
his power and something like Angelo's inner nature signals a central tension in the play's epistemology.[19] The Duke explains that his choice of
Angelo is a result of what he has seen: "There is a kind of character in thy
life, / That to th' observer doth thy history / Fully unfold" (1.1.27–29).[20]
And Angelo's response is similarly expressed in terms of figure: "Let
there be some more test made of my mettle / Before so noble and so
great a figure / Be stamped upon it" (1.1.48–50). This brief dialogue introduces one of the play's most important themes: the relation of invisible character to outward appearance. The comparison to the impression
of the monarch's figure on the coin—common in Shakespeare—takes
on additional force here in the context of the previous dialogue, raising
the question: Which is more important, the mettle (metal) to be stamped
or the figure that results from the impression?[21] It would seem that the
Duke's test, if that is what it is, rests on the assumption that even the
most well defined of public personas are no guarantee of true character.[22]

   In a subsequent scene, the Duke describes Angelo to Friar Thomas
as "precise": he "Stands at a guard with envy; scarce confesses / That
his blood flows, or that his appetite / Is more to bread than stone . . ."
(1.3.50, 51–53). But rather than the expected conclusion—Bassanio's lament in *The Merchant of Venice* that "the outward shows be least themselves" (3.2.1)—in *Measure for Measure* the dynamic between inner
character and outward appearance is not so clear. The Duke's suggestion
that Angelo's inner character is available to all who look on him would
seem to prove false as the action proceeds, yet epistemologically it is the
same suggestion that he makes (apparently accurately) to Isabella later in
the play.[23] Rather than a simple dichotomy (external/internal), the play
offers a more subtle articulation of the relationship between appearance
and truth, figure and its invisible referent. When Angelo succumbs to
the material world—recognizing for the first time that he too has bodily
desires—his soliloquy turns on the rhetoric of visible form:

O place, O form,
How often dost thou with thy case, thy habit,
Wrench awe from fools, and tie the wiser souls
To thy false seeming! Blood, thou art blood.
Let's write "good Angel" on the devil's horn,
'Tis not the devil's crest.

(2.4.12–17)

Later, as his plan begins to consume him, he turns again to form with the recognition: "This deed unshapes me quite" (4.4.18). Yet in his emerging self-awareness Angelo recognizes that his constitutional transformation is not mirrored in his outward appearance. In the same soliloquy he muses that his "authority bears so credent bulk / That no particular scandal once can touch" (4.4.24–25). What is "unshaped," we learn, is his spirit—"when once our grace we have forgot, / Nothing goes right" (4.4.31–32). The static image of the severe judge remains despite his actions, but the state of his soul now "unshaped" mars the outcome of his experience in time: "nothing *goes* right."

Isabella is introduced with a similar emphasis on form, but rather than outward appearance, it is the lack of emphasis on her figure that is striking (especially considering the action to follow):

. . . in her youth
there is a prone and speechless dialect
such as move men. Beside, she hath prosperous art
When she will play with reason and discourse,
And well she can persuade.

(1.2.177–81)

The use of *prone* here has been something of a puzzle. Shakespeare consistently uses the word in the sense "apt" or "inclined to," and it has been glossed thus by many editors.[24] But it is not clear how the word so defined modifies *dialect*, unless the syntax is manipulated: "her dialect is prone to move men." The Arden editor J. W. Lever claims that Claudio uses the word to indicate "the abject posture of submission or helplessness." While this is linguistically plausible, the Isabella we soon meet is hardly submissive or helpless, even when faced with a lecherous and powerful adversary. More to the point, neither reading of *prone* explains the paradoxical "speechless dialect," which it seems can refer only to visual appearance, for as we find out when Isabella appears, her dialect (her language) is not inclined to moving men (except Angelo, of course).[25] The natural conclusion is that Claudio is describing her looks: men are moved without words—youthful beauty is a universal language.

Lucio's words upon first seeing Isabella further complicate the play's epistemological stance on the relation of visible appearance to ontological status: "Hail, virgin, if you be, as those cheek-roses / Proclaim you are no less" (1.4.16–17). In another play, perhaps, the assumption that all young women are virgins could be taken on its face (sorry), but spoken by Lucio and in the Vienna of *Measure for Measure*, the comment points to significant epistemological questions. It is true that the play's central conflict is generated in part by the visual proof of Juliet and Claudio's indiscretion—"the stealth of our most mutual entertainment / With character too gross is writ on Juliet" (1.2.149–50). But proof of virginity is not available visually.[26] Lucio's slightly hesitant "if you be" signals that he is aware of the epistemological problem, despite the likelihood that he is correct (he is, after all, at the gate of a nunnery).

As Lucio's qualified observation suggests, the belief that knowledge of a person's invisible character can be derived from outward form is complicated in *Measure for Measure* at the same time that a rhetorical emphasis on the body, visible form, and perceptual intuition suggests that invisible character is intertwined with outward appearance. Isabella confirms as much in her description of Angelo:

> This outward-sainted deputy,
> Whose settled visage and deliberate word
> Nips youth i'th' head, and follies doth enew
> As falcon doth the fowl, is yet a devil:
> His filth within being cast, he would appear
> A pond as deep as hell.
>
> (3.1.88–93)

Where is the essence and where the appearance here? The question is complicated further by Isabella's explanation: "O 'tis the cunning livery of hell, / The damnedest body to invest and cover / In prenzie guards" (3.1.95–97).[27] Here it is the "damnedest body" rather than the inner character that is concealed, "cover[d]" by the clothing of authority, or the appearance of virtue. If it were possible to "cast" his "filth within" in outward form, Isabella suggests, his evil would "appear": we would be able to see his true essence. Importantly, this revelation is deferred to an undetermined future. Isabella's understanding of the relationship between Angelo's appearance and his inner character relies not on a dualism but on an understanding of body and soul as existing in a chiastic relationship. Similarly, in the Duke's first overture to Isabella he offers the same account of the soul-body relationship, but in positive terms: "The hand that made thee fair hath made thee good. The goodness that is cheap in beauty makes beauty brief in goodness; but grace, being the soul of your complexion, shall keep the body of it ever fair" (3.1.179–83). The Duke's speech is a complex chiasmus, signaling the intertwining of world and mind, body and soul, appearance and essence. But as with Isabella's description of Angelo, the key to the relational model's explanatory power is missing. Angelo appears virtuous to all who look on him, despite his iniquity. Isabella is desperate to protect her virtue, even though her beautiful appearance is proof enough for Vincentio that grace is the soul of her complexion; she confirms to Claudio that chastity is all: ". . . were it but my life, / I'd throw it down for your deliverance / As frankly as a pin" (3.1.102–4).[28] The intertwining here of visible beauty and invisible grace relies on the Duke's use of chiasmus, that most temporal of tropes: the hand that made you good produced your beauty, and your beauty is proof that the hand made you good. The sense of doubling back to move forward is most clear in the outcome, which is to exempt Isabella from the instability of temporal existence: her state of grace "shall keep the body of it *ever* fair" (3.1.182–83; emphasis added). The deployment of a temporal figure to shore up faith in the possibility of an atemporal state highlights the difficulty of representing the ethical, a difficulty that Shakespeare's play brings into sharp relief.

Temporality is also at the heart of Angelo's insistence on a precise demarcation of the line between abstraction and lived experience (ideas and actions): "'tis one thing to be tempted, another to fall" (2.1.17–18). Angelo would not have to look far to find a counterargument from the highest authority. In the Sermon on the Mount Christ dissolves the distinction on which Angelo's argument relies: "I say unto you, That whosoever looketh on a woman to lust after her hath committed adultery with her already in his heart" (Matt. 5:28). Nevertheless in the context of earthly rather than spiritual law, there is no recourse to the internal thoughts of others. Angelo, like any legal authority, is bound to what can be seen. He explains his empirical justice to Escalus:

> 'Tis one thing to be tempted, Escalus,
> Another thing to fall. I not deny,
> The jury, passing on the prisoner's life,
> May in the sworn twelve have a thief or two
> Guiltier than him they try. What's open made to justice,
> That justice seizes: what know the laws
> That thieves do pass on thieves? 'Tis very pregnant,
> The jewel that we find, we stoop and take't
> Because we see it; but what we do not see
> We tread upon, and never think of it.
> You may not so extenuate his offence
> For I have had such faults; but rather tell me,
> When I, that censure him, do so offend,
> Let mine own judgment pattern out my death,
> And nothing come in partial.
>
> (2.1.17–31)

Angelo's pragmatic approach to the law clearly defines the visible as the purview of earthly justice. Though by his own report Angelo was never tempted before meeting Isabella—"Ever till now / When men were fond, I smil'd, and wonder'd how" (2.2.186–87)—he makes no effort to answer Escalus's question: If you had the desire and opportunity, is it possible that you would make the same mistake as Claudio? Escalus is clearly in tune with Christ's message in the Sermon, which is concerned not with material offenses but with spiritual comportment: don't feel better about not having committed adultery if you yearn internally to commit it.

Of course, the prohibition against judgment in the Sermon on the Mount is a prohibition against the judgment of individuals rather than actions. Elsewhere in the sermon, Jesus is quite clear about actions deserving of negative judgment. For example, correcting the notion that he has come to reject the law, Jesus extends the law to heaven: "Whosoever therefore shall break one of these least commandments, and shall teach men so, he shall be called the least in the kingdom of heaven: but whosoever shall do and teach them, the same shall be called great in the kingdom of heaven" (Matt. 5:19). But the judgment of individuals is a matter of judging another's soul, and this must be left to God. Put in slightly different terms, this logic in no way contradicts the law that defines some actions as morally wrong, but it reserves judgment on the status of the individual guilty of committing the act: "Hate the sin, not the sinner."

While this axiom makes sense in the context of Christian theology, Shakespeare reminds his audience that the difficulty comes in the application of earthly justice, as the presumed restraint of hatred for the sinner runs counter to the retributive violence of judicial punishment. It is not possible to punish the sin, as Angelo rightly points out in his juridical debate with Isabella:

> Condemn the fault and not the actor of it?
> Why, every fault's condemned ere it be done:
> Mine were the very cipher of a function,
> To fine the faults whose fine stand in record,
> and let go by the actor.
>
> (2.2.37–41)

Isabella's response, "O just but severe law!" (2.2.40), acknowledges the clarity of Angelo's logic here, but without addressing the larger temporal problem left out of Angelo's account. His claim that the fine for "the faults" stands "in record" is based on the assumption that right and wrong are always known rather than elicited through reflection on the situation at hand.[29] The play's later rejection of strict retributive justice provides the critique of Angelo's conclusion without actually denying its logic. The faults are still wrong, but the role of the judge in punishing those faults is not simply to insist on the principle of "measure for measure" or "an eye for an eye." Shakespeare briefly offers the satisfaction that retributive justice delivers in the Duke's performative declaration of Angelo's sentence:

> The very mercy of the law cries out
> Most audible, even from his proper tongue:
> "An Angelo for Claudio; death for death.
> Haste still pays haste, and leisure answers leisure;
> Like doth quite like, and Measure still for Measure."
> Then Angelo, thy fault's thus manifested,
> Which, though thou woulds't deny, denies thee vantage.
>
> (5.1.405–11)

The sequence of events here is particularly interesting for the present discussion of the temporal dimension of ethics. The Duke's claim that Angelo would deny anything is peculiar considering that some forty lines earlier Angelo was the one to witness the manifestation of his fault:

> O my dread lord,
> I should be guiltier than my guiltiness
> To think I can be undiscernible,
> When I perceive your Grace, like power divine,
> Hath looked upon my passes. The good Prince,
> No longer session hold upon my shame,
> But let my trial be mine own confession.
> Immediate sentence, then, and sequent death
> Is all the grace I beg.
>
> (5.1.364–72)

Angelo makes good on his earlier claim to Escalus that if he were to be discovered committing a crime he would accept the punishment. But the crime for which the Duke sentences him to death is not the same as that for which he judged Claudio. According to the Duke, the "fault" for which he is condemned is his treatment of Claudio: his "double violation / Of sacred chastity and of promise-breach" (5.1.402–3). Having just pardoned Angelo for wronging Isabella's "well defended honor"

(5.1.399), in referring to the violation of "sacred chastity" the Duke suggests that Angelo violated his own chastity by harboring lecherous intentions. The second charge also turns the judgment away from the tangible effects of Angelo's actions to his spiritual condition. He is indeed guilty of "promise-breach," but by this point in the play the audience already knows that Claudio has been spared.

It is here that the play returns to the Sermon as its guiding scriptural reference. And clearly, the Sermon fails to support the application of the law in this manner: "Ye have heard that it hath been said, An eye for an eye, and a tooth for a tooth: But I say unto you, That ye resist not evil: but whosoever shall smite thee on thy right cheek, turn to him the other also" (Matt. 5:38–39).[30] Thus at the very moment that the play offers satisfaction in the form of retributive justice, it recalls Jesus's plea to eschew this urge and internalize the retribution for sin—to turn from the judgment of the other person to the submission of the self to the judgment of an absolute and unknowable Other. In redirecting the urge for external justice to the internal self, the Sermon might be seen to undercut the law. What function does the law serve if not to adjudicate human action and meet out punishment? Seeking an answer to this question was a concern for medieval and Reformation political theology alike, and as the previous discussion suggests, Shakespeare's play engages with the question directly.

Huston Diehl suggests that Shakespeare's representation of the law in *Measure for Measure* owes its logic to Calvin: "For Calvin, the law . . . serves a vital function: by revealing our inherent sinfulness, it produces dissatisfaction with the self, a dissatisfaction that, because it initiates the process of repentance, is essential for salvation."[31] Central to Calvin's account is the penitent's renunciation of the earthly self in favor of an eternal judge. Submission to an absolute other is contingent upon a process of self-effacement. And it is ultimately this process of self-effacement that will have the natural consequence of cultivating a Christian society in which mercy governs judgment.

Clearly Shakespeare's meditations on questions of ethics and judgment reflect his understanding of this system of political theology, but they also suggest his skepticism regarding this seamless wedding of earthly and spiritual judgment. *Pace* Portia in *The Merchant of Venice*, the quality of mercy is indeed strained in that play. And in *Measure for Measure* Shakespeare risks a representation of Christian mercy that is strained beyond the breaking point. The Duke's sensible declaration that "the very mercy of the law cries out" for Angelo to be punished is followed by the implausible scene of Isabella's plea for the life of the man responsible (she thinks) for her brother's death and the intention to deflower a would-be nun.[32] Rather than parrot Christian views on repentance, ethics, justice, and mercy, Shakespeare reserves judgment on every system that would proscribe, or prescribe, a particular course of action. By staging the dilemmas inherent in the opposition between old and new, law and mercy, earthly and spiritual justice, Shakespeare makes visible an array of coherent images that will be shattered in the course of time. The new replaces the old (even though the new relies on the old for its newness), law must yield to mercy, and earthly justice will give way to spiritual justice at the Day of Judgment. Time is critical in the movement between these terms, as the temporal resolutions to these dilemmas are simultaneously inevitable (they will come to pass) and withheld (they have not yet done so).

Penitential Ethics

What then, if anything, can *Measure for Measure* say about ethics? Rather than a helpless lament for the world's irredeemable corruption, *Measure for Measure* represents an extended reflection on human action in time, one with important insights into the place of ethics in our experience of the world. In the remaining space, I will argue specifically that *Measure for Measure* presents a "penitential ethics" in which the penitent is concerned not with his or her responsibility to the law or a concept of justice but with the situation at hand, acknowledging that judgment of any course of action must be deferred to an inaccessible future. Viewed in this manner, ethics might look entirely secular and material. Such is the view put forward by Alain Badiou in *Ethics: An Essay on the Understanding of Evil*.[33] For Badiou, true ethics relates to a radical fidelity to a truth event. The truth event is recognizable only in retrospect for its alteration of the course of human history (Einstein's theory, for example, but also the moment one falls in love). What Badiou ejects from ethics is any form of absolute other, even a supposedly desacralized version of the absolute other, as in Levinas: radical alterity.[34] In the case of Shakespeare, it would be going too far to suggest that the playwright evacuated ethics of its religious content. Shakespeare, like Levinas, retains a form of radical alterity in his emphasis on time. And if one accepts Badiou's argument that "every effort to turn ethics into the principle of thought and action is essentially religious," it is in the continual reference to time as the ultimate judge that Shakespeare's play becomes a play about religion (as opposed to being a play about doctrinal or theological disputes). Rather than presenting a play that seeks to represent a compromise between Puritanism and Catholicism, Calvin and Luther, or the Old and New Testament articulations of law and mercy, I suggest that Shakespeare engaged with the foundations of ethical thought in a way that requires the spectator to set aside conclusions about proper judgment (always to come) and focus on one's experience of the world in time.

Now this might sound patently absurd, given the contours of a Christian penitential theology in which retribution, satisfaction, and restitution loom large. In each case the act of penance is intended to amend the past: accepting punishment in the case of retribution, offering to make up for an injury against another in the case of satisfaction and restitution. But if we bracket the material acts of penance developed in medieval penitential theology and consider the penitent in terms of orientation, as a state of existence, the aneconomic kernel of penitential comportment comes into focus. Mercy is offered to the penitent not as absolution but as a *figure* for salvation, a form to be contemplated in anticipation of the penitent's possible future redemption. Only the repentant are open to salvation. Considered in this way, it is easier to make more sense of the mercy granted to the seemingly irredeemable characters that populate Shakespeare's play. The question, of course, is how to determine penitential comportment if not for some outward show of contrition. William Tyndale addressed precisely this question in *The Obedience of a Christian Man*: "Penance is a word of their own forging, to deceive us withal, as many others are. In the Scripture we find *poenitentia*, 'repentance:' *agite poenitentia*, 'do repent'; *poeniteatuos*, 'let it repent you': *metanoite*, in Greek, 'forthink ye,' or 'let it forthink you.' Of repentance they have made penance, to blind the people, and to make them think they must take pains, and do some holy deeds, to make satisfaction for their sins; namely such as they enjoin them."[35] Penance as the penitential act is the institutional solution to the problem of spiritual penitential comportment, but it is a solution, according to Tyndale, that relies on a misunderstanding of the nature of sacrament: "Repentance is no sacrament: as faith, hope, love, and knowledge of a man's sins, are not to be called sacraments. For they are spiritual and invisible. Now must a sacrament be an outward sign that may be seen, to signify, to represent and to put a man in remembrance of some spiritual promise, which cannot be seen but by faith only."[36] As reformers like Tyndale argued, the reliance of medieval penitential theology on the material, visible acts of penance drew attention away from the scriptural emphasis on the orientation of the individual toward God. The solution of prescribed acts quickly became the problem. But the rejection of outward acts of penance, while mitigating the threat of a preoccupation with the material sign, failed to offer an alternative for determining the penitent's spiritual condition. Contrition—whether or not the penitent is truly repentant—is a matter between the individual and God. Tyndale explains that "contrition and repentance are both one, and nothing else but a sorrowful and a mourning heart. And because that God hath promised mercy unto a contrite heart, that is, to a sorrowful and repenting heart, they, to beguile God's Word and to stablish their wicked tradition, have feigned that new word attrition, saying 'Thou canst not know whether thy sorrow or repentance be contrition or attrition, except thou be shriven. When thou art shriven, then it is true contrition.' O foxy Pharisee!"[37] The Reformation insistence on repentance as a state rather than an act (or series of actions) returns me to the temporal dilemma with which I began. Tyndale's attempt to rescue repentance from medieval penitential theology rests on a temporal distinction: "Repentance goeth before faith, and prepareth the way to Christ, and to the promises. . . . Repentance, that is to say, this mourning and sorrow of the heart, lasteth all our lives long."[38] The argument might be reframed in more recent theoretical language as "The true Christian always already repents." Thus Christian virtue is predicated on a penitential orientation toward the world. Importantly, the relation of God's atemporal truth to the temporally bound individual is conceived in spatial terms: the true (penitent) Christian has turned toward God, the heathen has turned away, and thus the penitential plea is always a call to "turn" and face the penitent sinner.

The call to turn brings me to a pivotal moment in *Measure for Measure*. The scene comes at the end of the first interview between Angelo and Isabella, after Angelo begins to fall but before he expresses his foul proposition. At just the moment when the "precise" substitute Angelo begins to recognize his devolution into sexual obsession, his interlocutor pleads for him to "turn back." Isabella's plea, "Gentle my lord, turn back" (2.2.144–45), at once refers to the visual scene presented to the audience at the point of Angelo's aside—he has turned his back on the conversation—and signals a "turning point" in the play, as well as in the ethical life of the character in question. Angelo does turn back—to invite Isabella for another interview—but in turning back, he has turned his back on the word (or the letter) of the law that was his world up to this moment in the play. In granting Isabella another interview, he has given over to something other than the word (the law), thereby allowing himself to embrace the unknown. But what is it that spurs the change?

Once moved—just after Isabella's plea to turn back—Angelo asks this very question: "Is this her fault or mine?" He is able to recognize after some reflection that she has said nothing to tempt him, but by this time it is too late. Having turned back, Angelo has set his course: he has refused to turn back from his chosen path, that which leads to his sexual coercion of Isabella. The ethical dilemma that Shakespeare stages in this scene is not whether Angelo should proposition Isabella (or even whether he should pardon Claudio). Rather, the moment for ethics is the moment when the visible crosses over into the realm of language; ethical recognition comes in the reconciliation of visible image and invisible word. Reasoned discourse on the application of the law crosses over into the living flesh, emphasizing that the law never exists outside individuals—singular embodied experiences; in other words, Jesus's claim in the Sermon that he is come to fulfill rather than destroy the law (that he is the Word become flesh).

"Gentle my lord, turn back." In this moment we witness a call to turn and thus we witness a turning point. The dramatic import of this plea is to emphasize the decision with which Angelo is faced: he is at a turning point, and the path he takes will determine his ethical fate. But Isabella's plea also closely follows the rhetorical pattern of the penitent, a pattern found repeatedly in the Psalms: consider, from Psalm 90, "Turne agayne O God (what, for euer [wylt thou be angry?) and be gratious vnto thy seruauntes," or from Psalm 6, "Turn thee, O Lord, and deliver my soul," or, from Psalm 26 as rendered in the Psalter of St. Jerome, "Hear, O Lord, my voice, with which I have cried to Thee. Have mercy on me and hear me. Turn not away Thy face from me; nor in Thy wrath turn from Thy servant. Be Thou my helper. Forsake me not, nor despise me, O God my Savior. Set before me, O Lord, the law in Thy way, and guide me in the right path, because of my adversaries. Deliver me not to those that persecute me."[39] The echoes of this very old tradition frame the plea for Angelo to turn back as a matter of a future yet to come: "I wait for you to turn back to me." The echo lends to the play's messianic atmosphere; even as the action darkens, one senses that there is a justice to come. But further, this call for justice is a call for the face-to-face encounter: "Turn back [to face me]," "Turn not thy face away from me." And it should thus be no surprise that the Sermon on the Mount is the play's central scriptural reference: Christ returned, confirming the prophecies to come face to face.

As I mentioned at the outset, once Angelo has yielded to Isabella's "prone and speechless dialect" his course is set; though he turns back in response to Isabella's plea he does not turn from his present course. The scenes that surround this turning—the first interview, in which Angelo is moved to transformation, and the subsequent interview, in which he makes his intentions known to Isabella—constitute the meditative center of the play and its reflection on the Sermon on the Mount. While the direct reference to the passage from Matthew is given to the Duke in the final act, the heart of the Sermon's lesson is more directly addressed here. Jesus's message on the mount is to attend to experience on earth with patience, avoiding the trap of dogma that is the product of looking back only or failing to look in the present:

> Judge not, that ye be not judged. For with what judgement ye judge, ye shal be judged: And with what measure ye mette, it shal be measured to you againe.

And why seest thou the mote that is in thy brothers eye, but perceiuest not the beame that is in thyne owne eye?

Or, how saist thou to thy brother, Suffer me to cast the mote out of thyne eye: and beholde, a beame is in thyne owne eye?

Hypocrite, first cast out the beame out of thine owne eye, and then shalt thou se clearely to cast out the mote out of thy brothers eye.

(Matt. 7:1–5)

The passage that drew Shakespeare's attention couches the problem of ethics bound to the exigencies of time in a language of the visual (the eye for an eye has become the eye blinded by splinter or beam). Isabella's repetition of her plea a line later emphasizes the need to see in order to judge. After Angelo has agreed to return to the topic ("I will bethink me; come again tomorrow" [2.2.144]), Isabella repeats the plea, this time unwittingly inviting Angelo to delve deeper into his fantasy: "Hark how I'll bribe you; good my lord, turn back" (2.2.145). Isabella's bribe is the promise of heaven should he show the mercy she imagines he will; but it highlights her own blindness to the situation at hand. She has apparently failed to notice Angelo's visible agitation, noted repeatedly by Lucio in his asides (such as "he will relent, he's coming, I perceive it" [2.2.125–26]). As they fail to see each other they also speak different languages. What she offers to the now changed Angelo, by this point entirely focused on his desire, is the image of "fasting maids whose minds are dedicate / To nothing temporal" (2.2.155–56). It is not until the second interview that Isabella comes to recognize Angelo's transformation, at which point she echoes her earlier call to turn back, but now with an understanding lacking earlier: "Let me entreat you speak the former language" (2.4.139). Interestingly, as far as Isabella is concerned the only language Angelo has spoken to this point has been the language of the law, the letter of the law that was the source of her pain, the condemnation of her brother Claudio. But with the revelation of Angelo's desire, the question of ethics rises to the surface, as there is no possibility of a return to the law, "the former language."

This epistemological Gordian knot at the heart of the play defines the pivotal scenes in which Angelo succumbs to the "temptation" presented by Isabella. At this moment Shakespeare employs another chiasmus:

When I would pray and think, I think and pray
To several subjects: heaven hath my empty words,
Whilst my invention, hearing not my tongue,
Anchors on Isabella: heaven in my mouth,
As if I did but only chew his name,
And in my heart the strong and swelling evil
Of my conception.

$$(2.4.1-7)^{40}$$

Disembodied thought and prayer are set against the bodily chewing mouth and lecherous intention, which are in turn associated not with evil thoughts but with the fleshy metaphor of "swelling . . . conception." Presented in the form of a chiastic reversal, invisible faith (heaven) is corporealized in the mouth, while the seat of faith (the heart) is occupied by Angelo's flesh: the "swelling evil of my conception." The heart is pre-occupied with the flesh rather than the flesh corrupting the heart; in the flesh Angelo still represents the law. And this revelation begins Angelo's conversion to the penitent, aware that outward actions cannot be the sole basis for judging the state of the soul. It is also here that Shakespeare's play reveals something of the depth of the epistemological problem nagging theological debates over the relation of world and Word. However immaterial the God of Christian desire, even the most pure spiritual desire remains mired in the material trappings of human existence. Thus, as Luther observed, both the iconoclast and the iconophile pay inordinate attention to the flesh.[41] Negotiating the intertwining of "heart and tongue" is a far more difficult task than trying to maintain their separation. This difficulty becomes clear to Angelo only as his personal crisis forces him from his absolute position on the side of the precise law.

Despite the play's emphasis on the visual throughout the various subplots, the text suggests that Angelo's "corruption" and fall are not brought on by his sensual experience upon *seeing* Isabella.[42] As the two trade arguments, and Angelo's desire grows, the pleasure of rhetorical debate—and Isabella's unwillingness to "put on the destined livery" (2.4.138) of woman—are the ostensible cause. Only after his transformation (his acceptance of bodily desire) does Angelo shift the dialogue from language to vision with the command "I do arrest your words":

> Be that you are
> That is, a woman; if you be more, you're none.
> If you be one, as you are well expressed
> By all external warrants, show it now,
> By putting on the destined livery.
>
> (2.4.134–38)

Again there is an oscillation between vision and language, "external" appearance and internal identity ("that you are"). The intertwining is evident in the problematic tension between what is seen and what is thought to be: (for example) I see that you are a woman, so show me what I see. Isabella's response turns back to language: "I have no tongue but one" (2.4.139). But her metonymy sustains the emphasis on the body. As Isabella continues to deny any value to bodily pleasure, her language becomes increasingly saturated with both visual and bodily references. The most striking of these is the oft-mentioned image she provides of herself under "threat of death": "Th' impression of keen whips I'd wear as rubies, / And strip myself to death as to a bed" (2.4.101–2). Perhaps more telling, though, is her later response to the Duke's proposition of the bed trick: "The image of it gives me content already, and I trust it will grow to a most prosperous perfection" (3.1.52–53). Surely Isabella's "content" (pleasure) derives from the appealing form of a well-conceived plan; and yet that well-conceived form leads her to find pleasure in the sexual deception of Angelo, in turn suggesting the generative rhetoric of success: What more prosperous perfection of conception can there be than procreation? Compare the obverse, coming at the height of the action brought about by the Duke's plan, when Angelo worries that his deed "makes [him] unpregnant" (4.4.18). While Angelo loses form—becomes unrecognizable to those expecting to see the precise ruler—Isabella gains a worldly body.[43] This process is akin to Marion's "kenosis of the image": the images created for the precise Angelo and the ascetic Isabella dissolve over the course of the play, leaving uncertainty and fallibility in their place. Both images borrowed divinity in material forms (the law as underwritten by visible proof and the trappings of saintly asceticism represented by choice of spiritual vocation), only to have that materially manifested divinity dissolve as a result of their actions over time.

At the personal level of individual penitential comportment, the dissolution and reconstitution of Angelo and Isabella recall the conversion of St.
Augustine as he recounts his sexual failings in the opening of the *Confessions*:

> I will call to mind the impurity of my life past, and the vncleane
> corruptions of my Soule; not for any loue that I beare to them,
> but for that which I owe to thee, O my God. For loue of thy loue,
> O Lord, I do it; recording my most wicked wayes, in the very bit-
> ternes of my soule, that thou mayst grow sweet to me; Thou who
> art no counterfait, but a happy and secure sweetnes; recouering me
> from that diuishon of my selfe whereby I was all torne in peeces,
> whilest being auerted from thee alone, I vanished away, upon the
> variety of thy creatures. For in my youth I did sometyms burne with
> a kind of hellish desire to be satisfied, and I presumed euen to grow
> wilde, with an appetite of strange and conceited pleasures; but in the
> meane tyme the beauty of my Soule was wholy blasted; and in thyne
> eyes, O Lord, I was putryfyed, whilest yet I took contentment in my
> selfe, and procured to please the eyes of men.[44]

Augustine describes his preconversion state as one in which he was
"averted from thee [God]" (*te aversus*). The primary meaning of *avert* in
the *OED* is "to turn away," either literally or figuratively, with early modern uses commonly describing the relationship with God. Augustine describes the result of being turned away from God as the "division of the
self," a "vanishing away" that resembles Angelo's lament that his deed
"unshapes" him (4.4.18). Augustine's language is saturated with bodily
figures at the very moment he seeks to turn away from the material to
embrace the spiritual. As a rejection of Manichean dualism, Augustine's
emphasis on the temporal quality of his embodied experience of conversion offers a middle way between moral law and ethical comportment.
The emphasis on the physical turning as simultaneously a spiritual turning is echoed in *Measure for Measure* as Shakespeare stages the difficulties
of sustaining either Angelo's strict adherence to earthly justice or Isabella's equally strict adherence to eternal justice.

What are we as readers and audience members to make of the fact
that the two characters most governed by strict restraint (either legal or

spiritual) fall equally for (erotic) visions born of the very antivisual rhetoric that allowed them to eschew the world of sense? Must we accept, as some critics have argued, that the play's movement away from order toward instability demonstrates that *Measure for Measure* is unsuited to any coherent ethical or theological position?[45] It is true that the play rejects the most obvious correctives to Vienna's morally depraved state—the Puritan Angelo's law, the ascetic Isabella's withdrawal, and ducal responsibility (Friar Thomas's suggestion that the law "rested in your Grace / To unloose this tied-up justice when you pleased" [1.3.32–33]). Does the debunking of every possible moral position confirm Diehl's position that the play offers a Calvinist worldview, in which the only personal growth comes in recognizing one's own imperfection? Both readings are compelling and not incompatible with my argument here. But to understand the play as a renunciation of the possibility of positive action or the need to give over to an absolute authority fails to account for the play's other guiding principle. As the action unfolds, the Duke's commonplace "All difficulties are but easy when they are known" (4.2.205) is perhaps the only axiom left standing. All speculation about Isabella's response to the Duke's proposal of marriage, of the happiness or despair of Angelo and Mariana's marriage, of the fate of Lucio, Claudio, Juliet, or anyone is meaningless without the movement of time.

The space between the word and image, judgment and action, is open in this play. This space and the instant it takes to traverse it sustain the hope for an ethics that resists settling for the limitations of image or word considered in isolation. For Shakespeare in this play, reversal opens the possibility for the penitential orientation we find in St. Paul, in the Psalms, in Jesus's words on the mount. Angelo's precise law, like Isabella's immaterial image of purity, cannot be sustained in ethical action. But penitential ethics are unlike the forms of penitential theology that prescribe specific actions as recompense for sin or wrong done to another. The ethics of *Measure for Measure* lie ahead paradoxically in what's behind. The play ends with the Duke's promise: "So bring us to our palace, where we'll show / What's yet behind that's meet you all should know" (5.1.535–36).[46] Returned to the world and to time, Shakespeare's characters and his audience alike await their fate in the unpredictable figure of the future.

Notes

A version of this essay also appears as chapter 6 of my *Image Ethics in Shakespeare and Spenser* (New York: Palgrave, 2011).

1. Unless otherwise specified, scriptural references are to *The Geneva Bible: A Facsimile of the 1560 Edition*, ed. Lloyd E. Berry (Madison: University of Wisconsin Press, 1969). On the significance of the title and the relation of the play to the Sermon on the Mount, see Paul N. Siegel, *"Measure for Measure*: The Significance of the Title," *Shakespeare Quarterly* 4, no. 3 (1953): 317–20; Stacy Magedanz, "Public Justice and Private Mercy in *Measure for Measure*," *Studies in English Literature* 32, no. 2 (2004): 317–32; and Andrew Barnaby and Joan Wry, "Authorized Versions: *Measure for Measure* and the Politics of Biblical Translation," *Renaissance Quarterly* 51, no. 4 (1998): 1225–54.

2. See Debora Shuger, *Political Theologies in Shakespeare's England: The Sacred and the State in "Measure for Measure"* (New York: Palgrave, 2001) and Julia Reinhard Lupton, *Citizen-Saints: Shakespeare and Political Theology* (Chicago: University of Chicago Press, 2005); see also the influential, though problematic, work of Carl Schmitt, *Political Theology: Four Chapters on the Concept of Sovereignty* (Cambridge, MA: MIT Press, 1985), and its elaboration in Giorgio Agamben, *Homo Sacer: Sovereign Power and Bare Life* (Stanford: Stanford University Press, 1998), and Jacob Taubes, *The Political Theology of St. Paul* (Stanford: Stanford University Press, 2004).

3. The play has been treated as a mirror for princes designed specifically for James I at the outset of his reign. Arden editor J. W. Lever identifies Edward Chalmers as the first to make the argument in 1799, followed by others including Louis Albrecht, David L. Stevenson, and Ernest Schanzer; see Lever, introduction to *Measure for Measure*, ed. J. W. Lever, Arden 2nd series (1965; repr., London: Thompson Learning, 2005), xlvii. All subsequent references to this work's text and scholarly apparatus are to this edition. For elaborations on this argument, some more recent examples are Josephine Walters Bennett, *"Measure for Measure" as Royal Entertainment* (New York: Columbia University Press, 1966); Alexander Leggatt, "Substitution in *Measure for Measure*," *Shakespeare Quarterly* 39, no. 3 (1988): 342–59; and Shuger, *Political Theologies*.

4. Lisa Freinkel, *Reading Shakespeare's Will: The Theology of Figure from Augustine to the Sonnets* (New York: Columbia University Press, 2002), 7.

5. The (1599) Geneva gloss on this passage reveals the difficulty of the comparison: "The applying of the similitude of our childhood to this present life, wherein we darkly behold heavenly things, according to the small measure of light which is given to us, through the understanding of tongues, and hearing the teachers and ministers of the Church; of our man's age and strength, to that heavenly and eternal life, wherein when we behold God himself present, and are

lightened with his full and perfect light, to what purpose should we desire the voice of man, and those worldly things which are most imperfect? But yet then, shall all the Saints be knit both with God, and between themselves with most fervent love, and therefore charity shall not be abolished, but perfected, although it shall not be shewen forth and entertained by such manner of duties as peculiarly and only and belong to the infirmity of this life."

6. Augustine, *De catechizandis rudibus* 4.8, quoted in Freinkel, *Reading Shakespeare's Will*, 22.

7. Freinkel, *Reading Shakespeare's Will*, 23.

8. Ibid., 217.

9. Maurice Merleau-Ponty, *The Visible and the Invisible*, ed. Claude Lefort, trans. Alphonso Lingis (Evanston: Northwestern University Press, 1968), 146.

10. Ibid., emphasis in original. On Merleau-Ponty's use of the term flesh, see *Chiasms: Merleau-Ponty's Notion of Flesh*, ed. Fred Evans and Leonard Lawlor (Albany: SUNY Press, 2000).

11. Jacques Lacan criticized Merleau-Ponty's concept of the flesh as another form of a primordial essence, an originary grounding category. See *The Four Fundamental Concepts of Psychoanalysis*, ed. Jacques-Alain Miller, trans. Alan Sheridan (New York: W. W. Norton, 1978), 81–82.

12. The term *kenosis* derives from Philippians 2:7, where Paul describes Christ's descent as an emptying (κένωσις) of his divinity: "But he made himself of no reputation, and took on him the form of a servant, and was made like unto men, and was found in shape as a man" (Geneva version). The Douay-Rheims translation of the passage is "But he emptied himself, taking the form of a servant." Christ's emptying of divinity is reversed for the Christian seeking God; where Christ emptied himself for man, man must empty himself for God.

13. Merleau-Ponty writes, for example, that "the chiasm is not only a me other exchange (the messages he receives reach me, the messages I receive reach him), it is also an exchange between me and the world, between the phenomenal body and the "objective" body, between the perceiving and the perceived: what begins as a thing ends as consciousness of the thing, what begins as a 'state of consciousness' ends as a thing" (*Visible and the Invisible*, 215).

14. Jorella Andrews, "Vision, Violence, and the Other: A Merleau-Pontean Ethics," in *Feminist Interpretations of Merleau-Ponty*, ed. Dorothea Olkowski and Gail Weiss (University Park: Pennsylvania State University Press, 2006), 167–82, esp. 167–68.

15. Ibid., 169.

16. Jean-Luc Marion, *The Crossing of the Visible*, trans. James K. A. Smith (Stanford: Stanford University Press, 2004), 60. See also Brian Robinette, "A

Gift to Theology? Jean-Luc Marion's 'Saturated Phenomenon' in Christological Perspective," *Heythrop Journal* 48 (2007): 86–108.

17. Marion, *Crossing of the Visible*, 61. Also see Marion's "'They Recognized Him; and He Became Invisible to Them,'" *Modern Theology* 18 (2002): 145–52. All bracketed interpolations are in the original.

18. The use of *elected* here is consonant with the theme of Angelo as a figure of the Elizabethan Puritan. The description of Angelo as precise has provided support for this position. For a recent discussion, see Maurice Hunt, "Being Precise in *Measure for Measure*," *Renascence* 58 (Summer 2006): 243–67. While the association seems clear, there is less agreement about what conclusions ought to be drawn from the characterization. The use of *elected* also emphasizes the theme of sovereignty. Consider another of Shakespeare's uses of *elected*, in *Richard II*, when Richard says, "The breath of worldly men cannot depose / The deputy elected by the Lord" (3.2.52–53); *King Richard II*, ed. Charles R. Forker, Arden 3rd series (2002; repr., London: Thompson Learning, 2005).

19. A positive reading of the Duke's decision to conceal his appearance relies on a distinction between what he is and how he is viewed. Katherine Eisaman Maus develops her reading of the play and its connection to a Renaissance notion of "inwardness"—an unavailable but important emerging element of human subjectivity—by stressing similar moments in the play. See Katherine Eisaman Maus, *Inwardness and Theater in the English Renaissance* (Chicago: University of Chicago Press, 1995), 157–81.

20. See also the Duke's comment to Friar Thomas concerning what he knows of Angelo (1.3.50–53). The Duke's preconception of Angelo is only complicated by the question of when he comes into the knowledge that Angelo has forsaken Mariana.

21. Of course this portends the eventual undoing of Angelo's identity—his "settled visage" (3.1.90) so fixed in the minds of all who know him.

22. In offering the commission, the Duke further invokes visible form in his admission: "I love the people / But do not like to stage me to their eyes" (1.1.67–68).

23. The Duke's comment is, "The hand that made thee fair hath made thee good. The goodness that is cheap in beauty makes beauty brief in goodness; but grace, being the soul of your complexion, shall keep the body of it ever fair" (3.1.179–82).

24. The *OED* identifies the following meanings for the adjectival form of *prone* as current around the beginning of the seventeenth century: "Having the front or ventral part downwards; bending forward and downward; situated or lying face downwards, or on the belly"; "Of a part of the body: So situated as

to be directed downwards; under, nether, ventral"; "*fig.* Said of action compared to following a downward sloping path: Easy to adopt or pursue; involving no difficulty or effort"; "Having a natural inclination or tendency to something; inclined, disposed, apt, liable"; "Ready in mind (for some action expressed or implied); eager" (*The Oxford English Dictionary*, prep. J. A. Simpson and E. S. C. Weiner, 2nd ed., 20 vols. [Oxford: Clarendon Press, 1989], *s.v.* "prone," 1.,1.a., 1.b., 5., 6., 7.). The word appears in Shakespeare five other times, always with the meaning "apt" or "eager," and in three cases with the additional connotation of sexual depravity. See *Henry VIII* (1.1.160), *The Winter's Tale* (2.1.108), *Cymbeline* (5.4.203), *The Rape of Lucrece* (98.5), and "Sonnet 141," (line 6).

    25. Eric Rasmussen and Jonathan Bate explicitly gloss "speechless dialect" as "silent communication (body language)"; see their *RSC Shakespeare: Complete Works*, ed. Bate and Rasmussen (New York: Modern Library, 2007), 164.

    26. Similarly, Othello's demand for "ocular proof" is by default a demand for proof of infidelity rather than marital chastity.

    27. The adjective *prenzie* is a mystery, the only use of the word in English. It could be an Italianate form of "prince's" as some editors suggest, or "proxy," but neither is entirely convincing, and the latter makes little sense in the passage quoted. I wonder if "apprentice" might not make more sense in the context of a theologically oriented reading of the play—a play seemingly focused on the question of how one might best practice/learn/model Christian virtue. In the Arden edition J. W. Lever amends the line by substituting *precise* for *prenzie*. See *Measure for Measure*, 3.1.93 and note.

    28. Lupton's argument centers on Isabella's decision to choose chastity over her brother's life. See Lupton, *Citizen-Saints*, 140.

    29. The "record" to which Angelo refers is the eternal record imputed to God but unavailable on earth.

    30. This passage extends Jesus's earlier reference to the eye: "And if thy right eye offend thee, pluck it out, and cast it from thee: for it is profitable for thee that one of thy members should perish, and not that thy whole body should be cast into hell" (Matt. 5:29).

    31. Huston Diehl, "'Infinite Space': Representation and Reformation in *Measure for Measure*," *Shakespeare Quarterly* 49 (1998): 393–410, esp. 404.

    32. It is important to remember that Angelo believed he had followed through on his intention.

    33. Alain Badiou, *Ethics: An Essay on the Understanding of Evil*, trans. Peter Hallward (London: Verso, 2001).

    34. See ibid., 18–29.

    35. William Tyndale, *The Obedience of a Christian Man* (1528; repr., London: Religious Tract Society, n.d.), 203.

36. Ibid., 204.

37. Ibid., 210.

38. Ibid., 204.

39. The first two quotes are from the Bishop's version (1568). The Psalter quote is to the translation of Psalm 26:7–12, which is translated thus in the Vulgate: "Ne avertas faciem tuam a me, et ne declinas in ira a servo tuo." Also consider Psalm 102, "Hear, O Lord, my prayer: and let my cry come to thee. Turn not away thy face from me: in the day when I am in trouble, incline thy ear to me." The Bishop's renders "turn not thy face" as "hide not thy face."

40. For a detailed reading of the linguistic conventions in this passage, see John L. Harrison, "The Convention of 'Heart and Tongue' and the Meaning of *Measure for Measure*," *Shakespeare Quarterly* 5 (1954): 1–10; also see G. K. Hunter, "Six Notes on *Measure for Measure*," *Shakespeare Quarterly* 15 (1964): 169–71.

41. See Freinkel, *Reading Shakespeare's Will*, 146.

42. In performance it is possible to put the emphasis on Angelo's reaction to Isabella's beauty, but the dialogue casts doubt on the interpretation (especially in the first encounter). Shakespeare was quite capable of staging the experience of visually inspired love: compare, for example, Claudio's first encounter with Hero in *Much Ado* or Bassanio's description of Portia in *Merchant*.

43. In Lupton's account, "Ruled by the counterfeit Angelo, the city has been in effect headless, or governed by a counterfeit head; in returning to power, in making his royal entry, the Duke must remarry the city, becoming its symbolic head and restoring order to the civil monster" (*Citizen-Saints*, 152).

44. St. Augustine, *The confessions of the incomparable doctour S. Augustine*, trans. Sir Tobie Matthew (St. Omer: English College Press, 1620), 2.1.D3–D3v.

45. See, for example, Ronald R. Macdonald, "*Measure for Measure*: The Flesh Made Word," *Studies in English Literature* 30, no. 2 (1990): 265–82.

46. In addition, his last words to Escalus are "There's more behind that is more gradulate" (5.1.526).

Contributors

SARAH BECKWITH, Marcello Lotti Professor of English, Duke University, has published on Margery Kempe, the literature of anchoritism, medieval theater, and sacramental culture in numerous essay collections and journals such as the *South Atlantic Quarterly* and *Exemplaria*. She is the author of *Christ's Body: Identity, Religion and Society in Medieval English Writing* (Routledge, 1993) and *Signifying God: Social Relation and Symbolic Act in York's Play of Corpus Christi* (University of Chicago Press, 2001). She is currently working on a book on medieval and Renaissance drama centering on Shakespeare and the transformation of sacramental culture, tentatively entitled *The Mind's Retreat from the Face*.

LISA MYŌBUN FREINKEL, associate professor of English and Director of Comparative Literature, University of Oregon, is the author of *Reading Shakespeare's Will: The Theology of Figure from Augustine to the Sonnets* (Columbia University Press, 2002) and articles on topics ranging from fetishism to usury that address authors as diverse as Shakespeare, Dante, Luther, Immanuel Kant, and the thirteenth-century Japanese monk Dogen Zenji. Along with Renaissance literature, her ongoing interests include Shakespeare, psychoanalysis, theology, the philosophy of money, performance studies, and literary theory. She is currently at work on two long-term and tangentially related projects: a book that situates Shakespeare's work in the context of early modern encounters with Buddhist Asia, and a series of articles on the literary trope called catachresis (or "the figure of abuse").

HANNIBAL HAMLIN, associate professor of English, Ohio State University, is the author of *Psalm Culture and Early Modern English Literature* (Cambridge University Press, 2004) and articles and reviews in *Renaissance Quarterly*, *Spenser Studies*, *The Sidney Journal*, *The Yale Review*, *The Spenser*

Review, and *Early Modern Literary Studies*, as well as book chapters in *Never Again Would Birds' Song Be the Same: New Essays on Poetry and Poetics, Renaissance to Modern* (ed. Jennifer Lewin) and *Sacred and Profane in English Renaissance Literature* (forthcoming). Current projects include *The Psalms of Philip and Mary Sidney* (forthcoming in 2009 from Oxford World's Classics), co-edited with Margaret Hannay, Michael Brennan, and Noel Kinnamon; commissioned chapters for *The Oxford Handbook to Tudor Literature* and *The Blackwell's Companion to the Bible and English Literature*; articles for *The Princeton Encyclopedia of Poetry and Poetics* (3rd ed.); and a book-length study of biblical allusion in Shakespeare's plays.

KEN JACKSON, associate professor of English and Director of Religious Studies, Wayne State University, is the author of *Separate Theaters: Bethlan (Bedlam) Hospital and the Shakespearean Stage* (University of Delaware Press, 2005) and of a number of essays on Shakespeare and early modern English drama. He is currently completing a book entitled *Shakespeare, Abraham, and the Abrahamic*, a study of Shakespearean drama in relation to postmodern philosophy and theology.

JAMES A. KNAPP, associate professor of English and Edward J. Surtz, S.J., Professor of English, Loyola University, Chicago, is the author of *Illustrating the Past in Early Modern England: The Representation of History in Printed Books* (Ashgate, 2003). His research focuses on aesthetics and the relationship between visual and verbal representation. Though specializing in the early modern period (roughly 1500–1660), his research interests extend to the entire history of reproductive media and to the history of the word and image relationship more generally. He is currently working on a book on the ethics of vision.

GARY KUCHAR, associate professor of English, University of Victoria, is the author of *Divine Subjection: The Rhetoric of Sacramental Devotion in Early Modern England* (Dusquesne University Press, 2005) and *The Poetry of Religious Sorrow in Early Modern England* (Cambridge University Press, 2008). His main research area is seventeenth-century religious literature. He is particularly interested in the relations among literature, theology, and devotion in the post-Reformation period. Secondary areas of research include Shakespeare and religion; psychoanalysis and literature; phenomenology of religion; contemporary critical theory; and the history of critical theory.

JOAN PONG LINTON, associate professor of English, Indiana University, is the author of *The Romance of the New World: Gender and the Literary Formation of English Colonialism* (Cambridge University Press, 1998). She has also written on the English Protestant martyr Anne Askew. Her current research is on trickster agency and trickster poetics in early modern England.

JULIA REINHARD LUPTON, professor of English and Humanities, University of California, Irvine, is the author of *Afterlives of the Saints: Hagiography, Typology, and Renaissance Literature* (Stanford University Press, 1996) and *Citizen-Saints: Shakespeare and Political Theology* (University of Chicago Press, 2005). She is currently completing a book entitled *Thinking with Shakespeare*.

ARTHUR F. MAROTTI, Distinguished Professor of English, Wayne State University, is the author of *Religious Ideology and Cultural Fantasy: Catholic and Anti-Catholic Discourses in Early Modern England* (University of Notre Dame Press, 2005), as well as two other monographs. He has edited *Catholicism and Anti-Catholicism in Early Modern English Texts* (Macmillan, 1999) and has coedited *Catholic Culture in Early Modern England* (University of Notre Dame Press, 2007). He is currently working on two books: one a study of the personal anthologizing of verse in manuscript in early modern England and the other a collection of essays on early modern English Catholicism.

RICHARD MCCOY, professor of English, City University of New York, Graduate Center, is the author of *Alterations of State: Sacred Kingship in the English Reformation* (Columbia University Press, 2002); *The Rites of Knighthood: The Literature and Politics of Elizabethan Chivalry* (University of California Press, 1989); and *Sir Philip Sidney: Rebellion in Arcadia* (Rutgers

University Press, 1979). He is currently at work on *Performative Grace in Shakespeare's Plays*, a study of links between Reformation liturgical theology and contemporary performance theory in early modern drama.

ROBERT MIOLA, Gerard Manley Hopkins Professor of English and professor of Classics, Loyola College, Baltimore, is the author of *Shakespeare's Reading* (Oxford University Press, 2003); *Shakespeare and Classical Comedy: The Influence of Plautus and Terence* (Oxford University Press, 1995); and *Shakespeare and Classical Tragedy* (Oxford University Press, 1992), among other works. He has also edited *Early Modern Catholicism: An Anthology of Primary Sources* (Oxford University Press, 2007).

Index

Abbot, Robert, 34

Abraham
  circumcision by, 171, 175, 186n22
  and Gaunt in *Richard II*, 16, 231, 238
  in Genesis 22, 229–30
  interpretations of, 230–31
  and Job, 16, 184n8
  Shakespeare's political theology and, 16, 245, 246
  and York in *Richard II*, 16, 242–43, 244–45
Abraham and Isaac, 230, 247–48, 249
absolution, 103, 105, 109, 110, 272. *See also* confession
Acts 19, 86
Adam and Eve, 145
Adams, William, 200–201
adiaphora principle, 54–55
Admiral's Men, 131
Admonition to the Parliament, 53, 57
Aeneid, The (Virgil), 63
Aers, David, 121n10
alienation, 47, 52
Allen, William, 51
Alleyn, Ned, 131
alterity. *See* otherness
Andrewes, Lancelot, 102–3
Andrews, Jorella, 261
Anglican Order for the Burial of the Dead, 62, 65
"Apologie of *Raymond Sebonde,* An" (Montaigne), 15, 136–37
Apology against the Defence of Schism, An (Garnet), 40

Apology for Poetry (Sidney), 82, 94n24
Aquinas, Thomas, 102, 120n1, 191
Arcadia (Sidney), 157n36
Aristotle, 75n16, 98, 225n23
Arte of English Poesie (Puttenham), 213, 225n21
Asquith, Clare, 25
Asymmetry in Buddha Faces (Empson), 196, 197, 204n16
As You Like It (Shakespeare), 79
Auerbach, Erich, 254n23
Augustine, Saint, 258, 279
  on lying and confession, 37, 119, 126n58
Austin, J. L., 107–8, 124n40
Axton, Marie, 88–89
Azpilcueta, Martin (Doctor Navarrus), 38

Badiou, Alain, 271–72
Bagshaw, Christopher, 26–27
Bakhtin, Mikhail, 157n36
Bancroft, Archbishop Richard, 28
Bate, Jonathan, 49, 61, 68–69, 74n3
Beckwith, Sarah, 13–14, 26, 48, 287
Becon, Thomas, 102, 123n22
Bell, Thomas, 40
Bellamy, Anne, 35
Bellarmine, Robert, 32
Benjamin, Walter, 18, 209
  differentiates *novel* and *story*, 219–20
  on miracles, 207, 217
  on redemption of history, 222–23
  on unrecorded past, 206, 216

291